MW00480035

FLORIDA

Contents

Original text by Gary McKechnie, Mitchell Davis and Jane Miller
Revised and updated by Becca Blond
Lodging and restaurant selection courtesy of AAA Publishing

Edited, designed and produced by AA Publishing, a trading name
of AA Media Limited, whose registered office is Fanum House,
Basing View, Basingstoke, Hampshire RG21 4EA. Registered
number 06112600.

Published in the United States by AAA Publishing,
1000 AAA Drive, Heathrow, Florida 32746.
Published in the United Kingdom by AA Publishing.

ISBN 978-1-59508-427-9

Cover design and binding style by permission of AA Publishing
Color separation by AA Digital Department
Printed and bound in China by Leo Paper Products

A04413
Maps in this title produced from mapping © MAIRDUMONT/
Falk Verlag 2011 (except pages 44-45, 146-147, 197 &
224-225)

The Magazine

A great holiday is more than just lying on a beach or shopping till you drop – to really get the most from your trip you need to know what makes the place tick. The Magazine provides an entertaining overview to some of the social, cultural and natural elements that make up the unique character of this engaging state.

WHEN DISNEY CAME TO TOWN

In cosmic terms, the arrival of Walt Disney World® Resort on October 1, 1971 was the Big Bang of Florida's tourism industry, and today, although many competing theme parks have followed in its footsteps, Disney remains Orlando's linchpin. There is just something enduring about its magic that keeps legions of smiling families returning time and time again.

Walt Disney's dream of bringing fairy tales to life began in Anaheim, California, with the opening of Disneyland® on July 17, 1955. The concept took off in a big way, forever changing how Americans view theme parks and beginning a legacy that would remain magical (and eternally popular) to this day.

However, because Disney couldn't afford more property to expand when he started out, cheap hotels and tourist traps quickly surrounded the resort, cashing in on his success. This irritated Disney, who felt these concessions were parasitic, taking away from the wholesome world he was creating inside its gates.

In 1965, after a secret four-year search, Disney purchased 43 square miles (111sq km) of Orlando area wetlands – purportedly chosen after

Walt Disney – innovator in animation and theme park design

Walt flew over central Florida, spotted the intersection of the Florida Turnpike and I-4, and proclaimed, "that's it." He then announced, in a press conference with his brother Roy and Florida's governor, his intent to open a second, far superior park. He envisioned it as a place families would spend their entire vacations, and where he could control every aspect of the experience – from the entertainment to the hotels, restaurants and even the parking.

"…Disney World remains the classic, drawing millions each year."

"Here in Florida, we have something special we never enjoyed at Disneyland… the blessing of size. There's enough land here to hold all the ideas and plans we can possibly imagine," Disney said about his dream park. He then set about winning over the Floridian legislature, promising them untold amounts of tourist dollars in exchange for full control of his Magic Kingdom. As a result, when Disney World® opened in 1971 it was exempt from a host of state laws and building codes other business were required to operate under. In effect, Disney World was largely self-governing.

Keeping the Dream Alive
Sadly, Walt never saw his dream completed. A year after the press conference he was diagnosed with cancer and died in December 1966.

Roy stepped in to oversee construction and changed the name from Disney World to Walt Disney World, so visitors would know that his brother was the resort's creator. Roy died shortly after the park opened in 1971, a bittersweet end to the story of Walt Disney World® Resort's early days.

Walt (left) and his brother Roy (right) discussing finance with banker Bernard Giannini (center)

Just over a decade after the grand opening, it appeared as if Walt's dream would die as well. By the early 1980s, Disney management was in disarray. Construction cost overruns and lower-than-expected attendance at Epcot® had created a drop in profits in 1982 and again in 1983. Start-up costs for The Disney Channel and a poorly performing film division also took their toll. On the other hand, the parks were taking in $1 billion a year, and company assets were worth far more than the $2 billion price tag created by market valuation. This made it a prime target for a takeover. One of the first to attempt it was Saul Steinberg who, in 1984, purchased nearly 10 percent of Disney's outstanding shares. Disney paid a premium to buy back Steinberg's shares.

As other bids surfaced there were major changes in the executive suites, including the replacement of Walt's son-in-law, Ron Miller, by Michael Eisner and Frank Wells. Their creative spark ignited Disney, and the company reestablished itself as the leader in animated features such as *Aladdin, Beauty and the Beast* and *The Lion King*.

The Legacy Lives On

Although Wells died in a helicopter accident in 1994, and Eisner left in 2005, by then Disney had the momentum to grow beyond belief. Today, The Walt Disney Company owns several publishing companies, television broadcasting groups, radio stations and film companies. And although other copycat parks have opened in this city – chiefly Universal Orlando Resort, which launched the much-hyped JK Rowling-approved Wizarding World of Harry Potter attraction in 2010 – Disney World remains the classic, drawing millions of visitors each year. It's an American icon on a par with the Grand Canyon or the Statue of Liberty, the only place in the world, some say, where adults can play like children again and children are not expected to act grown-up.

DISNEY'S EXPANSION

Walt Disney World® Resort in 1982 was two theme parks, two hotels and a campground. In 1988, two new resorts opened. Disney-MGM Studios (now Disney's Hollywood Studios®) premiered in 1989, as did Disney's Typhoon Lagoon and Pleasure Island, and in 1990 there were more resorts (Yacht and Beach Club, Swan and Dolphin hotels), followed in 1991 by Port Orleans and Old Key West resorts and in 1992 by Dixie Landings resort. By 1995, Walt Disney World® Resort boasted a new wedding pavilion, 1996 saw the premiere of the Disney Institute, and 1997 saw the grand opening of Disney's Wide World of Sports® complex, Downtown Disney® West Side and the Coronado Springs resort. In 1998, the fourth theme park, Disney's Animal Kingdom® Park, came to life. In 2010, Fantasyland in Magic Kingdom® Park began a three-year overhaul; when the facelift is completed in 2013 the park will include a new ride-through attraction and grotto greeting location for Ariel the mermaid, called Under the Sea – Journey of the Little Mermaid.

Florida's
SPACE
PROGRAM

When the Americans placed a man on the moon on July 21, 1969, beating the Russians in the Space Race (as the press called it), Floridians felt especially proud. The lunar-bound spaceship had blasted off from their Cape Canaveral spaceport four days earlier, and when Neil Armstrong spoke those immortal words, he was talking

The Race for Space

Florida's space industry was born in the years following World War II, when the Russians launched the Sputnik I satellite in October 1957, and accelerated the Cold War. If Russia could launch a satellite that could circle the Earth at 17,400mph (28,000kph), it could also drop missiles on the United States. The Space Race was on, and Cape Canaveral became its American epicenter. The military had first begun quietly launching missiles from the scarcely developed 15,000-acre (6,070ha) sandy strip of Atlantic coastline – today called the Space Coast – in 1949.

The Birth of NASA

America tried to match Russia by launching a satellite in December 1957, but its Vanguard rocket rose only 2 feet (0.6m) before it tumbled to the ground in a huge fireball. The failure led President Eisenhower to give Wernher von Braun, a rocket scientist captured by the Americans during World War II, the full support of the government. Shortly after, Americans witnessed two successful launches, and the government's purse strings were opened. Through the National Aeronautics and Space Act the National Aeronautics and Space Administration (NASA) was born on October 1, 1958, setting up shop at Cape Canaveral.

As the 1950s came to a close, Russians and Americans were battling for space firsts. Monkeys were rocketed into orbit, new discoveries were made, and men from the armed forces of both nations were recruited for space service.

On April 12, 1961, the Russians achieved another victory when Yuri Gagarin was launched into orbit atop a Vostok rocket and circled the globe five times before safely returning to earth. If Sputnik had demoralized Americans, they were in disbelief over Gagarin's feat.

Man on the Moon

On May 25, 1961, President Kennedy announced to Congress a challenge that would surpass anything the Russians could attempt. To regain superiority in the Space Race, America would "land a man on the moon and return him safely to the Earth." And it would do it before the decade was out. A new space facility on Merritt Island, just north of Cape Canaveral, opened nine months later (it was renamed the Kennedy Space Center a few years later after the president's 1963 assassination). And in February 1962, America had an orbital victory when John Glenn circled the Earth three times.

On July 16, 1969, with five months to spare, NASA achieved victory when Apollo 11, rose from Cape Canaveral's Launch Pad 39A and began its three-day journey to the moon.

Left: Astronaut Mark C Lee floats 130 nautical miles above the earth
Right: Buzz Aldrin's footprint on the moon

While Michael Collins circled the moon in the command module, Neil Armstrong and Buzz Aldrin descended to its surface in the lunar module, a flimsy contraption known as the Eagle. As the world watched, Armstrong spoke his now immortal phrase: "That's one small step for man, one giant leap for mankind."

NASA had done it. Despite the deaths, setbacks and disappointments, they had transformed a region of Florida marshland into America's doorway to space and beaten Russia to claim the moon.

The Shuttle Years

The American public, however, was fickle. Following the successful Apollo 12 trip to the moon, few bothered to watch Apollo 13's mission until an oxygen tank exploded, putting the lives of the astronauts at risk. By the time the program came to a close in 1972, NASA needed another project to capture the public's imagination. So they built the space shuttle, and introduced it to a live television audience.

Instead of disposable rockets, NASA would launch a reusable spacecraft comprising an orbiter, two solid rocket boosters and an external fuel tank that could transport up to eight astronauts and a cargo bay filled with satellites and scientific experiments, in a 17,322mph (27,876kph) orbit around the Earth. When its mission was complete, the spacecraft would glide back to Earth and land on a runway – like an airplane.

For years after the 1981 maiden voyage, America had a fleet of four space shuttles that did everything NASA claimed, and soon the missions into space became routine. But then, on January 28, 1986, everything changed. A shocked America watched their television screens in schools and houses across the country as an O-ring that sealed the fuel inside the solid rocket booster gave way just seconds after the Challenger space shuttle launched. The flame ignited the external tank and Challenger disintegrated, killing all seven astronauts on board. It would be another 17 years before a shuttle encountered a similar fate: On February 1, 2003, the Columbia broke apart on reentering the earth's atmosphere, killing the crew of seven.

Opposite and above: The space shuttle Atlantis carried out its final scheduled mission to the International Space Station in May 2010

Sunset for the Shuttle

It was the beginning of the end for manned spaceflight. Two more successful multi-day missions were flown in 2005 and 2006, but in 2009 President Barack Obama announced NASA would be retiring its space shuttle fleet to make way for future space exploration programs aimed at sending astronauts to asteroids by 2025 and then to Mars. It's part of the president's space exploration proposal, which also includes canceling development of new rockets and spaceships slated to return astronauts to the moon.

NASA has now stopped running manned space operations. The final shuttle run was made by the Endeavour, which blasted off in February 2011 carrying a $1.5 billion astrophysics experiment to the international space station. Ironically, America now has to rely on its former Cold War enemy, Russia, and its Soyuz spacecraft, to shuttle its astronauts into outer space.

Best of the Best:
THE TOP BEACHES

Be it searching for seashells, scuba diving, sunbathing or watching sunsets, when it comes to the perfect place to slather on lotion and play in the sand, Florida indulges all types of holiday whims with hundreds of beaches spread across 1,200-plus miles (1,930km) of coastline and two bodies of water. Following are some of the most popular.

Best of the Keys: Bahia Honda
The Keys aren't known for having good beaches (too many sand flies), but Bahia Honda State Park, on Big Pine Key, is one of a handful of exceptions. The long stretch of white sand juxtaposed against the Gulf of Mexico's emerald twinkle is picture perfect and, best of all, the view under the clear sea is as good as above. An extensive reef system right offshore has excellent snorkeling opportunities, and tours can be arranged from the beach.

Best for Surfing: Cocoa Beach
On the Atlantic Ocean's Space Coast, south of Cape Canaveral, Cocoa Beach is home to eight-times world champion surfer Kelly Slater and some of Florida's best waves. Board rentals and lessons are easy to arrange.

Best for Seashells: Sanibel Island
Thanks to a quirk of current, Sanibel Island is home to the USA's best shelling. Seashells of all shapes and sizes are deposited regularly on this

BEST SUNSET VIEWS

For a romantic sunset drive, take the A1A between Miami and Key Biscayne. The sun's final salute sets the deep-blue water of the bay on fire, making it glow orange and gold as the sky turns pink then purple before sliding slowly into black. You can turn around and return, or spend the night camped out by the beach in Bill Baggs Cape Florida State Recreation Area at Key Biscayne's southern end.

eccentric barrier island's shore. Look for Sanibel's prize – the Junonia, a rare shell with speckles on it. If you're lucky enough to find one you'll get your photo in the local newspaper.

Best for the Trendy Set: Miami's South Beach
Far and away the most fabled stretch of sand in Florida (and the likeliest place to spot a celebrity) is South Beach (SoBe), an art deco bastion of cool on Miami Beach between 1st and 15th streets at Lummus Park. The gay community has staked its claim to the portion between 11th and 13th streets, while all along the shore topless sunbathing is acceptable.

Best for Quirky Natural Beauty: Grayton Beach
Grayton Beach State Park is the jewel of the Panhandle – a hauntingly beautiful, still wild place where windswept marble-colored dunes roll into the Gulf of Mexico's incandescent waters. Don't miss the Dog Wall, a wacky only-in-Florida mural on which locals have painted their favorite canines' portraits.

Best for Camping Out: Cayo Costa State Park
You'll have to catch a boat to reach it, but this Gulf of Mexico island jewel between Venice and Naples (Florida, of course) is worth the commute. Pristine beaches and frequent manatee sightings await overnight campers.

Top: One of the many colorful lifeguard stations on Miami's South Beach
Above: Kayaking at Bahia Honda State Park, Big Pine Key

river of grass

A few generations ago, the Everglades was viewed as a vast, alligator-infested wilderness of swamps and marshes. Ever hungry for development, Floridians naturally thought the water of this region needed to be channeled, diverted and directed to the thirsty people of Miami.

It was an honest mistake. If you had driven through the Everglades in the 1940s on one of the few roads that traversed the southern end of the state, you would have been stung by giant mosquitoes or eaten by alligators. It was (and still is) an inhospitable place for humans to live.

But the Everglades was never designed for humans. Few people realized that this morass of marsh was in reality a fragile ecosystem that masked a nearly 50-mile-wide (80km) river, less than a foot (0.3m) deep, that began south of Orlando and worked its way slowly to the state's southern tip at Florida Bay.

An airboat skimming the waterways

Although the Everglades was seen as a "useless" mucky swamp grass region, it was the largest natural filtration system in the country, and the seemingly dead landscape was teeming with wildlife. For centuries, the southern tip of Florida had been subjected to alternating periods of flood and drought, a natural cycle that helped produce thriving shrimp beds as well as mangrove swamps and the formation of coral reefs. Sportsmen found the best fishing in Florida in Florida Bay, the terminus of the Everglades, where the brackish water supported an abundance of sea life.

Destruction

It was a perfect climate to foster the needs of wildlife and sportsmen, but it was too good to last. A "flood control" system was begun to divert water to the more populated coasts. The move started a three-ring circus of special-interest groups competing for what they thought was best for Florida.

In one corner were developers who wanted to use the waters of the Everglades to fill the reservoirs of Miami and sustain its growing population. Then there were the farmers. Tomatoes, strawberries, oranges, mangoes, sugarcane and other crops needed the water of the Everglades. And finally the environmentalists, who recognized the dangers posed to the state's future if the Everglades was claimed for development or drained for farming.

The unofficial spokesperson for the last group was Marjory Stoneman Douglas, a former society columnist for the *Miami Herald* and a native of Miami. She saw that the limited resources of the Everglades could not support the dreams of developers.

In 1947, she published *The Everglades: River of Grass*, a book that correctly defined the Everglades not as an endless source of water to be diverted for farmers or developers, but as a "river of grass" fed by rivers hundreds of miles to the north, a natural, national treasure that needed to be preserved and protected.

Preservation

From the early 1920s, local residents recognized the need to preserve the Everglades. In 1929, Congress authorized a feasibility study, and by 1947 the national park became a reality. It covers an area of more than 1.5 million acres (607,000ha), and is now America's largest national park east of the Rocky Mountains.

Yet, although the Everglades is protected on paper, special interests and a lack of resolve on the part of the state government continue to erode the natural beauty and importance of the region. Canals distribute water to the

Left: A flowering bromeliad (air plant), one of many species of plants in the Everglades
Right: The beautiful but rare Florida panther (Puma concolor coryi)

EVERGLADES WILDLIFE

The best spots to see wildlife are the Anhinga Trail at Royal Palm, and Eco Pond. Rent a canoe and paddle around Snake Bight or Chokoloskee Bay. North American Canoe Tours (107 Camellia Street, Everglades City, tel: 239/695-3299; www.evergladesadventures.com; Nov to mid-Apr) rents out boats from $25 per half-day. A ranger-led tram tour (tel: 305/221-8455; www.sharkvalleytramtours.com; $18.25 adult, $11.50 child) leads to Shark Valley's 65-foot (20m) tower for a good bird's-eye view of the sawgrass prairie's birds and alligators.

Once endangered, the American alligator (Alligator mississippiensis) is now thriving

Miami coast and slowly drain the Everglades. More than 90 percent of the bird life has disappeared since the 1940s, and the Florida panther (ironically Florida's official animal)

> "Few people realized that this morass of marsh was in reality a fragile ecosystem…"

is near extinction. Florida Bay is now being infiltrated with salt water and mercury pollution. Both threaten the delicate ecosystem.

Rejuvenation

It's heartbreaking, but there is hope. Legislation against development and pollution has achieved a number of goals, among them the establishment of an Everglades Trust Fund.

In 1998, the Clinton administration released a draft $7.8 billion plan to restore the Everglades (filling in back-country canals, leveling water control, restoring natural water flows and reservoirs). Since then, Congress has approved the 30-year re-engineering project, and today cleaning up the Everglades remains America's largest, most ambitious project. The result will be a rejuvenation of the river of grass.

ERNEST F COE VISITOR CENTER

Eleven miles (18km) southwest of Homestead on Route 9336. Take US 1 south out of Miami, turn right at S.W. 344th Street/State Road 9336 and follow signs ☎ 305/242-7700; www.nps.gov/ever/planyourvisit/coedirections. htm 🕐 Daily 9–5 💲 Inexpensive

The Best of
OLD FLORIDA

Florida is a large state full of cultural diversions, and once the sand gets into your shoes, you'll want to head away from the shore and explore what locals refer to as "Old Florida" – the state's backroads, old-fashioned attractions and historic villages.

Above: A trolley bus at Fernandina Beach on Amelia Island
Left: The Flagler College in St Augustine was once a hotel

St Augustine

Without a doubt, St Augustine (➤ 180–181) is Florida's most beautiful and historic village, 120 miles (193km) northeast of Orlando. Although it's a popular part of Florida folklore, Spanish explorer Ponce de León never actually landed here in 1513, but he paved the way for future explorers, and by 1565, St Augustine had been established, making it the oldest permanent European settlement in the United States.

Today, the town is a popular getaway for romantics and a vacation destination for families. With its European flair, stylish architecture, artsy alleyways and intimate bed-and-breakfast inns, it's a perfect place for walking or taking a spin in a horse-drawn carriage. Brimming with art and antiques showrooms, gift shops, courtyard cafes, microbrew pubs and ice-cream parlors, it is also home to stunning Flagler College (formerly Henry M Flagler's grand Ponce de León Hotel), as well as America's oldest school, house and pharmacy.

A wide, white sandy beach lies a few miles south of the Bridge of Lions, which spans Matanzas Bay and overlooks the 17th-century fortress, Castillo de San Marcos. Fortunately this scenic city has not been overrun by development, and a historical tour should not be missed.

Amelia Island

About an hour north of St Augustine, Amelia Island (➤ 187) is the only place in America that has been ruled under eight flags. In the early 1900s, the island's colorful cast of characters ranged from bawdy ladies to salty sailors, and a Northern newspaper dubbed the town "a festering fleshpot." Nowadays, it's home to oceanfront horseback riding, deep-sea fishing and the downtown shopping district of Fernandina Beach. On Centre Street there's a trendy collection of antiques and art shops, specialty stores, candy counters and casual cafes.

The wonderful Palace Saloon is believed to be Florida's oldest bar and is definitely haunted, say employees. This charming town is a neighborhood of vintage homes and small inns. For a larger-than-life piece of history, Fort Clinch hosts tours featuring character guides who adopt the persona of Union soldiers from 1864.

Mount Dora

The picturesque hillside town of Mount Dora (► 91), 30 miles (48km) northwest of Orlando, is the home of the historic 1883 Lakeside Inn, a relaxing retreat on Lake Dora's shores. Take a stroll along Donnelly Street, pausing to peek into antiques stores and galleries, boutiques, jewelers and candle-making shops. Stay awhile and smell the orange blossoms, catch a concert or festival at Donnelly Park, play shuffleboard or a game of tennis, or enjoy a nature walk on Palm Island.

Micanopy

A tiny town (population 700) tucked away between I-75 and US 441 just south of Gainesville (about two hours north of Orlando), Micanopy has received an unusual amount of attention. With its dirt roads, ancient oak trees and Spanish moss, it welcomes droves of curious tourists every weekend. They come to browse around the antiques shops, bookstores and craft stores that surround the town square. You can visit this well-preserved slice of Old Florida for an afternoon, or stop over at the local bed-and-breakfast, and get back to doing what sometimes needs to be done – absolutely nothing (tel: 352/466-3121 for information).

The imposing portico of the neoclassical Old Capitol, Tallahassee

Tallahassee

Tallahassee was the only Southern capital spared in the Civil War, and no other Florida city rivals its ability to let time pass by in such a graceful, old Southern way. Visit the Old Capitol, built in 1842, where there are several rooms devoted to museum displays on Florida's political history, or the new State Capitol, which has a great observation tower on the 22nd floor, with an outstanding view of Leon County. On a clear day, you might see Georgia, about 15 miles (24km) to the north, or the Gulf of Mexico, 30 miles (48km) to the south.

To really understand the Tallahassee spirit, you'll need to get off the Main Street and head to the country. Here canopy roads lead to an old-fashioned environment of general stores and fishing holes.

VISITOR INFORMATION

St Augustine Visitor Information Center
✉ 10 Castillo Drive, St Augustine 32084 ☎ 904/825-1000; www.oldcity.com
Amelia Island Convention and Visitors Bureau
✉ 102 Centre Street, Fernandina Beach 32034 ☎ 904/277-0717; www.ameliaisland.com
Mount Dora Area Chamber of Commerce
✉ 341 Alexander Street, Mount Dora 32757 ☎ 352/383-2165; www.mountdora.com
Tallahassee Convention and Visitors Bureau
✉ 106 E. Jefferson Street, Tallahassee 32301 ☎ 850/606-2305, 800/628-2868; www.visittallahassee.com

72 HOURS
on the Gulf Coast

From hand-rolled cigars to circus culture and Jimmy Buffett, Florida's Gulf Coast between Tampa Bay and Naples packs a lot of punch into 225 miles (360km). If you only have three days, you could try the following three adventures.

Roll Your Own

Before anything Cuban was banned in 1950, Tampa Bay's Ybor City was home to the state's largest cigar industry. Although it went through a period of decline in the second half of the last century, one decade into the new millennium sees Ybor City buzzing again. An ongoing revitalization project has brought life back to the cobblestoned historic district that still firmly embraces its smoking legacy and strong Cuban-Spanish roots (► panel opposite).

Cheeseburger in Paradise

Anyone in need of a tasty burger with a view will know to take a water taxi across the Gulf from near Fort Myers (► 166) to Cabbage Key, where Jimmy Buffett, king of American beach ballads, found his "Cheeseburger in Paradise" decades ago. Buffett penned his hit after dining at the Cabbage Key Inn. Have your own cheeseburger in paradise moment or spend the night at this small guest house on a 100-acre (40ha) private barrier island where Ernest Hemingway, Julia Roberts and JFK Jr have also stayed. Check out the restaurant's walls as they tell a ballad of their own. Plastered with more than $20,000 of real greenbacks (dollars), many date back to the 1940s when commercial fisherman would autograph bills after payday, then use the walls as an improvised savings account by exchanging them to pay for food and drink when they were broke.

From Venice to Naples...With Love

Florida's southwest Gulf Coast seemingly loves legendary Italian capitals, with a town called Venice and another named Naples. While the Floridian versions aren't known for either their gondoliers or their pizza, both are famous for romance. Included in the Florida package are psychedelic pink, purple and inferno-red sunsets, picture-perfect china-white sand and warm, marbled turquoise sea, and delicious fresh seafood – try the stone crabs, a regional specialty.

Naples, the more affluent of the two communities, is filled with beautiful mansions and boutique shops, and has managed to weather the recent recession. Visit The Boathouse (990 Broad Avenue S., tel: 239/643-2235), right on the beach, for a romantic date. Locals say this waterfront joint with a big deck is the town's best bet for sunset cocktails and seafood.

Further north, ultra-relaxed Venice is Florida's shark tooth capital, thanks to a current that has been depositing the teeth here for centuries. They can be bought from shops in town, or you can search for them yourself. Try the southern two-thirds of Caspersen Beach on Harbor Drive, just south of downtown.

Bottom: Sunset at Anna Maria Key on the Gulf Coast

CIGAR SCOOP

Learn to roll your own cigar at the Gonzalez y Martinez Cigar Company (2025 E. 7th Avenue, Ybor City, tel: 813/247-2469), which offers demonstrations Monday to Saturday. There are also a number of cigar emporiums, such as Metropolitan Cigars (2014 E. 7th Avenue, Ybor City, tel: 813/248-3304), where you can watch master rollers at work.

FLORIDA'S CHARACTERS

Throughout its history, Florida has had its share of characters whose personalities have run the gamut from extravagant and innovative to dangerous and cruel.

Panfilo de Narvaez

Consider Spanish explorer Panfilo de Narvaez, who arrived in Florida in 1528 accompanied by 400 soldiers and their war dogs. Narvaez claimed the land near Tampa for Spain. In a show of force, the callous conquistador cut off the nose of a Tocabago chief and threw the chief's protesting mother to the dogs.

Determined to discover the New World's non-existent gold, Narvaez sent his ships up the coast, while he and the rest of the soldiers marched north in an unsuccessful search. Fed up with the foreigners, Apalachee warriors attacked, chasing the Spanish to the Gulf, where they were forced to build rafts and set sail for Mexico. Narvaez died at sea.

Julia Tuttle

Julia Tuttle, daughter of homesteader and state senator ET Sturtevant, visited the state during the 1870s. Two decades later she moved south and forever changed the area. Tuttle recognized that South Florida's potential rested on reliable transportation. Railroad titans Henry Plant and Henry Flagler were running railroad lines and building hotels for sunseeking Northerners, but neither had plans for the Biscayne Bay area.

Tuttle purchased property along the Miami River and led a comfortable life. After a major freeze hit the rest of the state, Tuttle had an idea. She plucked a few fresh orange blossoms from a tree and mailed them to Henry Flagler, who was building a line down Florida's Atlantic coast.

Flagler, a former grain dealer-turned-cofounder of Standard Oil, was impressed by the proof of Miami's frost-proof climate and agreed to run his trains farther south – provided Julia gave him the land on which he

---

RON RICE

In the late 1960s, Ron Rice was a Daytona Beach high school biology teacher who, after school, spent his time mixing natural oils together in a garbage can, which he bottled and sold at pools along the beach. It was an inauspicious beginning, but Rice's Hawaiian Tropic proved to be popular with sun lovers everywhere.

could build one of his opulent hotels. She agreed, and 300 Miami residents cheered the arrival of the first train in 1896.

Thomas Alva Edison

Down in Fort Myers, prolific inventor Thomas Alva Edison built a winter retreat, one of Florida's first prefabricated homes. He had sections of his home built in New England and shipped to Fort Myers, where the pieces were patched together. And after a hard day's work, he could splash around in his swimming pool, one of the first modern pools in Florida, built in 1910.

Edward Leedskalnin

When Leedskalnin, a Latvian immigrant, came to America, he began his 20-year labor of love: a 1,100-ton "coral castle" built using only simple chains, pulleys and recycled auto parts. He worked alone at night to create his home, which includes an 8-foot-high (2.5m) wall made from huge blocks of coral rock, a 2-ton rocking chair so delicately balanced it moves with the touch of a finger, and a 9-ton gate that a child can push open. How he managed to move coral rocks weighing up to 35 tons without the use of machinery remains a mystery. Coral Castle (28655 S. Dixie Highway, Homestead, tel: 305/248-6345) is open daily 8–6.

Ray Charles

One of America's most celebrated recording artists grew up in Greenville, Florida. When he left the St. Augustine School for the Deaf and Blind, Charles played piano in the dives and gin joints of many Florida towns for a few dollars a night. In 1949, realizing his career was at a dead end, he asked a friend to look at a map and find the largest city that was the farthest distance from Orlando. A few weeks later, he was on his way to a new life and the dawn of stardom in Seattle, Washington.

From the top:
Julia Tuttle;
Thomas Alva Edison;
Ray Charles

Bienvenida a
MIAMI

Want to spend the morning drinking sugary thick Cuban coffee in Little Havana, the afternoon shopping in Haiti and the evening drinking mojitos and dancing tango in Argentina? Welcome to Miami, where you can travel around Latin America in a day, where languages, countries and cultures collide in an explosion of exotic music, spicy food and fun.

America's Latin Heart

Miami is a cutting-edge city – a progressive urban wonderland. With a greater mix of Cubans, Haitians, El Salvadorans, Hondurans, Brazilians, Dominicans, Puerto Ricans and Mexicans than any single Central or South American country, it's been dubbed the "Latin Capital of North America," a place where new frontiers are forged and racial and sexual stereotypes are broken down. Gay or straight, black or white, Miami welcomes all. It's also a city where Spanish is still the first language (along with others, such as French and Creole) and where up-and-coming Hispanic musicians, soap-opera starlets and young politicians can cut their teeth before making their global stage debut.

One such success story is Pitbull, the Cuban-American hip-hop artist

who grew up on the streets of Little Havana. He is responsible for launching a mainstream revival of Cuban music not seen since Gloria Estefan and the Miami Sound Machine mixed beats in the 1970s and 1980s.

Cubans are the city's most dominant Latino group (many arrived as political refugees from Castro's Cuba), with the strongest influence on local and national politics and trade. As a whole they tend to be politically conservative, prosperous Catholics who vote politically conservative. Their neighborhood, Little

Pitbull at the Latin Music Awards in Miami

Havana, is famous for its hand-rolled cigars and thick, sugary coffee served tableside at sidewalk cafes. To hear traditional Cuban ensemble band music, with groups of up to 20 musicians and singers performing at once, check the lineup during one of Miami's many cultural performances, including Carnaval Miami, which is held over nine days in early March.

Play Me Some Latin Music

Latin American music is the rhythm that pumps Miami's heart, and from salsa to tango, mambo to hip-hop and Mexican pop, this red-hot city is full of sexy boys and girls shaking their hips and swinging their partners to a musical roll call as diverse as the population. You can do the same. For an authentic Cuban music scene try Hoy Como Ayer (2212 S.W. 8th Street, tel: 305/541-2631), a Little Havana local hot spot where the wood paneling is refreshingly unstylish and cigar smoke pervades the air. The dance floor is small and always packed with Cuban transplants moving to the beats of *son*, a Cuban salsa-style dance, or Spanish *boleros*, along with the year's top Cuban pop and hip-hop hits.

ENTERTAINMENT CENTRAL

Considering the red-hot Latin music scene, it's little wonder that Miami is also the center of America's Latin American music and entertainment industry. Most of the major labels and television broadcast stations – Mexico's Televisa, MTV Networks Latin America, Universal Music Group Latin America and Telemundo, one of the biggest Spanish-language broadcasters in the USA – have based their international headquarters here. In addition, the city hosts the hugely popular Latin Music Awards in July.

Dancing the night away in a high-energy club in South Beach

Miami is famous for the beauty of its residents, and South Beach is where they go to show off. Miami's most glittering art deco beach jewel is home to the city's hottest nightlife, period. And that includes the high-end Latin scene. You're more likely to see Latin stars partying in South Beach than hanging out back in their old neighborhoods (if you get past the velvet club ropes, that is; dress to impress and look confident for the best chance at getting past the lines and bouncers). Skybar (Shore Club, 1901 Collins Avenue, tel: 305/695-3900) is the pinnacle of beautiful Miami, packed with more models and movie stars than any other place. Try to gain entrance into the coveted all-crimson Red Room, where the A-list crowd chills, but if you can't convince the sullen-faced bouncer then head to the equally imaginative (and frankly less stuffy) area outside, under colossal wrought-iron Moroccan lanterns. Grab a mojito and watch the beautiful people come and go.

> "…it's been dubbed the Latin Capital of North America"

GAME OF JAI ALAI?

Roughly translating from Spanish as "merry festival," jai alai (pronounced high aligh) is actually a game. It originated in the 17th century in the Pyrenees Basque region as a cross between lacrosse and racquetball, and first became a Miami phenomenon in 1924. The game is played by hurling a small rubber ball wrapped in goat skin – it's called a pelota and is capable of speeds of more than 170mph (270kph) – at opponents, who try to catch the flying missile with a woven reed basket that's attached to a hand glove. To score, the pelota must be thrown against the front wall of the court with enough speed that opposing players cannot catch it or return it upon first bounce. It's quite a sight, although the spectators at the Miami Jai-Alai (3500 N.W. 37th Avenue, tel: 305/633-6400; inexpensive; matches Wed–Sun 12–5, Mon, Fri–Sat 7pm–midnight) where matches take place, include many chain-smoking, South Florida retirees making small bets. Still it's a fun experience, and you'll never forget the sound of that goatskin ball zipping through the air at high speed.

Finding Your Feet

First Two Hours

Orlando International Airport

If your destination is Walt Disney World® Resort in Florida, here's a relatively simple way to get from plane to luggage to transportation at Orlando International Airport (OIA), tel: 407/825-2001; www.orlandoairports.net.

- Domestic flights arrive at all gates from **1–99**, except gates **30–89**, which are usually but not always reserved for international flights.
- All halls lead to a **free electric shuttle** that takes you to the third level of the main terminal. Straight ahead is a fountain, and beyond the fountain to the left is an information booth.
- Take the escalator down one flight to **claim your bags**.
- There are **three currency exchange counters** – one in the East Hall, one in the West Hall and one at Baggage Retrieval on the B side of the airport. Each is open from 8am to 7pm.
- Take another escalator down another flight to find the **rental car counters, taxis and buses**. Some rental cars are parked at OIA.
- If your rental car is at the airport, descend another level to reach a tunnel that leads to the **multilevel parking garages**. Otherwise, just outside are buses and taxis to hotels, and shuttle buses and vans to rental car centers.
- Orlando's own buses, the **Lynx** system (tel: 407/841-8240), depart from the A side of the terminal on Level One, but they have no provisions for luggage.
- As you leave, look for **Route 528** (the Bee Line Expressway, toll), following signs to Walt Disney World® and the attractions. Route 528 heads west to **I-4**, access point to International Drive, Universal Orlando and Walt Disney World®.

Orlando Sanford International Airport

Orlando Sanford airport (tel: 407/585-4000; www.orlandosanfordairport. com) is about 30 miles (48km) northeast of OIA, is popular with smaller charter airlines, and is halfway between the ocean and Orlando.

- **American Coach Shuttle** (tel: 407/826-9999; www.americancoachforlando. com), across from the terminal, dispatches vans to pick up and deliver passengers wherever they are staying.
- If driving from Sanford, **Route 417 (the Greeneway)** is best. It's a toll highway (you'll need some quarters). Alternatively, **I-4** is about 8 miles (13km) away.

Miami International Airport

Miami's airport (MIA) (tel: 305/876-7000; www.miami-airport.com) seems more crowded and confusing than OIA, but is in fact fairly easy to navigate. (MIA is undergoing a $5.2 billion expansion of terminals and concourse.)

- The first level is arrivals, the second level is departures, and the third level features a **long moving walkway** that wraps nearly all the way around the horseshoe-shaped terminal with exits at Concourses B–H.
- Use the walkway on Level Three to save your feet; go to Level Two if you need a shuttle bus or the **Main Tourist Information Center** at Concourse E; and go to Level One to retrieve your bags, rent a car or hail a taxi.
- When you leave MIA, the most direct route to South Beach is **Route 836** (also called the Dolphin Expressway), which heads east to the MacArthur Causeway and directly to the southern end of the Art Deco District.
- If your destination is north of South Beach, **Route 112** (Airport Expressway) is a straight shot to the Julia Tuttle Causeway and mid-Miami Beach.
- When you rent a car, ask the clerk to give you a map and mark your route for you. The city has a **"Follow The Sun" system**, which marks the safer routes to popular destinations with huge sunburst logos on directional signs.

- Cab fares from the airport to South Beach, the Art Deco District and destinations as far as 63rd Street are reasonable. **Yellow Cab** is a safe bet.
- **SuperShuttle vans** (tel: 305/871-2000) run 24 hours a day. They pick up at the ground level of each concourse.
- The last option is an inexpensive Miami-Dade Transit Agency **Metrobus** (tel: 305/770-3131), which picks up on the lower level of MIA.

Tampa International Airport
Tampa International Airport (TIA) (tel: 813/870-8700; www.tampaairport.com) is small and easy to handle. Passengers arrive on the third level.
- Although the airport is divided into two sides **(red and blue)**, everyone descends to the first floor to retrieve their bags.
- Here you'll find rental cars, taxis, buses and courtesy vans (clearly marked) to hotels. **Yellow Cab** charges a reasonable fare to take three people downtown, about 15 minutes away. You can get details of shared-ride services at the first-floor information counter.
- The corners of the airport are numbered 1 and 2 on both the red and blue sides, and is where shuttle buses and limos pick up, but the city bus system, **HARTLine** (tel: 813/254-4278), picks up from Red 1. Look for Route 30.
- Again, rent a car. When you leave TIA, look for **I-275** north to reach Tampa or **I-275** south to reach St Petersburg.

Tallahassee Regional Airport
Tallahassee is a small town, and the airport (tel: 850/891-7802; www.talgov.com/airport) is easy to navigate. TLH is about 5 miles (3km) southwest of downtown. Car-rental services and ground transportation are located at the terminal.
- Leaving the airport, **I-10** and **US 90** are to the north of the airport terminal. Turn left onto **Capital Circle/FL 263** and drive north to **Route 20, US 90** and **I-10** at Exit 196. I-10 runs east to Lake City and Jacksonville and west to Marianna and Pensacola.
- From the airport **turn right onto Capital Circle**. Turn left on Springhill Road for downtown, Florida A&M University and Florida State University.

Pensacola Regional Airport
The airport (PNS, tel: 850/436-5000; www.flypensacola.com) is less than 6 miles (10km) northeast of downtown Pensacola near the west shore of Escambia Bay, and just minutes from the Alabama border. Rental cars and ground transportation can be arranged at the main terminal.
- **I-10**, which leads to Tallahassee and Jacksonville (as well as Mobile, Alabama and Santa Monica, California), is a short distance north of the airport. **US 98**, which skirts the Gulf of Mexico, is to the south.

Jacksonville International Airport
Landing in Jacksonville (tel: 904/741-2000; www.jaa.aero) puts you midway between Daytona Beach and Savannah, Georgia – and right on the Atlantic Ocean. JAX is about 14 miles (22.5km) north of downtown Jacksonville. Car-rental services and ground transportation are located at the terminal.
- **Route 102/Airport Road** connects the terminal area with **I-95** at Exit 363. I-95 runs north to Georgia, and south through downtown Jacksonville to St Augustine, Daytona Beach, Melbourne and other points to Miami.
- From I-95, take **Highway A1A/FL 200** eastbound at Exit 373 to Amelia Island and Fernandina Beach.
- **I-295** (a ring road) connects with I-95 at Exit 362 to bypass Jacksonville to the west. I-295 connects with I-10, which runs west from Jacksonville to Lake City, Tallahassee and the Florida Panhandle.

Getting Around

Orlando

If your entire vacation is on Walt Disney World® property, you could just use their transportation (➤ 48–49). If driving, you may find the road layout difficult to follow. For the most part, you'll need to be concerned only with I-4.

- I-4 is an east–west highway that takes a diagonal northeast–southwest route through Orlando. It's busy during **weekday rush hours (7–10am, 4–6pm)**, but it's the main artery from Walt Disney World® Resort to SeaWorld, Universal Orlando, International Drive and downtown Orlando.
- The distance from **Disney to downtown** is only about 12 miles (19km).
- **Route 528** (the Bee Line Expressway), which skirts the airport, and **Route 408**, which edges through downtown, are Orlando's two major east–west roads.
- Tolls on each range from 25¢ to $1, and the **Bee Line Expressway** is best to reach Port Canaveral, the Kennedy Space Center and Cocoa Beach.
- **Route 408** delivers you to **Highway 50**, which leads to Titusville and Cape Canaveral – but only after dealing with city and suburban traffic.

Miami

The fastest way to get to the far north and south of Miami is via I-95. I-75 leads into the city from the northwest, and **Route 836** (the Dolphin Expressway) connects the airport to downtown, lower Miami Beach and the Art Deco District. A map is necessary (obtainable from airport bookstores), but when in Miami you can take advantage of four sources of inexpensive transportation. An **EASY Card**, available from metrorail stations, EASY Card outlets or online (www.miamidade. gov.com), lets you put money on a card, which is deducted automatically for each journey you make. It saves having to find change each time.

- **Metrobus** has an extensive route system around Miami.
- **Metrorail** runs from downtown Miami north to Hialeah and south along US 1 to the Dadeland Mall.
- **Metromover**, a free elevated electric tram, runs through downtown Miami.
- The **South Beach Local** buses ride around SoBe, taking passengers to all the things worth seeing. Pay just 25¢ for buses on Route 123. For schedules and information, call 305/770-3131.

Tampa

Most of the city is on a peninsula and the layout is like a grid. When you need to reach St Petersburg, Clearwater or any of the beaches, it's easy.

- To get to St Petersburg from south Tampa, take **Highway 92** across the Gandy Bridge or, from north Tampa, via I-275 and the Howard Frankland Bridge.
- Once you're in St Petersburg, the beaches are easily reached by taking **Central Avenue** due west to Treasure Island. From here, **Highway 699** goes south and north along the coast.
- You can use **HARTLine** buses in Tampa (➤ 33).

The Panhandle

Florida's Panhandle, between Jacksonville on the Atlantic Coast and Pensacola on the state's western border, is fairly easy to navigate since there are only a few major highways to deal with and each has its own merits.

- **I-10** is the fastest route between the two cities, and is intersected at Lake City by **I-75**, which leads south to the Florida Turnpike and eventually Miami.
- **US 90** was the original east–west highway and is still a charming back road that runs through several rural counties and into county seats along the way.
- **US 98** is the road along the Gulf that is the best route for reaching coastal cities such as Panama City and Apalachicola.

- **Route 399** between Pensacola Beach and Navarre Beach takes you down Santa Rosa Island, a popular swimming and sunbathing beach.
- A few north–south highways intersect the Panhandle between St Marks and Tallahassee **(Route 363)**, between Panama City and Marianna **(US 231)**, and **Route 85**, which connects Fort Walton Beach to Crestview.

Rental Cars

- If you live outside the United States, you will need a **valid driver's license** (written in English), you must be at least 25 and carry a major credit card. Before you go, check if your own insurance will cover your rental.
- All passengers have to **wear seatbelts**; headlights need to be used when it's raining; and you have to drive on the right side – no exceptions.
- If you have kids age three and under, they need to sit in a **child's safety seat**, which can be rented from $5–$8 per day.
- Ask for the **mileage allowance**. Some rental fees are based on keeping the car in Florida, or they'll add extra fees if you exceed your limit.

Buses

- **Greyhound Lines** (tel: 800/231-2222; www.greyhound.com) serves major cities.

Tourist Information Centers

Visit Florida ✉ 661 E. Jefferson Street, Suite 300, Tallahassee 32301 ☎ 888/7FLA-USA; www.visitflorida.com

Orlando Official Visitor Center
✉ 8723 International Drive
☎ 407/363-5872;
www.orlandoinfo.com

Kissimmee/St Cloud Convention & Visitors Bureau
✉ 1925 E. Irlo Bronson Memorial Highway, Kissimmee 34744
☎ 407/847-5000 or 800/327-9159 for a vacation guide;
www.floridakiss.com

Greater Miami Convention & Visitors Bureau
✉ 701 Brickell Avenue, Suite 2700, Miami 33131 ☎ 305/539-3000; www.miamiandbeaches.com

Key West Chamber of Commerce
✉ 510 Greene Street, Key West 33040 ☎ 305/294-2587;
www.keywestchamber.org

Tampa Bay Convention & Visitors Bureau
✉ 401 E. Jackson Street, Suite 2100, Tampa 33602 ☎ 813/223-1111 or 800/826-8358;
www.visittampabay.com

St. Petersburg/Clearwater Area Convention & Visitors Bureau
✉ 13805 58th Street N., Clearwater 33760 ☎ 727/464-7200 or 877/352-3224;
www.visitstpeteclearwater.com

Discount Passes

At shopping plazas surrounding Disney, and along International Drive, you will see ticket kiosks where you can buy discounted tickets to theme parks and attractions. The catch is you will have to agree to visit a timeshare resort.

Admission Charges
The cost of admission for museums and places of interest mentioned in the text is indicated by price categories:
Inexpensive up to $15 **Moderate** $16–$30 **Expensive** $31–$50
Very expensive over $50

Accommodations

Hotels and Resorts

Although most properties in Florida have some sort of pool, hotels and resorts differ from other accommodations by the scope of amenities they offer and their size. In general, resorts offer the most, the idea being that you need never leave the property. Golf and tennis are common themes, but Disney has broken the mold by introducing themes such as Polynesia, pop culture, Atlantic City, old Florida, New Orleans, the Caribbean and more.

- **Access to a beach** is always a plus. Check if the hotel is right on the water, or whether you will need to travel. Keep in mind that waterview is not waterfront. Neither is waterfront – sometimes it's a street.
- Generally, **rooms are large**, and two double beds are standard. Suites, with two or three separate rooms, are increasingly common and offer an affordable alternative for families traveling together.
- The more services the property offers, the more opportunity there is to add hidden charges onto your bill, especially the use of telephones. **If you're on a budget**, make use of pay phones in the lobby, even when making local calls.
- Parking, in-room movies, laundry, room service and other amenities may also **come with exorbitant prices**. Look for a menu of services in the room or quiz the front desk before making arrangements.

Disney

- With your guest ID, **perks include** free parking at theme parks, package delivery, early admission to parks, planned activities and free transportation.
- Even with approximately 25,000 rooms at nearly 20 on-property locations, **lodgings can still be hard to find**. Make reservations well in advance.
- Staying at one of the "deluxe" resorts such as Disney's Grand Floridian Resort® Spa, Disney's Polynesian and Disney's BoardWalk Inn will cost around $350 per night plus tax; from $75 per night plus tax for "value" resorts; and between $100 and $300 per night plus tax for "mid-range" accommodations. **Rates vary depending on season and availability**.
- Every resort has a pool, food service and free transportation, and there are **more services at the higher-end resorts**.
- **For reservations** at any Walt Disney World® hotel, tel: 407/934-7639 or the Walt Disney Travel Company on 800/828-0228; www.disneyworld.com.

Motels and Motor Inns

Motels and motor inns are distinguished from hotels by having a small or nonexistent lobby and direct access to your room. There is the advantage of being able to park your car close to your room. The only drawback is security – because the door to your room opens to the outside world, there is less of a buffer between you and unsavory types who target visitors.

Bed-and-breakfasts

In some historic or rural areas of the state, there is the option of staying in a bed-and-breakfast. B&Bs and small inns offer a more authentic sense of local life and the opportunity to meet and interact with people.

- During the season, many properties insist on a **minimum length of stay** and require advance payment.
- A helpful **list of inns** is available at www.florida-inns.com.

Apartment Rentals

An excellent and often economical option is to rent an apartment. Many people from the north own vacation condominiums in Florida, and there are a lot of vacant apartments available for rent outside the high season (January–March). Since apartments have full kitchens, you can prepare your own meals, which may suit you. Many also have swimming pools and other facilities.

Self-catering

Self-catering is popular. Rooms with cooking facilities, "efficiencies," can be found in most budget and moderate hotels and motels.

Camping

Camping can be an economical and fun option. Some campgrounds offer amenities, such as swimming pools and shops, typical of small hotels. Others simply allocate a plot of land to pitch your tent on.

■ **Renting an RV** (recreational vehicle) also gives you some increased freedom and the opportunity to see parts of the state you might not otherwise visit. A popular nationwide service is at www.cruiseamerica.com.

■ For information about where you can **camp or park your RV**, contact Florida's Department of Environmental Protection, Parks and Recreation (tel: 850/245-2157) or the National Park Service (www.nps.gov/parks. html). Reserve America (tel: 877/444-6777; www.reserveamerica.com), a nationwide central reservations system, covers 13,000 campsites. For Florida state parks with campgrounds check www.myflorida.com or www.floridastateparks.org.

Youth Hostels

For information about hostels in Florida, check out www.hostels.com. Or try Hostelling International USA (tel: 888/464-4872; www.hiusa.org).

Tipping

The amount you tip depends on where you are staying. In the finest hotels, doormen, bellmen, room-service staff, concierges, housekeepers and anyone else who performs a service for you should be tipped between $1 and $5, depending on the service; and usually $1 per bag. A few hotels include a daily service charge to cover tipping; make sure you ask at reception before you hand out tips.

Diamond Ratings

AAA field inspectors evaluate and rate lodging establishments based on the overall quality and services. AAA's diamond rating criteria reflect the design and service standards set by the lodging industry, combined with the expectations of our members.

The one (◈) or two (◈◈) diamond rating represents a clean and well-maintained property offering comfortable rooms, with the two diamond property showing enhancements in decor and furnishings. A three (◈◈◈) diamond property shows marked upgrades in physical attributes, services and comfort and may offer additional amenities. A four (◈◈◈◈) diamond rating signifies a property offering a high level of service and hospitality and a wide variety of amenities and upscale facilities. A five (◈◈◈◈◈) diamond rating represents a world-class facility, offering the highest level of luxurious accommodations and personalized guest services.

Accommodations Prices

Expect to pay per room per night:
$ under $125 $$ $125–$250 $$$ over $250

Food and Drink

Climate, immigration and tourism drive Florida's vast, colorful and tasty food scene. The state serves as the test market for nearly every fast-food or theme-restaurant concept, and a cadre of award-winning chefs oversees nationally acclaimed restaurants. In between, you can get good food at good value.

■ Restaurants throughout Florida **are more casual** than in other East Coast cities such as New York. Although the fancier places require jackets, most other places will let you eat in T-shirts and sometimes even shorts.
■ Service is **almost always welcoming and friendly.** Waiters are used to helping people from other places navigate their way through the menus and pricing systems. Don't forget to tip.
■ Florida is a place for cars, and consequently all restaurants **have ample parking.** The more chic eateries offer valet service.

Orlando
Orlando is overrun with dining spectacles where food is an afterthought – medieval jousting, car racing and mystery are among the main attractions. That doesn't mean there are no quality options.
■ Perhaps the **biggest gastronomic strides** in the area have been made by Walt Disney World® Resort, which has upgraded its dining facilities. Every October, Epcot® hosts a month-long international food and wine festival that brings chefs, restaurateurs and vintners from around the world to taste each other's fare.
■ The restaurants in and around Orlando cater primarily to a captive tourist audience, so the **prices are generally high.** Perhaps more concerned with quantity than quality, people generally eat early and fast. If you stray off the beaten path, you can find a more authentic local experience.

Miami
The restaurants of Miami run the full gamut. There are great gastronomic temples and hole-in-the-wall dives. A number of chefs creating what's known alternately as Floribbean (for Florida and Caribbean) or New World cuisine mix tropical ingredients and classic techniques to produce an exciting style of fusion cooking characterized by bold flavors and striking presentations.
■ The **fashionable crowds of South Beach** have sparked a restaurant boom. The attitude is sometimes as important as the cooking, but the results are nevertheless impressive. Sushi restaurants are becoming popular.
■ The **streets of Little Havana** are lined with authentic Cuban restaurants, where you can have a delicious and satisfying home-cooked meal for very little money. And Miami still has its early-bird eaters, most of them elderly, who dine from 4:30 to 6pm to take advantage of bargain-priced dinners. Late-night diners will find plenty of places that stay open late.

Tampa
Route US 19 in Pinellas County, outside Tampa, is home to one of the densest restaurant populations in the country. If a concept can make it there, among so much competition, it can make it anywhere. As a result, there are some great dining experiences in Tampa. Steak and Italian are among the best options, and there's certainly great wine.

Tipping
Bars (standing up) $1–$2 per drink; (sitting down) 10–15 percent. Restaurants 15–20 percent. Valet parking attendant $1–$2.

Citrus Capital

Florida is the citrus capital of the world. Although most of the oranges are turned into juice, truck stops (laybys), fruit stands in season and souvenir shops often have bags of them for sale. The best grapefruits come from Indian River County. Be careful not to buy juice oranges, which are difficult to peel and slightly bitter. On your travels, why not try Key limes or kumquats? You can also ship cases of citrus home.

Specialties

Fish and seafood are another specialty of the region. Though overfished and polluted in parts, the Gulf of Mexico still yields some delicious specimens. With their sweet, white, flaky flesh, red snapper and pompano are perhaps the most common. Escolar is more difficult to find. Often served chilled with a tangy mustard sauce, large stone crab claws are worth seeking out. Only one claw is harvested, and within two years the crab generates a new one.

Vegetarian Food

Although Florida is more often associated with fruits than vegetables, vegetarians will have an easy time finding suitable dishes. Restaurants always have at least one vegetarian appetizer and entrée, and many of the better establishments offer complete vegetarian *dégustation* menus.

Glossary of Florida Food

Café con leche – strong, rich Cuban coffee mixed with hot milk.
Cherimoya – also known as custard apple, this tropical fruit has very sweet, creamy white flesh and black seeds.
Cuban sandwich – a hot, pressed sandwich of roast pork, ham, cheese and pickles.
Dolphin – be assured it's the fish of the same name, not the mammal.
Early-bird specials – special bargain-priced dinners available in the late afternoon and early evening.
Key limes – juicier and sweeter than their more common cousins, these yellow-green limes (named for the Florida Keys) provide the juice that makes the state's favorite dessert, Key lime pie.
Mangoes – the sweet, fleshy fruit is a south Florida specialty.
Stone crabs – only the large meaty claws of these crabs are eaten.

Pan-Asian Cuisine

Many Florida chefs cook in a pan-Asian style, blending the ingredients and techniques of Asian countries to create a vibrant cuisine that sounds and tastes Asian, but is uniquely American. Results are sometimes more interesting than they are delicious.

Diamond Ratings

As with the hotel ratings (► 37), AAA field inspectors evaluate restaurants on the overall quality of food, service, decor and ambiance – with extra emphasis given to food and service. Ratings range from one diamond (💎) indicating a simple, family-oriented establishment to five diamonds (💎💎💎💎💎) indicating an establishment offering superb culinary skills and ultimate adult dining experience.

Restaurant Prices

Expect to pay per person for a meal, excluding drinks:

$ under $15	**$$** $15–$30	**$$$** over $30

Shopping

Like just about anywhere in the United States, shopping is a major cultural pastime in Florida. High-school students meet in shopping malls after class, elderly people walk along pedestrian promenades to catch some sun, and tourists hunt for mementos and souvenirs to take back with them.

Malls
The principal venue for shopping is the mall, with its large "anchor" **department stores** (such as Saks Fifth Avenue, Neiman Marcus, JCPenney and Sears), smaller chain stores (such as Gap, Pottery Barn, Crate & Barrel, Victoria's Secret and Barnes & Noble Booksellers) and sometimes a few locally owned independent boutiques with eclectic collections of goods for sale. Because of Florida's warm weather, there are also **pleasant outdoor malls** that offer a range of stores and restaurants.

Factory Outlets
Shopping at factory outlets is now a major part of the picture. These stores are often owned by the manufacturers themselves and can offer **discounted prices on merchandise** (some of it last season's styles, some are seconds or flawed items). It is not unusual to see merchandise being sold simultaneously at a retail mall and an outlet store with as much as a 50 percent difference in price. Outlet stores are often located alongside major highways and thoroughfares.

Superstores
Superstores have made their presence felt in Florida. These giant stores (such as Home Depot, Borders Books & Music, Bed Bath & Beyond) **specialize in one type of merchandise** (hardware, books, bathroom and kitchen accessories, respectively) and offer reasonable prices.

Food
The best option for food shopping is the large **grocery store often attached to a strip mall**. You can also try the local bakery, delicatessen or butcher shop, though it may cost more than the supermarket. Grocery stores often carry other items (such as pharmaceuticals) and many open 24 hours a day.

Specialty Shopping
■ **Miami is often the place to find unique things to buy** because of its large residential population and cosmopolitan nature. South Beach is filled with urban and avant-garde boutiques offering everything from fashion to crafts to eyewear. The most exclusive stores abound in the affluent neighborhoods of the city – international brands such as Cartier, Prada and others are all represented. You are less likely to find specialty items outside Miami.
■ Orlando is one of the most tourist-laden cities in the United States, so **souvenirs are available all over**, especially at Walt Disney World® Resort's huge range of shopping opportunities (➤ 98).
■ In Tampa **look for cigars**, which are often rolled before your eyes (➤ 24, 25), and **sporting goods**.

Opening Times
In residential areas, stores are generally open from 9 or 10am until between 6 and 9pm. On Thursdays and Fridays many stay open later. In tourist areas, stores often have extended hours to accommodate busy sightseeing schedules.

Entertainment

Florida has always been one of America's premier tourist destinations, long before the opening of Walt Disney World® in 1971, and there is truly something for everyone to do, from the good clean family fun of Disney theme parks to Miami's steamy club scene.

A high demand among Floridians for cultural events means there are many high-quality venues for everything from opera to foreign film. In addition, the influx of large numbers of Northerners to the state has resulted in a greater demand for sporting events not readily associated with Florida: ice hockey and basketball have become extremely popular. Following is a partial calendar of the more unusual and interesting annual festivals, parades, parties and other goings-on around the major Florida cities. This is by no means a complete listing of all there is to do around Florida. For more information contact the visitor center or tourism bureau for the specific city with dates of your stay. October through March is high tourist season in Florida, so many events that cater to visitors happen during this time.

January

- **Orange Bowl:** Usually held on January 1, the Orange Bowl is one of the premier bowl games in college football, and takes place at Miami's Pro Player Stadium. Following a long-standing tradition, the King Orange Jamboree Parade kicks off the festivities the day before. Pro Player Stadium is 15 miles (24km) north of downtown Miami, which is the parade's location. For tickets, tel: 305/371-4600; www.orangebowl.org.
- **Capital One Bowl:** Another exciting college bowl game, this one is held in Orlando's Capital One Bowl, complete with a parade and a New Year's Eve celebration. For information, tel: 407/423-2476; www.fcsports.com.
- **Outback Bowl:** A week's worth of parties, parades, breakfasts and firework displays heralds in Tampa's own bowl game, the Outback Bowl. See two tough college teams battle it out at Tampa's Raymond James Stadium. For tickets and information, tel: 813/874-2695; www.outbackbowl.com.

February

- **Silver Spurs Rodeo:** Since 1944 the Silver Spurs Rodeo, held on weekends in late February and October in Kissimmee, has provided rodeo fans with a chance to see bronco riding, bull riding, roping and more. Spectators can attend one day, or see and participate in a weekend's worth of events. For more information, tel: 407/67-RODEO; www.silverspursrodeo.com.
- **Gasparilla Festival:** The name of this annual Tampa event originates from the infamous pirate José Gaspar, who terrorized the Tampa area 200 years ago. Since 1904 Ye Mystic Krewe of Gasparilla has staged a mock attack on the city, and in recent years the event has evolved into a month-long series of attractions including parades, races, firework displays, art shows and more. The highlight is the pirate attack, usually in February. For information call Ye Mystic Krewe of Gasparilla on 813/251-4500; www.gasparillapiratefest.com.
- **Miami Film Festival:** The premier film festival in Florida since its inception in 1984, the Miami Film Festival is particularly noted for introducing many Spanish and Latino filmmakers to America. In addition to the 10 days of screenings, there is a host of parties and seminars where attendees can rub shoulders with actors and filmmakers. For more information call the Film Society of Miami on 305/237-3456; www.miamifilmfestival.com.

March

- **Arnold Palmer Invitational:** This PGA-sanctioned tournament at the Bay Hill Club (9000 Bay Hill Boulevard, Orlando) is hosted by Arnold Palmer. Spectators at the week-long event will have the chance to see many of the country's top golfers in action. For more information and tickets, tel: 407/876-2888; www.bayhill.com.

April/May

- **Fringe Festival:** Held at a wide range of indoor and outdoor venues around Orlando, the Fringe Festival is a diverse assortment of performances that lasts for 10 days starting in late April. During the festival you can see everything from Shakespeare's plays to circus acts. Prices vary. For information, tel: 407/648-0077; www.orlandofringe.org.
- **Florida Folk Festival:** Up in White Springs by the Suwann.ee River is a three-day celebration of the music, dance, stories, foods and old-fashioned crafts that defined pre-Disney Florida. For information, tel: 877/635-3655; www.floridastateparks.org/folkfest.

June

- **Coconut Grove Goombay Festival:** Celebrate Florida's Caribbean heritage at this day-long party in Miami's Coconut Grove. The event is free and thousands of people show up to sample ethnic food and hear live music.

July

- **Hemingway Days Festival, Key West:** Celebrating the Key West days of novelist Ernest Hemingway, this multi-day event features a Hemingway look-alike contest, arm wrestling and celebrations of his literary works.

October

- **Fantasy Fest:** The wildest event of the year takes place in Key West, Florida's wildest town. The Mardi Gras-style celebration features drag queens, naked parties, public drunkenness, Caribbean balls and tattoo shows. For information, tel: 305/296-1817; www.fantasyfest.net.
- **Halloween Horror Nights:** During weekends and the last two weeks of October, Universal Orlando is transformed into a ghoulish party designed to shock and scare attendees. There are monsters, gremlins and walking dead all over the park, as well as haunted houses and live concerts. Not recommended for young children. For tickets, tel: 407/363-8000; www.universalorlando.com.

November

- **International Film Festival:** Independently produced films premiere at this annual film festival in Fort Lauderdale. For information, tel: 954/760-9898; www.fliff.com.

December

- **Mickey's Very Merry Christmas Party:** One of the highlights of Disney's Christmas festivities is the annual Christmas Party held in the Magic Kingdom. December in Walt Disney World® Resort is full of other holiday events including concerts, firework displays and storytelling. For more information, tel: 407/824-4321; www.waltdisneyworld.com.

There are thousands of festivals across the state. For more information check out www.visitflorida.com, www.myflorida.com or the local convention and visitors bureaus. For information on other entertainment in Orlando, Miami, Tampa, St Petersburg and the Panhandle, see the individual chapters.

Orlando

Getting Your Bearings

Until October 1, 1971, Orlando was a sleepy town surrounded by orange groves, cattle ranches and a few military bases. Then Walt Disney ushered in a whole new world. Orange groves were frozen out in the 1980s, and tourism took root. In their place evolved a universe of new worlds: Flea World, Hub Cap World, Liquor World, Lobster World, Speed World… Orlando is World Headquarters.

Drop by a theme park and you have instant access to Alaska, the South Pacific, the Canadian wilderness, the streets of New York, the hills of San Francisco, London, Paris, Morocco, China and all points east.

Not only does the diversity of the theme parks make Orlando the world's favorite tourist destination, the city's cleanliness, friendliness and climate make it a perfect getaway for families, honeymooners, seniors and solo travelers. Another draw is the city's strategic location: Atlantic Ocean beaches are 50 miles (80km) east; the Gulf of Mexico is just 60 miles (96km) west; there are small villages filled with antiques; suburban enclaves where hip college students watch art films; and freshwater springs that are perfect for picnics, snorkeling and canoe trips into a forgotten Florida.

Despite appearances to the contrary, Orlando and its surrounding towns do have a history. If you take time to look, you will find historic museums, older neighborhoods displaying wonderful architecture, and pockets of Greater Orlando that survive without dependence on theme parks and the tourist dollar.

★ Don't Miss

1 Magic Kingdom® Park ► 50

2 Disney's Animal Kingdom® Park ► 56

3 Disney's Hollywood Studios® ► 60

4 Epcot® ► 65

Page 43 (left to right): Kraken, SeaWorld Orlando; Spaceship Earth, Epcot; Atlantis space shuttle

At Your Leisure

Farther Afield

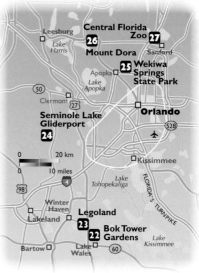

In Seven Days

If you're not quite sure where to begin your travels, this itinerary recommends a practical and enjoyable seven days exploring Orlando and its surrounding sights using the Getting Your Bearings map on the previous pages. For more information see the main entries.

Day 1

Visit the **❶ Magic Kingdom® Park** first (➤ 50–55), whether or not you have children. If there are fireworks, stick around. If not, have a late dinner at Downtown Disney.

Day 2

Rise and shine for an early half day at **❷ Disney's Animal Kingdom® Park** (➤ 56–59), since the wildlife retreats to cooler habitats by noon and may be difficult to spot. After lunch spend a lazy afternoon at one of **❺ Walt Disney World® Resort's water parks** (➤ 69–70). Later, return to Disney's Animal Kingdom® or, if you have a Park Hopper pass, to **❹ Epcot®** (➤ 65–68) for dinner at one of the World Showcase restaurants. Stick around until closing – there'll be a fantastic display of fireworks and lasers in the park's grand finale.

Day 3

Take a break down the road at **❻ SeaWorld Orlando** (left, ➤ 71–73). It's more casual and easier to tackle than Disney. The park's Makahiki Luau is a fun dinner show.

Day 4

Make this a **❸ Disney's Hollywood Studios®** day (➤ 60–64). Stay for an early evening parade followed by dinner at the Hollywood Brown Derby (➤ 63).

Day 5

7 Universal Orlando (above; ➤ 74–82) is home to Universal Studios, Islands of Adventure and the new Wizarding World of Harry Potter. Try dinner at the world's largest Hard Rock Café and, if you have the stamina, party till the wee hours at the nightclub-rich CityWalk (➤ 101–102).

Day 6

With your energy dwindling, this may be the best day to see **4 Epcot®** (➤ 65–68) since there are fewer "must-see" attractions.

Day 7

Use today to revisit your favorite Disney attractions, the parts of Universal Orlando you missed, or get away from the theme parks for a canoe trip down the **25 Wekiwa** River (➤ 91), a visit to the **8 Kennedy Space Center** (left, ➤ 83–84), or a day at an Atlantic or Gulf Coast beach (➤ 14–15). Wrap up the night at Downtown Disney – and make it count.

Visiting Walt Disney World® Resort

Walt Disney World® Resort is not an amusement park, it is a 47sq-mile (120sq km) fiefdom with all the features of a major city. It is large, sprawling, exciting, crowded, peaceful, noisy, tranquil, confusing and obvious. If you ignore the plentiful extraneous offerings of Walt Disney World® Resort, you'll have a better chance of seeing what's important.

Once you've settled into your hotel, return to the lobby to get some insider information from Guest Services. Now is the best time to buy tickets, since buying at the gate is crowded and confusing; or you can purchase tickets in advance by phone (tel: 407/824-8000), online (www.disneyworld.com) or by mail (Walt Disney World Guest Communications, PO Box 10000, Lake Buena Vista, FL 32830), although each method adds a surcharge and takes a few weeks to deliver.

Which Ticket?
There are more than a dozen types of ticket, and selecting just one can be daunting. Make your choice based on your length of stay, how many parks you will hit in a day (be realistic), and which parks you want to see. Below is a small selection of options available. Keep in mind tickets don't need to be used on consecutive days and unused tickets will never expire. Remember also that prices and ticket details can change so check ahead. Disney World uses a rather complicated pricing scheme, but the following might make things easier.

■ You can purchase a **Magic Your Way Ticket** for unlimited entry into a single park (i.e. Magic Kingdom® Park, Disney's Animal Kingdom® Park, Epcot®, Disney's Hollywood Studios®) for one to ten days, with prices dropping significantly the longer you stay (a seven-day ticket is only $20 more than a three-day one). A one-day ticket costs around $75 for adults and $65 for a child, a three-day ticket costs around $200 for an adult, $175 for a child, while a seven-day ticket costs around $220 for an adult and $185 for a child.

■ The Magic Your Way Ticket grants unlimited entry into a single park, but check online for all the mix-and-match combinations. One of the most popular is the **Park Hopper** (for an additional $5–$50 per day), which allows **unlimited entry to all four parks** (instead of just one) for the duration of your base ticket.

Navigating the Park
For resort guests it's far easier to park your car and take advantage of Walt Disney World® Resort's Transportation System. The most common mode of transportation is **buses**, which run about every 15 minutes from roughly an hour before park openings to half an hour after they close. Buses go to each resort area, picking up from each hotel. It can take up to an hour to travel between resorts. If you're in a hurry, take your car as buses can take a circuitous route to your destination.

- If you drive your own car or are entering from off-property, ask for directions before leaving your hotel. Highly traveled routes are well marked with bright signage, and some street lines are color-coded to lead you to your destination. **Parking** is easy and attendants will direct you to the massive parking lot outside each park. Walt Disney World® Resort guests do not pay for parking.
- For practical or pleasurable reasons, you can **board a monorail** at the Transportation and Ticket Center (TTC), across the Seven Seas Lagoon from the Magic Kingdom® Park. It has two loops: one leaves TTC and goes to the Polynesian Resort, Grand Floridian, Magic Kingdom and Contemporary Resort; the other goes to Epcot® and back.

Epcot® is easily accessed by monorail

Top Tips

- **Guest Relations** is your best bet for a full range of assistance. Located near the entrance of every theme park, this is where you can leave messages, pick up foreign-language guide maps, exchange foreign currency, make reservations for hotels and priority seating for dining, and get information on behind-the-scenes tours.
- **FASTPASS** is an ingenious virtual line system that "stands" in line for you. Just swipe your park ticket at the automated machine at the ride entrance and the slip will tell you the time to return. Then show the FASTPASS at the entrance to be escorted past the waiting crowds to the front. The most popular rides stop printing FASTPASS tickets by midday if it's crowded.
- It's hot in spring, and very hot in summer with temperatures into the 90s °F (30s °C). **Bring sun hats, sunglasses, sunscreen and a water bottle**.
- Some thrill rides have **height and health requirements**.
- If you are traveling with kids, you can attend a **character breakfast** at the theme parks and resorts. For information, tel: 407/939-3463.
- On one monorail journey, ask to **sit up front with the driver**. It's worth waiting for the next one.
- From any park, you will need a **handstamp and ticket** for re-entry.
- Resort designers have sprinkled the parks with abstractions and symbolic representations of Mickey Mouse's head. Finding these **Hidden Mickeys** has become an obsession for some Disney aficionados, an amusement to others. Look up, down and around. For the most extensive list of Hidden Mickeys, check www.hiddenmickeys.org.

OPENING TIMES

Opening times vary depending on season, but in general **Magic Kingdom** is open 9–7; **Epcot®** 9–9 (Future World at 9 and World Showcase at 11), **Disney's Hollywood Studios®** 9am to about an hour after dark, and **Disney's Animal Kingdom** 7 or 8am to an hour after dusk. For information on all parks ☎ 407/939-6244 or (for UK guests) 0870 242 4900 or 407/939-7718 (in the US); www.disneyworld.com.

❶ Magic Kingdom® Park

If you only have time (or cash) to visit one Walt Disney World® Resort theme park, mythical Magic Kingdom makes the choice easy. It has traces of the other three parks and is the most imaginative, fairest and truest to Disney's original fantasy of them all.

There's no "right way" to hit the Magic Kingdom, although there are several ways you can take advantage of what others don't know. Disney's cornerstone park is a masterpiece of design. From the plaza (or "hub") in front of Cinderella Castle, seven "lands" branch off like the spokes on a wheel (left to right, they are Adventureland, Frontierland, Liberty Square, Fantasyland, Mickey's Toontown Fair, Tomorrowland and Main Street, U.S.A.). It's easy to navigate and much easier if you arrive early, since lines will be significantly longer by mid-morning. The most popular regions are included here, but there is much more to this park, so stop at anything that catches your fancy. It's likely to be good.

Town Square and Main Street U.S.A.

Stepping into **Town Square** for the first time is a magical experience no matter what your age. This is the Walt Disney World® Resort image probably burned into your memory when you were a child. It reflects a wholesome version of the American Dream, stuck in a time and place that never really existed but giving an idea of what could be that will always be cherished. The smell of fresh popcorn fills the air, flowers burst from planters, marching bands parade on the street and horse-drawn streetcars wait for passengers. Don't rush, just take it all in.

From the center of Town Square, look down **Main Street U.S.A.** to the very end, where the dazzling **Cinderella Castle** dominates the distant skyline. No matter how many times you see it, you'll never forget its beauty. The Main Street Gazette, heading down the street toward the castle, is an information board listing show times, ride wait times and park hours. A cast member is usually on hand there to answer any questions you may have.

Tomorrowland

Based on the hugely popular animated feature about the misadventures of a wild (but lovable) alien, **Stitch's Great Escape** is one of Tomorrowland's top two rides. It features cutting-edge, audio-animatronic technology and high-energy escapades that recruit visitors to provide additional security when the Galactic Federation learns of Stitch's whereabouts.

© Disney

Cinderella Castle is the focal point of the Magic Kingdom® Park

Magic Kingdom's most legendary ride is also here, **Space Mountain**. No aliens here, it's just a screaming fast roller-coaster ride through a dark void that lasts nearly three minutes and hits speeds of up to 28mph (45kph). Use the FASTPASS option (➤ 49) to do it again when you're done as this is one of Disney's most revered rides for speed geeks.

Although the **Tomorrowland Indy Speedway** is meant to make children's dreams of driving a grand-prix race car come to life on a giant figure-eight track, it's minimum height requirement of 52 inches (1.32m) to drive solo eliminates much of its target audience. That said, the ride is strangely popular with adults who don't have kids. They wait in long lines to squeeze into the tiny cars, which are not only affixed to the track, but also never exceed speeds of 7mph, and race each other around the track.

Also in Tomorrowland, **Buzz Lightyear's Space Ranger Spin** transports you, laser cannon and all, directly into a spin-off of the *Toy Story II* video game. You'll get to steer your own Star Cruiser in a race through the galaxy with the Evil Emperor Zurg in fast pursuit.

If you just need a good chuckle, check out the absolutely hilarious interactive **Monsters, Inc. Laugh Floor movie**. It changes with each showing and manages to incorporate audience members by projecting their images and voices onto the big screen, and is completely devoted to making you laugh yourself silly with the monsters.

Main Street U.S.A., the hub of the Magic Kingdom

Liberty Square, Frontierland and Adventureland

Don't miss the wonderful **Haunted Mansion** ride in Liberty Square. After being greeted by a cadaverous host, you are ushered into the portrait gallery (look up when the lights go out), then board a "Doom Buggy" to travel down darkened hallways, past the ghostly ballroom, up to the creepy attic and through a graveyard. It's one of Disney's greatest classic haunts and well worth the wait.

Frontierland is home to two legendary Disney attractions. Finding the first, the epic **Splash Mountain** wet-water ride is easy: head toward the sound of screaming guests. Don't worry too much about following the storyline (Disney's film *Song of the South*), just be ready for the log you are riding in to take some fast drops and big splashdowns. Close by, **Big Thunder Mountain Railroad** whips through tight turns, over high hills, past possums, goats and a cowboy in a bathtub. It's not as fun as Splash Mountain, but nearly as famous and still worth a ride.

If the thrills, chills and special effects have you wiped out, then watching a group of hillbilly bears perform at the

Country Bear Jamboree in Frontierland makes a change. It's hard not to love these banjo-, jug-, guitar- and washboard bass-strutting bears, actually all gifted musicians, singing corny country songs and dancing around on stage. The concept may be weird, but it's a fun, frivolous, cool escape from the ordinary, and it's almost certain you'll lose your heart to Big Al.

In Adventureland, Johnny Depp's Captain Jack Sparrow narrates the **Pirates of the Caribbean** ride, which is perfect on a hot day. After entering a darkened cave, you will board a boat and head out on a ransacking, rum-swilling adventure. The cannon shells, burning villages and repetitive theme song ("Yo Ho, A Pirate's Life for Me") make this 10-minute tour one of the Magic Kingdom's better attractions. **Jungle Cruise**, narrated by a comedian/skipper, is a 10-minute tour down the mysterious rivers of the world that's also amusing. Watch out for everything from hippo attacks to cute Indian elephants bathing in a sacred pool.

Fantasyland and Mickey's Toontown Fair

If you're with young kids, these two areas are filled with the most child-friendly attractions. Fantasyland, which announced the start of a three-year overhaul in 2010, will

© Disney

look different when it's completed in 2013, although a few revered kids' attractions, including Ariel's Grotto, will be closed in the interim. The good news is Ariel will be back with a brand-new grotto greeting location, and her very own ride-through attraction, entitled **Under the Sea: Journey of the Little Mermaid**, when Fantasyland finishes its expansion.

If you miss Ariel, you can still experience plenty of magic on **Peter Pan's Flight**, which remains open during reconstruction. It takes you on an aerial tour above nighttime London and past Captain Hook's ship, using old-fashioned special effects like glow-in-the-dark paint, with fantastic results. You really feel as if you are flying above the city.

Also open during renovation is Fantasyland's most quintessentially old-fashioned Disney ride of them all, **It's a Small World**, which has been delighting children since it first debuted at the 1964 New York World's Fair. Transferred to and opened at the Florida park in 1971, it takes guests on a whimsical boat ride around the world, pausing in different exotic lands to watch hundreds of animated dolls dressed in national costume sing and dance to the song "It's a Small World" in representations of their native country. It's a sweet experience that takes you back to a time when entertainment was simpler, more folk artsy than digitized robotic (although you may find that the song is likely to get annoyingly stuck in your head afterwards).

Cinderella's Golden Carrousel, a beautifully restored 1917 carrousel, which plays bouncy Disney songs, is another good option for younger kids. Explore the world of Pooh and Tigger, Piglet, Eyore, Kanga and Roo on **The Many Adventures of Winnie the Pooh**. Be prepared for a long wait, but the animation is fantastic and even adults will be charmed by its cuteness.

Connected to Fantasyland, Mickey's Toontown Fair is a small area filled with whimsical architecture, a kid-sized roller coaster, **The Barnstormer**, and the chance to meet Mickey. For an audience with the famous mouse, walk through his country house, out the back door and into the **Judge's Tent**. No matter what their age, fans of Mickey, Donald Duck and other well-loved Disney cartoon characters will dig the 3D **Mickey's Philharmagic** film. Catch the show on a 150-

The Magic Carpets of Aladdin ride takes you aboard a flying carpet

foot-wide (46m) screen; in addition to 3D effects, it has
4D sensations like water splashing, gusts of wind and even
pleasing scents.

Character Experiences

Having breakfast, watching fireworks or going on safari with
your child's favourite Disney characters is an experience they
will cherish. Here's the scoop on meeting some of them.

For free meetings with characters check out the *Times
Guide*, which lists the specific spots in each park where the
characters hang out, then you can hop in line and have your
picture taken. Alternatively, you could try a character dining
experience like **Cinderella's Royal Table**, or the prestigious
My Disney Girl's Perfectly Princess Tea at the Disney Grand
Floridan Hotel. This glamorous affair is also Disney's priciest
– $250 for one adult and one child – but it's also a little girl's
dream, with high tea served on silver, a visit from Aurora and
a goodie bag that includes a princess bracelet and a doll.

Get a group together and take part in one of four **Grand
Gathering Magical Experiences**, which also happen at the
other Disney parks. A top adventure at Magic Kingdom is the
Magical Fireworks Voyage, an evening boat cruise hosted
by Mr Smee and Captain Hook that includes storytelling and
songs as Disney's nightly firework extravaganza explodes
overhead. The **Good Morning Character Breakfast** is
another excellent choice, especially for the youngest kids who
won't be awake late enough for the fireworks, but are usually
raring to go early in the morning.

➕ 225 A3 ☎ 407/939-6244 or 407/939-7718 (for UK visitors);
www.disneyworld.com 🕐 Daily 9–7, varies according to season
📖 See Which Ticket?, ➤ 48, for information on prices

MAGIC KINGDOM: INSIDE INFO

Top tips If you are a Walt Disney World® Resort guest **save the Magic Kingdom for
Sunday or Thursday** when you can enter an hour earlier than everyone else.
■ The best spot for a photograph of you and Cinderella Castle is from **the
sidewalk near the Tomorrowland entrance.**
■ The **Disney Dreams Come True Parade** – featuring all the best-loved characters –
marches down Main Street U.S.A. daily at 3pm.
■ Depending on the season, **SpectroMagic** lights up the Magic Kingdom once
or twice an evening. The parade features 600,000 miniature lights and
72,000 watts of sound, plus lots of special effects – from holographic to
smoke and liquid nitrogen.
■ **Wishes** is a firework show extraordinaire. It's best seen from Main Street
U.S.A., with Cinderella Castle as the backdrop. During the 12-minute
show, Jiminy Cricket launches more than 650 fireworks, timed to explode
in sync with a music track. For the best view, get to the second floor of the
train station.

One to miss Unless you are returning for a second day, you can forget the
Liberty Belle riverboat around the Rivers of America and the **raft ride to Tom Sawyer
Island**. The time you will spend on these is greater than the fun returned.

2 Disney's Animal Kingdom® Park

Animal Kingdom® was the fourth theme park to be built, but in terms of enjoyment it outperforms earlier arrivals Epcot® and Disney's Hollywood Studios®.

Despite the themed architecture, shows, storylines and thrill rides, this is really a safari park at heart. You will have to see it at the animals' pace, so adjust your schedule accordingly. The biggest mistake is arriving late and rushing to the premier attraction, Kilimanjaro Safaris. After mid-morning, lines are ridiculously long and animals are taking cover to escape the heat, so you may not see much.

How To Do the Park

Since Disney's Animal Kingdom® Park opens before the other parks (sometimes at 7am or earlier), plan to safari early (or much later) in the day and fill in the middle hours with shows, rides and indoor attractions. Don't think you are missing everything as you scurry from place to place. As in other parks, you will retrace your steps after hitting the highlights.

To simplify things, the park is divided into two major sections: Africa to your left and Asia to your right (other "lands" include **The Oasis, Safari Village, DinoLand U.S.A.** and **Camp Minnie-Mickey**). From the bus stop or parking lot you will arrive at the ticket booths of the Entrance Plaza. Lavatories, lockers and a mail drop are on your far left, with phones, lavatories, an ATM (cashpoint) and pet-boarding facility on your right.

The Oasis and Tree of Life

Near the entrance is **The Oasis**, an area of banana trees and waterfalls that delights and distracts with flutes, steel drums, brightly colored birds, orchids and hidden tunnels and a good place to get orientated. Nearby, the impressive **Tree of Life** is a towering 14-story-tall baobab with more than 325 different images of animals carved into its trunk. If you think the outside's cool, wait until you step inside. **It's Tough to Be a Bug!**, a movie experience inside the tree. This isn't for kids who are scared of the darkness or creepy crawlies, but adults and older children will appreciate the funny commentary and full-on sensory effects of this awesome eight-minute, 3D experience. It features characters from the Disney-Pixar film *A Bug's Life*, along with a host of supporting insects and arachnids. Sit near the back for the greatest impact.

Africa

Disney puts on quite a realistic magic show with **Kilimanjaro Safaris**, the star attraction in this part of the park. It almost

Plummeting down the Forbidden Mountain on Expedition Everest

feels like going on a real safari across the African savannah, replete with travel in a rickety jeep, potholed roads and washed-out bridges, and scores of rhinos, giraffes and zebras roaming the well-stocked reserve. There are even a few scary poachers you have to duck from thrown in for good measure. Make sure to bring a camera.

Festival of the Lion King is another popular African attraction. Inside a huge open-air theater, it is a multicultural carnival of music and motion as acrobats, singers, dancers and fire-jugglers put on a colorful stage show.

Asia

Visitors are reminded just how destructive slash-and-burn logging is on the eco-conscious **Kali River Rapids** ride through a mock-Asian rain forest. Expect to get wet on this watery adventure that includes riding a circular raft to the top of a hill then bouncing down it at breakneck speed through the dripping forest and past a logging camp. It's a great ride.

Tracking down Africa's wildlife with Kilimanjaro Safaris

Expedition Everest is the other supersized attraction (lines can be stupendously long, so try to arrive early), which begins in a reconstructed Nepalese village authentic enough to feel as if you're close to the summit of the world's highest peak. In the Disney version of the epic climb, you'll board a steam train that chugs slowly to the top, but once you reach the "summit" and start the descent, you'll be gasping for air. Not because of the altitude though: this is a roller coaster and you will find yourself plummeting down the mountainside at ultra-fast speed.

DinoLand U.S.A.

Although this area sticks out like a sore thumb, with its rather garish large plastic dinosaurs wedged between the live animals in the Africa and Asia regions, it includes some exciting rides and one of the best shows in Walt Disney World® Resort. **Finding Nemo – The Musical** is a 30-minute live theater spectacular with a narrative that mimics the movie, visionary special effects and larger-than-life puppets. For a bit more seat-of-your-pants excitement, board a jeep-like vehicle and travel back in time millions of years to retrieve a dinosaur for a scientist three minutes before a meteor shower rains down on the exciting **DINOSAUR!** ride.

➕ 225 A2 ☎ 407/939-6244 or 407/939-7718 (for UK visitors); www.disneyworld.com 🕐 Daily 9–about an hour after dusk, but varies according to season 💷 See Which Ticket?, ➤ 48, for information on prices

DISNEY'S ANIMAL KINGDOM: INSIDE INFO

Top tips Walt Disney World® Resort guests can enter Animal Kingdom an hour earlier than other guests on a **Monday or Friday**.
- As you explore the park, look for the **subtle touches Disney is famous for**: leaf imprints in cement; details hidden within the Tree of Life; silks and brass bells hanging in the prayer trees of Asia; and literally thousands of other artistic secrets.

© Disney

③ Disney's Hollywood Studios®

With Hollywood Studios, Walt Disney World re-creates the spirit of Hollywood's Golden Age of film, the mythical 1930s and 1940s, through the use of neon lights and lots of chrome, art deco architecture and bouncy Disney movie scores. The park also brings the glitz and glamor of modern-day television to life, with updated attractions that highlight the most popular small-screen shows of today. From *High School Musical* and *Hannah Montana*, to auditioning for *American Idol*, Hollywood Studios is particularly appealing to 'tweens, teens and anyone with a passion for fame.

Arrive early to get the most out of your Disney movie day that includes a behind-the-scenes look at movie sets, backstage tours and special Disney-only events dedicated to the showbiz industry. It's a good idea to have the big four attractions finished before noon, allowing time for an early lunch and a mellow afternoon. Guests who arrive late may very well end up spending half their time waiting in line and the other half waiting to get out!

Twilight to Terror: Top Attractions

It is attractions such as **The Twilight Zone™ Tower of Terror** that make Hollywood Studios worth visiting. After you snake through the entrance and lobby of the abandoned hotel, you will be ushered into a library where you will get the story line: this grand hotel was struck by lightning in 1939, and an entire wing – as well as five hotel guests trapped in an elevator – vanished. A secret door opens, you enter the boiler room and snake through another line until you are seated in an elevator. It's worth the wait. You will be hoisted to a hallway where the doomed guests appear, your car drifts through a mysterious dimension, a door opens and you see the park 150 feet (46m) below. Then the doors close. What happens next is worth every cent you spent to get here. The cable breaks, your car plunges straight down – stops – rises again – and takes yet another dive down the elevator shaft, then again and again for good measure. It's scary to say the least, and you will want to do it again. Remember seeing a bright flash when you fell? At the exit, you can buy a picture of yourself screaming like a baby.

On Sunset Boulevard, near The Twilight Zone™ Tower of Terror, is Disney's state-of-the-art **Rock 'n' Roller Coaster Starring Aerosmith**, featuring the music of the Grammy-winning rock band. Here, guests board a Limotrain and, after an Aerosmith recording session, are launched from

Disney & Co.: "Clothing Hollywood's Elite since 1923"

0 to 60mph (96kph) in 2.8 seconds (as fast as an F-14 Tomcat) and reach forces of 5 Gs as they speed through twists, turns, loops, corkscrews, hills and dips. A special Aerosmith soundtrack is pumped through a total of 900 speakers with more than 32,000 watts of power.

The **American Idol Experience** is the latest hot new attraction at Hollywood Studios, and lets aspiring stars (age 14 and older) audition for the chance to perform live on stage during the end-of-the-day Finale Show. If the audience votes you the day's best singer at this show, you'll receive a "dream ticket" to audition for an upcoming season of the popular reality TV show! It's a fun experience.

Mann's Chinese Theatre houses **The Great Movie Ride**, a guided tour where you board a large vehicle and enter scenes of famous films (*Singin' in the Rain*, *Casablanca*, *Mary Poppins*). In a few moments you will be accosted by gangsters, watch desperadoes blow up a safe, enter an alien-infiltrated spaceship, travel to Munchkinland and witness the frightening arrival of the Wicked Witch of the West. Scary for kids, but satisfying for adults who love the movies.

The next must-see is **Star Tours** – cross the plaza and head toward a small boat/expensive ice-cream stand at tiny Echo Lake. The venue **Sounds Dangerous Starring Drew Carey** (a sound effects-based attraction) is on your right, but pass this by and head straight to Star Tours.

With the return of George Lucas's *Star Wars* prequels, the ride has been upgraded to include effects from the films. You will recognize droids R2D2 and C3PO, who are working on a spacecraft. Then you will climb aboard your own star speeder for a voyage to the Moon of Endor. You start your trip smoothly but it soon goes wrong – of course. This is not for sissies. The ride pitches, rolls, banks and dodges giant

You can't miss the Rock 'n' Roller Coaster Starring Aerosmith

ice crystals and lasers fired by enemy fighters. You will need stamina, a strong back, a healthy heart and an iron stomach for this one.

And so on to the **Indiana Jones™ Epic Stunt Spectacular**. This is easily the most exciting live performance in the park. Why go to California for earthquakes, explosions, rock slides and fights when you can see the highlights of *Raiders of the Lost Ark* performed right here? It is edge-of-your-seat entertainment made even more fun when they reveal a few tricks of the trade.

Best of the Rest

The sights listed earlier are the most popular, but far from its only attractions. Don't miss Jim Henson's **Muppet*Vision 3D**, which stars nearly every Muppet you can remember in an all-star, sensory-overload performance that kids (and adults) will enjoy – especially since it ends with a bang.

While the streets of New York play host to the oversized world of **"Honey, I Shrunk the Kids" Movie Set Adventure**, around the corner, on Mickey Avenue, is the **Studios Backlot Tour**. This takes you through an actual working studio, including the wardrobe department and prop shop, before exiting into **Catastrophe Canyon**, famous for its display of special effects. It's startlingly real – especially when the ground buckles beneath the tram. Around the corner, the **Lights, Motors, Action! Extreme Stunt Show** is a fast-paced, thrill-filled performance imported from Disneyland Paris, with explosions and minicars, high-torque motorcycles and jet skis racing, jumping and careening (almost) out of control in a demonstration of movie stunt skills.

From here there are two types of attractions left: those revealing how movies are created and those that capitalize on Disney movie hits. Back on Mickey Avenue, **Who Wants To Be A Millionaire – Play It!** brings you an exact replica of the game-show set, showing how the game is played and produced. **Walt Disney – One Man's Dream** is an overview of the man's life, with stories from his childhood and intriguing items such as his original animation camera. Before you reach the final section, **Animation Courtyard**, you may be lucky and catch a presentation on Disney's latest movie release or hit TV show.

Voyage of the Little Mermaid is a kid-friendly stage show featuring songs and stars from the animated movie. Sit farther back and kids can see the stage better.

On **The Magic of Disney Animation** tour you can watch Disney animators creating upcoming animated films. This is a great way to see how the cartoons are developed, and an animator also answers guest questions. The Robin Williams/Walter Cronkite preshow is as good as any attraction here.

From the Animation Courtyard you are in the perfect position to enjoy a leisurely dinner at the **Hollywood Brown Derby** (having arranged priority seating earlier). This California icon was re-created here, complete with celebrity caricatures, private booths and the "Cobb Salad" (created by original owner Bob Cobb), as well as featured meat and fish dishes.

© Disney

After Dark

Wrap up the day after sunset with two more shows. **Beauty and the Beast – Live on Stage** is a 20-minute performance that captures the essence of the animated movie. It's a terrific stage show that stars singing silverware, a beautiful Belle and a thrilling finale; fun for young and old.

The grandest grand finale is next door at **Fantasmic!**, which is based on the wild dreams of Mickey Mouse. Like most Disney extravaganzas, this is filled with lasers, lights, fireworks and characters. Seating begins an hour before show time. The amphitheater seats 6,900 guests and 3,000 standing, so you don't have to rush it. Just sit near the back so you have a great overall view of Mickey battling the forces of evil.

IllumiNations: Reflections of Earth at Epcot

🔢 225 A2 ☎ 407/939-6244 or 407/939-7718 (for UK visitors); www.disneyworld.com 🕐 Daily 9–about an hour after dark, but varies according to season 💲 See Which Ticket?, ➤ 48, for information on prices

---

DISNEY'S HOLLYWOOD STUDIOS: INSIDE INFO

Top tips If you are a Walt Disney World® Resort guest, **save this park for Tuesday or Saturday** when you can enter the Disney's Hollywood Studios® an hour before opening time and see selected major attractions.

■ Here, as in any Disney park, if it's too crowded in the afternoon return to your hotel and cool off with a swim. In peak season, **the parks are open later**, and you can always come back. Have your hand stamped and keep your ticket for readmission.

■ The **Hollywood Boulevard parade** is usually themed to Disney's latest movie release (*Aladdin, Mulan, Pocahontas,* etc.) and takes place at 3pm. Stake your claim on the sidewalk at least half an hour earlier.

■ If you decide to put off the highlights for later, you can usually hit all the major attractions, **often without waiting**, in the 90 minutes before closing.

4 Epcot®

Epcot, not the Magic Kingdom® Park, was Walt Disney's greatest dream. In his mind, Epcot® (an acronym for Experimental Prototype Community Of Tomorrow) would be a utopian community where citizens would develop solutions to the world's ills. It didn't quite work out the way Walt pictured it.

The concept is simple: you enter Future World and visit pavilions where mega-corporations present their latest products. Next comes World Showcase, where 11 nations display their country through detailed architecture, gift shops and restaurants – with perhaps a ride or a movie. This park is twice the size of the Magic Kingdom and there's a lot of walking. Be prepared. Although Epcot is adding a few more exciting rides, it's a mixture of science fair, video arcade and travelog. Here's the best way to see it.

Future World

As always, get an early start. You will arrive by car, bus or monorail and be channeled to the Entrance Plaza. Lavatories and a currency exchange are on your right, just before the turnstiles. You are in **Future World** now and approaching its focal point, **Spaceship Earth** (it looks like a big golf ball). There's a ride inside, but you can skip it for now. And forever.

The iconic giant golf ball that is Spaceship Earth

Since it usually doesn't open until 11am, don't race toward World Showcase. Instead, walk past Spaceship Earth and the two semicircular buildings to your left and right (**Innoventions East** and **Innoventions West**) and turn left for **Test Track**.

After seeing how new cars are tested on banked curves, high-speed curves, with special brakes, without special brakes, over bumpy roads and in crash tests, you board a six-passenger vehicle (minus a steering wheel and brakes) and experience what you just saw. There are 65mph (105kph) straight stretches, hairpin turns and near-collisions. You will exit into a make-believe assembly line, a showroom for GM (General Motors) cars and then a gift shop.

Next head for **Honey, I Shrunk the Audience**. Located inside **Journey into Imagination**, this is a 25-minute presentation that begins with a brief pre-show before you step inside to watch Professor Wayne Szalinski, star of *Honey, I Shrunk the Kids*, demonstrate his latest inventions. The 3D special effects include mice invading the theater, a cat clawing at you, and then, after you are shrunk to the size of an insect, a giant kid picking you up.

In order to keep up with the competition, Disney has been adding rides that inject a burst of adrenaline. In 2005, **Soarin'**, which borrowed from Disney's California Adventure™ Park, opened. Here you'll sit under the wings of a hang glider, be hoisted 40 feet (12m) high inside a giant projection screen dome, then glide around California, all the while smelling

At Mission: Space you are as close as you'll get to blasting off without leaving Earth

pine forest, orange blossoms and the ocean. In October 2009, Epcot unveiled its newest attraction, **The Sum of All Thrills**, which uses the same kind of robot-arm, high-tech, simulator technology that Universal used on its Harry Potter ride six months later. Guests can design, then ride their own jet planes, roller coasters and even bobsleds.

Mission: Space is a high-tech, high-thrill attraction. Created in conjunction with former NASA advisors, astronauts and scientists, the simulated space adventure will launch you from a pulse-racing lift-off to a rendezvous with weightlessness. Exercise caution; it's very easy to get nauseous.

The remaining attractions in Future World don't offer that much. The only borderline attraction is **The Living Seas**, which begins with a short film and then takes a brief tram ride past an artificial reef and into Sea Base Alpha. The two-level aquarium is filled with moray eels, barracuda and bonnethead sharks.

World Showcase opens at 11am, but if you want to beat the lunch crowds, walk next door to **The Land**. This pavilion features **Living With the Land**, a boat ride that drifts past experimental gardens.

World Showcase

After lunch, walk to the **World Showcase Lagoon**, the start and end of a 1.2-mile (2km) circular walk. This half of the park is far more inviting, with native flowers and trees, entertainers, craftspeople and gourmet restaurants at nearly every pavilion. There is no right way to go, just visit those that interest you most. If you start counterclockwise, the first pavilion is **Canada**, highlighted by a reproduction of Ottawa's Chateau Laurier. The attraction here is *O Canada!*, an 18-minute, Circle-Vision 360-degree movie that puts you in the middle of Canadian prairies, cities, rivers and wilderness. Next, **United Kingdom**, with no movies or rides, presents street performances by an improv comedy troupe and a Beatles soundalike band. Many guests here prefer a pint and a meal at the Rose and Crown pub.

Just past the International Gateway is **France**, which has the most beautiful movie (*Impressions de France*), the most delectable pastries (Boulangerie Patisserie) and the finest gourmet dining (Chefs de France) at Epcot.

Morocco is next and, without a movie and ride, makes do with craftspeople, street performers, a restaurant and several stores. Next door, **Japan** follows the route of Morocco and adds koi ponds, rock gardens, a pagoda, a small cultural gallery and a very large department store with Japanese gifts.

The American Adventure is the halfway point and features perhaps the best show in the World Showcase. An audio-animatronic Mark Twain and Ben Franklin introduce America's historical

highlights in an inspiring, patriotic show. There is a busy counter-service restaurant next door, but unless you are starving it's best just to grab a snack from one of the many food stands.

The Neon Walkway at Epcot®

Italy is next. No rides or movies, just more stores, street musicians and a restaurant. **Germany** is the same, but its Biergarten features lively entertainment – oompah bands, yodelers and dancers who perform as you eat.

Although **Africa** doesn't have a complete pavilion, it's represented by street performers and a store. **China** is recognizable by the towering Temple of Heaven, which houses a Circle-Vision 360-degree theater showing a movie shot by the first Western crew granted access to previously off-limit sites. There is also a store and a restaurant. **Norway** has a 14th-century castle, Akershus; a gift shop filled with trolls; a restaurant; and the Maelstrom, an occasionally scary boat ride through a troll-filled forest, and the raging North Sea. The last pavilion, **Mexico**, has stores, two restaurants, and a boat ride – El Rio del Tiempo – similar to Norway's Maelstrom.

The park's grand finale is the fantastic **IllumiNations: Reflections of Earth**, a 13-minute synchronized symphony of fireworks and lasers. The big show kicks off at closing time and can be seen from anywhere in the World Showcase.

➕ 225 B2 ☎ 407/939-6244 or 407/939-7718 (for UK visitors); www.disneyworld.com 🕙 Daily 9–9 (Future World opens at 9, World Showcase at 11), but varies according to season; summer "extra magic hours" three nights a week (10pm–1am) 💷 See Which Ticket?, ➤ 48, for information on prices

EPCOT: INSIDE INFO

Top tips If you are a guest at Walt Disney World® Resort, **save Epcot® for Wednesday** when you can enter an hour earlier than everyone else and see selected Future World attractions.

■ Can't wait to see your snapshots? The **Camera Center** near the Entrance Plaza and World Travel in the International Gateway has two-hour processing.

■ A **Guest Relations counter** is next to Spaceship Earth. Stop here if you want to make reservations for dinner. Alternatively, call 407/939-3463.

5 Water Parks in Walt Disney World® Resort

With the Atlantic Ocean on Florida's east coast and the Gulf of Mexico to the west, why would you go to a Walt Disney World® Resort water park?

There are two good reasons: they are closer and cooler, and on a hot day they can be terrific fun. You may not have time to devote a full day to diving and splashing around, and if it's wintertime even the bright Florida sun won't warm up the waters much, but the water parks are a fun place to spend a few hours relaxing. At their core, **Typhoon Lagoon** and **Blizzard Beach** are roughly the same. Each is themed and has waterslides, lockers, a beach, a central lagoon, children's pools, snack bars and other concessions. On closer inspection, however, you'll find that Blizzard Beach is better for speed rushes and adrenaline-pumping thrills, while Typhoon Lagoon boasts a far superior wave pool and better overall ambiance. Families with small kids will want to spend their time at Typhoon Lagoon, as its lazy river and children's play area provide hours of entertainment for small ones, and parents can get a little downtime on the beach.

Toboggan Racers – an eight-line waterslide at Blizzard Beach

© Disney

It's best to bring essentials like toys, bottled drinks, snacks and towels, along with plenty of sunscreen, for moments between slipping down watery slides and the wave pool.

Typhoon Lagoon

The 56-acre (23ha) Typhoon Lagoon – perhaps the most attractive water park in the USA – is centered on the **Wave Pool**, which re-creates the appeal of the ocean by adding a sandy white beach and big waves. At twice the length of a football field, the massive pool generates 10-foot (3m) waves that ripple across its surface every 90 seconds. It's quite an experience – you hear the roar as the wave is generated far across the lagoon, then the screams and laughter as it approaches and people dive and run as it breaks above their heads. There are a number of islands along the lagoon's shoreline that break up the waves and provide calm and shallow inlets for small children to play. Less intense is **Castaway Creek**, where a very relaxing 45 minutes begins when you hop into an inner tube and drift on a lazy river beneath a misty rain forest and through caves and grottoes. Some of the most harrowing few seconds of your life may be on the **Humunga Kowabunga**, where you will reach speeds of up to 30mph (48kph) as you take a sheer drop on this very long waterslide inside Mount Mayday.

Blizzard Beach

Although Blizzard Beach is actually newer than Typhoon Lagoon, the water park feels outdated when directly compared, especially in the wave pool department. Blizzard Beach's version of the pool is the snowcapped **Mount Gushmore**, which spits out waterslides rather than lava. There are several different ways to get down the mountain, but taking **Summit Plummet** is the most fun. Riders sit directly on the slide (no tube or sled) and zoom down 360 feet (110m) at speeds of around 55mph (88kph) to the bottom. If you don't have the nerve to plummet off the summit take the slightly less speedy Slush Gusher or Teamboat Springs, which speeds down the mountain in a five-person raft over a series of waterfalls.

Castaway Creek at Typhoon Lagoon

Typhoon Lagoon
⊞ 225 B2 ☎ 407/560-4141; www.disneyworld.disney.go.com/parks/ 🕐 Daily 10–5, but varies according to season

Blizzard Beach
⊞ 225 A1 ☎ 407/560-3400; www.disneyworld.disney.go.com/parks/ 🕐 Daily 10–5, but varies according to season

6 SeaWorld Orlando

SeaWorld Orlando is based on the sea and its inhabitants, and man's relationship with them. Though there's no flash and thunder in the manner of Disney and Universal, this oceanic theme park is worth at least the better part of a day and probably longer. You'll find yourself getting an education even if you aren't aware of it.

Blue Horizons has something for everyone – acrobatic dolphins, soaring birds and amazing stunt actors

After winding your way to the toll plaza ($10), you will park and then be taken by tram to a seaside village where you can purchase tickets at one of three kiosks. Once inside, go straight ahead to the information desk for a park map and schedule of the day's shows. Take a moment to review show times and plan your day. Keep in mind that (a) SeaWorld's design involves backtracking; and (b) the major attractions are not rides but shows. Most shows' finishing times conveniently allow you about 10–15 minutes to reach the next performance venue. The best bet is a clockwise sweep of the park. Begin by passing through the park's version of Key West, where street performers are the featured attraction, and areas where you can feed and touch a stingray or a dolphin.

Rides and Shows

Manta, a world-first combined roller coaster and marine-life attraction, captures the speed, power and grace of the mysterious manta ray. Floor-to-ceiling aquariums give close-up views of rays, rare leafy sea dragons and thousands of schooling fish, then you can find out what it's like to spin, glide, skim and fly at speeds approaching 60mph (95kph) face down on a giant manta ray on steel rails.

Adding an ethereal twist to dolphin shows is **Blue Horizons**. With its Cirque du Soleil-style costuming and acrobatics, it's a must. Divers, flying gymnasts, leaping dolphins and whales, and a pleasing musical score make this 30-minute performance worthwhile.

Journey to Atlantis is a water coaster based on a battle between Hermes and Allura. It's great if you don't have to wait long, otherwise you may be disappointed by the lack of steep drops. Warning: you will get soaked either by the ride or by guests who fire water cannons at you when you float by.

SeaWorld's second coaster, **Kraken**, is named for an underwater beast kept caged by the Greek god Poseidon. This is the tallest (151 feet/46m) and only floorless roller coaster in Orlando. You go through seven inversions – including a Cobra roll, zero-gravity roll and numerous vertical loops and flat spins.

Continuing on, bypass **Penguin Encounter** and **Pacific Point Preserve** (unless you like penguins and seals). The show at the **Sea Lion and Otter Stadium** is fun, and you should arrive early to catch the excellent pre-show performance by the mime artists.

By now you should have covered nearly half the park. If time is tight, forget **Terrors of the Deep** but consider dining on Floribbean and Caribbean cuisine at **Sharks Underwater Grill**. The cavernous restaurant, with its underwater grotto, is reminiscent of the lair of a James Bond villain. Three tiers of booths and tables front five bay windows that expose a large aquarium filled with multiple species of sharks.

SeaWorld's exciting **Shamu** shows feature the park's family of killer whales performing awe-inspiring choreography set

Shark Encounter takes you through the world's largest underwater viewing tunnel

TICKET OPTIONS
Adults (10 and over) $74.99 plus tax, children (3–9) $64.99 plus tax. Validate your ticket before leaving the park and exchange it for an "Any Time" pass, valid for complimentary admission to SeaWorld for the next seven days. See Universal Orlando (▶ 76) for details of the Orlando FlexTicket.

Manta – a blend of close-up animal encounters and face-down thrill ride

to music. Although the trainers no longer work alongside the whales in the water, the shows are as popular as ever.

The park's **Animal Rescue & Rehabilitation Team** is on call 365 days a year, 24 hours a day and to date has rescued more than 18,000 sick and injured or orhpaned animals. Take a 90-minute behind-the-scenes tour to discover how the experts care for rescued manatees and sea turtles. You can also interact with a small shark, explore one of the hidden polar bear dens and touch a penguin.

✚ 225 C3 ☎ 407/351-3600 or 800/423-3688; www.seaworld.com 🕐 Daily 9–7; extended hours summer, holidays and weekends 💲 See Ticket Options, ➤ 72, for information on prices

SEAWORLD ORLANDO: INSIDE INFO

Top tips Perhaps the best way to wrap up the day is a night of entertainment at **Makahiki Luau** (tel: 800/327-2420). The evening begins with a welcome drink, a hula lesson, and the arrival of the Grand Kahuna. The family-friendly stage show includes sing-alongs and displays of fire-torch twirling.

■ **Discovery Cove**, next to SeaWorld Orlando, is a man-made creation of colorful coral reefs teeming with thousands of tropical fish, underwater ruins, tropical rivers and gleaming white sands. The big draw is the chance to swim and play with Atlantic bottle-nosed dolphins. Tel: 877/434-7268 for advance reservations; www.discoverycove.com.

■ If you are traveling with kids, you may want to **bring along bathing suits and towels** for the inevitable visit to Splash Attack.

■ **Aquatica™** is SeaWorld's whimsical, one-of-a-kind water park, just across the street on International Drive. It includes Dolphin Plunge, which will send you racing through an underwater world past black-and-white Commerson's dolphins, to tranquil and rapid rivers, and white sand beaches for relaxing.

Getting there From Walt Disney World® Resort, travel 10 minutes east on I-4, take Exit 71 and follow the signs. From downtown, head 15 minutes west on I-4 to the Bee Line Expressway (Exit 72), take the first exit on the right and follow the signs.

⑦ Universal Orlando

Universal Orlando is still a working movie studio, a point it goes out of its way to prove by incorporating elaborate big-city set designs as backdrops for its predominately blockbuster film-inspired and special effects-heavy rides. Although Disney is the most famous park in Florida, many argue Universal, with its impressive motion-simulator fantasy rides is less dated and more entertaining, especially with the new Wizarding World of Harry Potter themed zone. Universal is an all-encompassing resort with two spectacular theme parks – Universal Studios and Islands of Adventure – its own restaurant and club district and luxury hotel collection.

In a quandary where to go? If time limits you to visiting one movie theme park (Universal Studios or Disney's Hollywood Studios™), pick Universal Studios – it's more energetic, more creative and more fun overall. It had a rocky start, but the bumps have long been smoothed out and the rides are in equal parts exciting, terrifying, exhilarating, sickening and fun. Here's one way to approach it.

UNIVERSAL STUDIOS
There are no trams here, just two massive multilevel parking lots (write down your space number) and a moving walkway to take you to CityWalk. From here you can walk straight ahead to reach Islands of Adventure (➤ 79–82) or to your right to reach the ticket kiosks of Universal Studios. Follow the lane to your right, over a bridge, under an arch and, after buying your tickets, walk through the turnstiles and you're in.

You may now feel crowded by other guests, but the lavatories and lockers to your left give you an excuse to duck out for a moment. Guest Services is to the right and can help make dining reservations, provide foreign-language maps, hold items for lost and found, and care for lost children.

In the summer of 2007, the Blue Man Group, the surreal musical/comedy performers, premiered in their own theater on the former site of Nickelodeon Studios. The performance requires a separate admission price from the park.

Unlike other theme parks, sections here are loosely defined and may be difficult to distinguish. Just ignore the section names and blitz the park, hitting the popular attractions as quickly as possible. This will mean circling the park twice, visiting premier attractions on your first trip and picking up the strays and revisiting your favorites on the second loop.

Early Start
If you arrived early, you will notice other guests are heading left toward Twister…Ride It Out. Resist temptation, walk to the next corner, turn right and go to **Terminator 2: 3D Battle**

The Hollywood Rip Ride Rockit reaches speeds of up to 65mph (110kph)

Across Time. This attraction, based on the films starring Arnold Schwarzenegger, is guaranteed to jump-start your day. A demonstration of law-enforcing robots goes awry and triggers a high-energy, 100mph (160kph), 12-minute series of 3D special effects, filmed scenes and live action that ends in a very loud and chilly grand finale. Better than a night at the movies, this attraction promises to have you buzzing all day.

If you are hungry, when you exit turn left and grab a quick pastry at the Beverly Hills Boulangerie, or turn right and pick up a snack (ice cream, soft drink or sandwich) at Schwab's Pharmacy. You may not want to wait, though, since you can hightail it to the far end of the park to **The Simpsons** ride. Here you will take a virtual-reality trip with the dysfunctional Simpson family through the fantasy amusement park called "Krusty Land," home of the show's Krusty the Clown. Experience a side of Springfield previously unexplored on this hysterical, high-speed, almost unimaginable adventure. It replaced the long-standing Back to the Future: The Ride in spring 2008.

One more must-see is **Men in Black: Alien Attack**, an interactive ride through dark city streets where you fire a laser gun at aliens who pop up from unexpected places. The only way you know if you've zapped an alien, however, is a readout on your "training vehicle" console.

The Universal globe and archway mark the entrance to Universal Studios

COMBINED PASSES

■ **Four-park Orlando FlexTicket** – up to 14 consecutive days of unlimited admission to SeaWorld Orlando, Universal Studios, Islands of Adventure and Wet 'n Wild water park. Tickets are non-transferable. Adult: $189.95, child (age 3–9): $155.95.

■ **Five-park Orlando FlexTicket** – same as above, but includes admission to Busch Gardens. Adult: $234.95, child (age 3–9): $199.95.

■ **Orlando Value Ticket** – includes one-day each at Busch Gardens in Tampa Bay and SeaWorld Orlando. Adult: $99.95, child (age 3–9): $89.95.

Midmorning

With another must-see attraction you have hit nearly half the park. Based on the film, **Jaws** starts as a gentle boat ride on the waters of Amityville…at least until a shark (surprise!) breaks the surface. Even though you know the fish is fake and the explosions are rigged, several surprise attacks by this monster will scare you silly. Adding to the effect, the heat of exploding fuel tanks and crackling electrical lines mean things can become uncomfortably warm.

At the ride's exit, turn right and bypass the midway games that suck kids in like a whirlpool. Your goal should be **Earthquake – The Big One**, a seriously scary experience just a few feet down the street. An audience participation pre-show demonstrates how special effects were created for the film, after which you enter a subway train that rolls into a darkened station. It's no surprise when things start to shake, rattle and roll, but wait for the adrenaline rush when the attraction starts falling to pieces above, below and all around you. A definite stop worth waiting for even if there is a line.

A few blocks ahead, is **Revenge of the Mummy**. Entering an Egyptian tomb, you'll walk past hieroglyphics and artifacts and then step into a roller coaster that takes you deeper into the realm of the dead. What follows is a jolting, twisting, turning, wrenching, back-and-forth ride in the dark where you're subjected to an infestation of beetles, flames, smoke and fog. Caution: leave all loose items behind; they'll all be thrown overboard.

Macy's Thanksgiving Day Parade re-creates the excitement of this New York City tradition

You'll have fun at **Twister…Ride It Out** – the attraction that everyone else raced for earlier in the morning. After the pre-show, you will be ushered before a bucolic country scene. It all goes crazy when an ominous funnel cloud appears on the horizon. The tornado takes center stage and kicks off a catastrophic cacophony of flying cows, lightning strikes and wails from kids who find the action too real.

It's probably around noon now and you've circled the entire park (and missed only a few major rides). After lunch you'll feel like tackling the next section.

Midafternoon

Straight down the street from the entrance are two rides. The first is **Jimmy Neutron's Nicktoon Blast**, a virtual-reality ride where the boy genius is joined by a large collection of Nickelodeon characters, including SpongeBob SquarePants and the Rugrats. The ride features computer graphics and high-tech, motion-based seats to give you the sensation of zipping through a cartoon universe with a large assortment of characters. On the right, **Shrek 4-D** is an animated saga starring the cartoon characters and their vocal counterparts – Mike Myers, Eddie Murphy, Cameron Diaz and John Lithgow. When Shrek and Princess Fiona leave for their honeymoon, the ghost of Lord Farquaad interrupts their plans. This puts you in the middle of an aerial dogfight between fire-breathing dragons and includes a plunge down a 1,000-foot (305m) waterfall. Avoid these if you have a weak stomach.

At the exit, head past **Twister** and **The Boneyard** (a collection of old props from forgettable movies) to reach the many refreshment kiosks and concession stands along the way. Also, check the show schedule inside your park map, and you may arrive in time for several shows presented on this side of the park. **The Blues Brothers** (actually two actors who look like them) perform outside Finnegan's. In an amphitheater off the streets of New York, **Beetlejuice's Graveyard Revue** is a popular, though offbeat, show that features classic monsters singing Motown songs.

While in the neighborhood, check out **Disaster**. In this attraction you are part of the cast of *Mutha Nature*, a disaster movie. It starts with a fast-talking Hollywood casting agent choosing a handful of folks from the audience and giving them acting directions. Everyone then heads to the "set" – an incredibly authentic replica of a San Francisco train station – and gets on a subway train. Just as you are about to exit, the big earthquake hits the city. The tracks buckle, the station crumbles and hysteria erupts. It's pretty intense!

Down the street, past Jaws, is **Fear Factor Live**, a re-creation of the American TV program where guests face their fears (and forsake their humility) in a stunt-filled show that pays off with prizes.

On nearly the opposite side of the park, **Animal Planet Live!** is based on the popular network's programming. The stars here are incredibly smart animals that push the limits on the cute-o-meter. When you leave Animal Planet Live!, you will notice kids are lured to the left by **E.T. Adventure**, **Fievel's Playland**, **A Day in the Park with Barney** and **Curious George Goes to Town**. If you don't have kids, there is no reason to be here. If you do, you have no choice. E.T. is the most popular ride here, a fantasy trip to the alien's home planet that concludes with a personal greeting. Barney's is a sing-along show, where you will be impressed by preschoolers' knowledge of the purple multibillionaire's song catalog. If it's a hot day, don't miss Curious George, a super, soaking, splashing water attraction. Fievel's is a colorful playground where kids can enjoy things to climb up, slide down and crawl through. Not only does it give you a chance to rest, it helps train them for a prospective military career.

The Pharos Lighthouse at Islands of Adventure, with the Incredible Hulk Coaster behind

Dusk

Now is a good time to drop in at the last attraction. **The Universal Horror Make-Up Show** is a definite must-see. If you are a fan of horror movies, this will be like visiting the Smithsonian. If not, you will still get a kick out of the blending of comedy and creepy special effects.

You've done it all now – and hopefully gone off schedule and wandered into the numerous gift shops, snack stands, unscheduled shows and back alleys. After a few miles of walking, resting by the lagoon with an ice cream may be more fun than being attacked by a shark.

ISLANDS OF ADVENTURE

Maybe it helped that creative consultant Steven Spielberg offered his advice, because Islands of Adventure's rides, creativity and presentation give Disney a run for its money.

The five separate "islands" comprising Universal Orlando's second theme park are geared toward different areas of interest, so your agenda will vary according to the age level of your group.

Unlike at Universal Studios, the layout here makes it extremely easy to get your bearings and navigate the park. The entrance is the most colorful and exotic of any theme

park – a montage of architecture, landscaping and music from Asia, Africa, India and Europe that takes you out of Florida and into the heart of an adventure. In the plaza, as in every single square inch of the park, there is a contrived storyline: You are an explorer who can buy provisions before embarking on your journey. Just know that you can find film, strollers (pushchairs) and wheelchairs as well as snacks to get started.

The Hogwarts Express steam locomotive arriving at Hogsmeade Station

Marvel Super Hero Island

You are walking beneath an extension of the **Incredible Hulk Coaster**, which, unlike slowly accelerating roller coasters, has a 150-foot-long (45.5m) glow-in-the-dark tube that catapults you from 0 to 40mph (65kph) in less than two seconds. After being shot out of the barrel, the coaster skims over the water and twists through five inversions before the two-minute ride leaves you frazzled.

Buildings in this surreal land are affixed with comic-book labels. Look to your left for **Doctor Doom's Fearfall** that rapidly hoists you 200 feet (61m) into the air and drops you down again. You will probably never find a ride as exciting or as fun as **The Amazing Adventures of Spider-Man**. Even when the rest of the park is quiet, the line here is usually long – and for good reason. It combines the technology of *Terminator* and pyrotechnics to fool your senses and put you in the middle of a search for the Statue of Liberty. A strange storyline and a very long wait, but it's worth it just to

experience the grand finale – a 400-foot (122m) sensory drop. There's far more than this going on during the few minutes you are inside, but you have to see it to believe it.

Ahead, a bridge leads to Toon Lagoon, inspired by the Sunday comics. **Popeye and Bluto's Bilge-Rat Barges** is a white-water rafting excursion that contends with obstacles, including octopuses, and kids firing water guns at passengers from Popeye's boat. Ahead on the left, **Dudley Do-Right's Ripsaw Falls** is a water-flume ride that drops 75 feet (23m) below the surface of the water and into the TNT shack as the Canadian Mountie tries to save his beloved Nell.

Jurassic Park, The Lost Continent and Seuss Landing

Camp Jurassic is the next island and the park's halfway point. Overhead, **Pteranodon Flyers** is a ski-lift-like aerial ride – except that passengers overlook Camp Jurassic from beneath the 10-foot (3m) wingspan. At this island's premier attraction, the **Jurassic Park River Adventure**, you drift past docile dinosaurs before taking a wrong turn and encountering aggressive "spitters" and a T. rex – and now your only escape is via a very steep 85-foot (26m) drop. Around the corner at **Jurassic Park Discovery Center**, an interactive area helps kids extract the last scintilla of information about dinosaurs.

From here, the bridge crosses to **The Lost Continent**, an intriguing blend of myths and legends. Music of old England, Arabic tents and the Alchemy Bar set the stage, and the hypercool Enchanted Oak Tavern (inside a massive oak tree) is like dining inside Sherwood Forest (shame about the food).

Stop at **The Eighth Voyage of Sindbad**, the fabled sailor embarks on a stunt show that includes water explosions, fire dives, shipwrecks and pyrotechnical effects, all staged in a shaded, 1,700-seat theater. Before leaving The Lost Continent, look for the feet of the Colossus of Rhodes and you are at **Poseidon's Fury**, a show that starts with a water vortex and concludes with a battle between Zeus and Poseidon.

The final island, **Seuss Landing**, is by far the most visually appealing. Nothing is linear and every image you've seen in the books is presented here in marvelous 3D to put you inside some of the best children's books ever written. From the Hop on Pop Ice Cream Shop to the Green Eggs and Ham Cafe to the Caro-Seuss-el, the presentation is a perfect tribute.

One Fish, Two Fish, Red Fish, Blue Fish lets kids guide their Seuss-style fish up or down – depending on the instructional rhyme they follow (if they don't get it right, they get squirted by a flying fish). **A Hat-Full of Fun** is a trip through the classic *The Cat in the Hat*, with 130 ride effects and 30 animated characters including, naturally, the Cat in the Hat, Thing 1 and Thing 2.

The Wizarding World of Harry Potter

Universal's latest attraction, **The Wizarding World of Harry Potter**, is a themed zone at Islands of Adventure devoted exclusively to Harry Potter and his gang. **Harry Potter and the Forbidden Journey** is the centerpiece ride. Sitting on an enchanted bench high in the sky, following Harry on his broomstick, it takes visitors on a stupendous adventure through his magical world and creates the feeling of high-speed free flight. The animation and computer-generated scenes projected on a 360-degree screen are what make this ride truly exceptional – the enchanted bench is manipulated by a robotic arm that moves along a track as simulated objects fly past. Despite being the hottest new attraction since it opened, waiting in line for rides has never been so enjoyable – Universal has created elaborately detailed scenes to entertain the queues. In **Hogsmeade Village** you'll find dozens of shops selling Harry Potter products that have been created especially for the theme park; they are great collectors' souvenirs (check out the broomsticks).

Join Harry and his friends on the thrilling new Forbidden Journey ride

---

🚌 224 C4; ☎ 407/363-8000; www.usf.com or www.universalorlando. com 🕐 Daily: Universal Studios 9–8; Islands of Adventure 9am–10pm, with extended summer, holiday and weekend hours 💲 Expensive; parking moderate

UNIVERSAL ORLANDO: INSIDE INFO

Top tips The "Orlando Magicard" is free and will save you money on hotels, lodgings, car rentals and so on. You can get your free card at the Orlando Visitors Center, 8723 International Drive (Gala Shopping Center). You can also print one out online (www.orlandoinfo.com). The Orlando tourism office can also mail you a card in advance if you call 407/363-5872 or 800/897-5439. The center is open daily 8–7; ticket sales close at 6.

■ If you can swing it, stay at one of Universal Orlando's resort hotels (Portofino Bay and Hard Rock Hotel). You'll save hours with **special privileges** such as early admission to the parks, VIP access to the front of some lines, character dining, priority seating at restaurants and the option of an unlimited-access ticket.

■ Use the **Universal Express system**: Pick up a free pass at any kiosk and you can reserve a place in line, which allows you to see other attractions, have a meal or take a break. Now you just have to return in time to claim priority admission to the ride – a major time-saver.

■ **For a great shortcut**, follow signs to "valet" and for around $12 (double regular parking), you can park next to the main ticket booth. Not only is your car safer, it's much closer if you need anything from it during the day.

■ Many of the motion rides have **height requirements of 40 inches (1m)**. If you are an expectant mother, have a weak heart or a back condition, don't plan on riding any of the motion simulators or roller coasters.

■ All rides have a **"baby exchange area"** where, after standing in line, one parent can ride and then take over parenting duties so the other can ride without having to wait in line again.

Getting there To reach Universal Orlando from Disney, head east on I–4 about a mile (1.6km) past the International Drive exit. Take Exit 75A on the right, and at the light turn left. From Orlando, head west on I–4 and take Exit 74B to the right. Follow signs.

8 Kennedy Space Center

The Kennedy Space Center represents the most successful space base on earth. If you are even remotely interested in space travel, engineering, discovery, daring or heroism you owe it to yourself to see this place.

The **Kennedy Space Center Visitor Complex** (➤ 199–201) offers a combination of tours, artifacts, IMAX films and ingenious attractions. Less than an hour from Orlando's theme parks, this is where Americans were first, and have ever since been, launched into space. Departing from the bus loop, just outside the entrance area and to your right, coach tours simplify most of the complex, almost immediately giving passengers close-up views of the enormous **Vehicle Assembly Building**. Built to accommodate Saturn V rockets, the VAB is 716 feet (218m) long, 588 feet (179m) wide, 525 feet (160m) high, and encompasses 129.5 million square feet (more than 12 million sq m) – the equivalent of nearly four Empire State Buildings.

Another stop is the **Launch Complex 39 Observation Gantry**. From the top of the six-story structure, you'll get a Hubble-perfect view of the space shuttle launch pads.

Outside the **Apollo/Saturn V Center**, you'll see stands that are reserved for media and family members during launches. If you know when you'll be visiting, call ahead and request special passes that may grant you access to these seats – they offer a great view of the launch pads. Inside, the first exhibit is the **Firing Room Theater**, where the simulation of the launch of Apollo 8 pulls you into the drama of the program's first manned lunar mission. Until 1968, astronauts

A Saturn V rocket in the Apollo/Saturn V Center

had only traveled 850 miles (1,370km) from earth and now Apollo 8 was aiming for a lunar orbit about 250,000 miles (400,000km) away. The Firing Room contains the actual launch control consoles used in 1968, and the drama is heightened by audiotapes from the launch. You'll actually believe you're witnessing the real thing when you hear "3, 2, 1…ignition…lift off!" followed by a ground-shaking, window-rattling launch of a Saturn V rocket, visible in the sky behind you. The show exits to a magnificent hall where you'll encounter the biggest space souvenir of them all: an actual Saturn V rocket. It's longer than two space shuttles, 2.4 Statues of Liberty, nine 40-foot-long (12m) tour buses, or a football field plus 20 yards (18m). Also in the hall is the transfer van that ferried astronauts to the launch pad, models of lunar modules suspended from the rafters, moon rovers on lunar dioramas and actual capsules from Apollo missions.

The **Lunar Surface Theater** presents an emotional re-creation of the lunar module Columbia landing on the moon.

Take the bus back to the main entrance and check out one of two **IMAX films** (daily 10–5:40) offered with admission: *Hubble 3D* or *Space Station 3D*. The former is KSC's latest production and tells the story of the Hubble Space Telescope and how its creation changed the way mankind views the universe; the latter is a journey of discovery from Earth to the International Space Station narrated by Tom Cruise.

Outside the theater is the **Rocket Garden**, a collection of spare rockets and parts, while a few feet away, a museum of **Early Space Exploration** focuses on the earl days of rocketry.

Before you go, make sure you participate in the **Astronaut Encounter** (➤ 201). Anyone who has ever dreamed of traveling through space or wondered what "blast off" really feels like with enjoy this experience, where a real astronaut appears for a free question-and-answer session with guests.

At the end, head over to the **Astronaut Memorial** where the names of those who have died are inscribed on the 60-ton marble mirror.

➕ 221 E3 ☎ 321/449-4444 (general information and inquiries), 866/737-5235 (ticket reservations); www.kennedyspacecenter.com 🕐 Daily 9–5:30; last regular bus tour 3 hours before closing; closed certain launch dates
NASA Space Shuttle and Satellite launch hotline ☎ 800/KSC-INFO (572-4636)
Space Coast Office of Tourism ☎ 321/868-1126 or 800/936-2326

KENNEDY SPACE CENTER: INSIDE INFO

Top tips The Space Coast is an easy shot from Orlando via Highway 50 or the Bee Line Expressway. Just head east for about 40 miles (65km) and follow the signs. About 6 miles (10km) from the KSC entrance is the **Astronaut Hall of Fame** (daily 9–dusk) now a partner with KSC. This houses the world's largest collection of astronaut memorabilia and features hands-on activities, including a simulated moon walk, a chance to land the space shuttle via a video screen, and a contraption in which you can pull 4Gs.

■ A **Maximum Access Badge** is a two-day ticket valid for both the KSC Visitor Complex and the Astronaut Hall of Fame (adult $38, child $28).

At Your Leisure

9 Gatorland

Gatorland bills itself as the Alligator Capital of the World. It has earned the right, considering it is also one of Florida's oldest attractions. Here since 1949, it is now a breeding farm. About 1,000 alligators crawl around these wetlands alongside crocodiles, reptiles and snakes, showing their strength in shows such as Gator Wrestlin' and Gator Jumparoo. For a native delicacy, go to Pearl's Smokehouse and try gator ribs or gator nuggets, then duck into the gift shop for a sampling of old-fashioned Florida souvenirs.

➕ 225 D2 ✉ 14501 S. Orange Blossom Trail (Kissimmee), US 441 north ☎ 407/855-5496 or 800/393-JAWS; www.gatorland.com 🕐 Daily 9–5 💲 Adults: moderate; children 3–12: inexpensive

10 WonderWorks

This unusual building is completely upside down. Inside, interactive games geared toward kids (but equally appealing to adults) let you experience the winds of a hurricane or sit in a diner as a 5.3 Richter scale earthquake hits. Virtual-reality games and hands-on science exhibits round out this educational/entertainment experience. One price is good for all exhibits, all day, with an additional fee if you want to play Lazer Works, a laser tag game.

➕ 225 C3 ✉ 9067 International Drive, Pointe Orlando, Exit 74A ☎ 407/352-0411; www.wonderworksonline.com 🕐 Daily 9am–midnight 💲 Inexpensive

11 Ripley's Believe It or Not!

It's hard to miss Ripley's Believe It or Not! Just look for the bizarre lopsided building dropping into the ground. The "odd-itorium" is filled with camp, kitsch, gross and bizarre novelties collected from around the world by Robert Ripley – all strangely entertaining.

➕ 225 C3 ✉ 8201 International Drive, Exit 74A ☎ 407/363-4418 or 800/998-4418; www.ripleys.com 🕐 Daily 9am–midnight 💲 Inexpensive

Welcome to the oddest place in Orlando – Ripley's Believe It or Not!

🔢 Wet 'n Wild

This theme park is a maze of water-slides designed for the thrill of slipping and sliding. Shallow areas have been set aside for kids, but bigger kids looking for adrenaline-pumping action will want to hit Bomb Bay, Der Stuka or Hydra Fighter, a thrill ride that combines the exhilaration of a bungee jump with the power of a water cannon. Changing facilities and snack bars are plentiful, but you can also bring a picnic.

➕ 225 C3 ✉ 6200 International Drive, I-4 to Exit 75A ☎ 407/351-1800; www.wetnwild.com ⏰ Hours vary seasonally 💲 Moderate (half price after 3). Parking and lockers inexpensive. See Universal Orlando, ➤ 76, for additional ticket options

🔢 SkyVenture

If you'd like to experience a skydiving thrill without the hassle of using a plane and a parachute, drop by SkyVenture, just off International Drive at I-4. In essence, it's a mammoth blow dryer that places you atop a column of air to keep you afloat like a real skydiver.

After watching a training video and getting outfitted in a jumpsuit, pads, helmet and goggles, you sit around the glass-enclosed column and watch other would-be aviators step in and over the rushing winds. When it's your turn, you'll be amazed at how extraordinary it is that your body can float like a ping-pong ball and how extremely difficult it is to balance yourself without being blown straight into the padded walls. While it may sound easier than the real thing, the reality of staying aloft on a column of air can be difficult – but fun.

➕ 225 C3 ✉ 6805 Visitors Circle ☎ 407/903-1150; www.skyventureorlando. com ⏰ Sun–Thu 11:30–9, Fri–Sat 11:30–10. Reservations suggested 💲 Expensive (discount coupons available along 1-Drive or online)

🔢 Premium Outlets

The idea is that you can buy brand-name merchandise at discount prices because manufacturers are selling items in a low-overhead store. If you believe you can find a deal, check out the two malls, four annexes and more than 180 stores of this enormous complex. It is possible to get discounts of 30 to 60 percent off regular prices. Although this is just shopping, it has become a tourist attraction in itself.

➕ 224 C4 ✉ 4951 International Drive (northern end), Exit 75A (eastbound) ☎ 407/352-9600; www.premiumoutlets.com/ orlando ⏰ Mon–Sat 10am–11pm, Sun 10–9

Experience the thill of skydiving in the wind tunnel at SkyVenture

The beautiful red pagoda in the gardens of Lake Eola Park, in the heart of downtown

ⓕ Orange County Regional History Center

If you want to know what Orlando looked like before the Mouse, check out the local archives, which contain a large selection of historic Central Florida photographs, souvenirs and relics rescued when the original City Beautiful was dismantled in favor of what you see today. In 2000, the old county courthouse was renovated to become home to this collection, which includes exhibits telling the story of the area's natural environment, Seminole Indian population, early settlers, the cattle and citrus industries, the advent of tourism, Florida's Space Age and the arrival of Disney.

➕ 224 D5 ✉ Downtown at Heritage Square Park (Central Boulevard and Magnolia Avenue)
☎ 407/836-8500; www.thehistorycenter.org
🕓 Mon–Sat 10–5, Sun 12–5 💲 Inexpensive

ⓖ Lake Eola Park

Lake Eola Park is the beauty mark of downtown Orlando. In vintage postcards you'll see families and lovers walking hand-in-hand around Lake Eola or sitting beneath the stars enjoying a band concert. Decades later, not much has changed. It takes about 30 minutes to circle the park, but slow your pace and soak up the scenery or pick up your pace and pedal one of the charming swan boats out to the fountain. This watery work of art lights up at night and changes color schemes, making a dramatic backdrop for the amphitheater where you can see Shakespeare in the Park, comedy shows or orchestral performances.

At the south end of the park there are plentiful oak trees where families and lovers relax, and to the southeast there's a playground. Across the street to the northeast is the trendy Eo Inn, which features the equally trendy sidewalk cafe of the Panera Bread shop. To the west, convenient concession stands are open year round from 10:30–6.

➕ 224 D5 ✉ Downtown, Rosalind Avenue and Central Boulevard I-4 to Exit 83 ☎ 407/246-4485 🕓 Daily 6am–midnight 💲 Inexpensive

17 Thornton Park

A few blocks east of Lake Eola, Thornton Park is a small business/ residential district of 1920s homes, sidewalk cafes and casual restaurants, where Orlando's young professionals are creating a quasi-Coconut Grove. It's a great place to take a walk, relax with a drink, enjoy an evening meal and see classic Arts and Crafts homes and beautiful Lake Eola Park (➤ 87).

➕ 224 D5 ✉ Washington and Summerlin avenues

18 Orange Avenue

Downtown stores and nightspots pop up and turn over faster than hot pastries. The trendy restaurants and fine clothiers have been replaced by fast-food restaurants, tattoo parlors and nightclubs that cater to post-teens, although the pendulum is swinging back. Most bars are large and dark and serve beer, but may be worth visiting if you want to see how the locals socialize.

➕ 224 D5 ✉ I-4 to Exit 83, east three blocks

19 Antique Row Shopping

The North Orange Avenue Antique District boasts an eclectic array of antiques and collectibles shops, vintage clothing boutiques, art galleries, outdoor cafes and blue-collar bars. For several blocks south of Princeton Avenue, the shops display a wide variety of goods. If you are a collector, it's worth a few hours.

A must-see is Rock 'n' Roll Heaven (1814 N. Orange Avenue, tel: 407/896-1952), an awesome record shop with venerable vinyl disks and an assortment of collectible toys.

➕ 224 D5 ✉ Orange Avenue (between Princeton and Magnolia streets), I-4 to Exit 85, east one block to Orange Avenue, right ⏰ Daily. Many shops closed Sun

20 Harry P. Leu Gardens

If it's a peaceful afternoon and photo opportunities you're after, this is as good as it gets in the city. This 50-acre (20ha) garden oasis in the heart of Orlando features the Harry P. Leu homestead, oak-shaded scenic walkways, an orchid conservatory, the largest camellia collection in eastern North America and the largest formal rose garden in Florida. The Garden House, near the shores of Lake Rowena, re-creates a Southern manor home and offers a quiet place to relax and enjoy a romantic view.

Along the pathways you'll find a huge variety of plants, including beautyberries, bottle brushes, bromeliads, firecracker plants, crinums, dogwoods, flame vines, impatiens, sweet alyssum and violas. Throughout the year, they host special events including the Friends of Florida Folk Concerts and seasonal displays that highlight winter-blooming annuals.

➕ 224 E5 ✉ 1920 North Forest Avenue, I-4 to Exit 85, head east to 17/92, right to Virginia Drive, left about 2.5 miles (4km) ☎ 407/246-2620; www.leugardens. org ⏰ Daily 9–5, longer hours in summer 💲 Inexpensive

A lavender-purple passionflower (Passiflora incense) in Harry P. Leu Gardens

The Orlando Science Center

21 Loch Haven Cultural Center

A few blocks east of Antique Row is a museum and science center that, depending on your interest, can keep you entertained for a few hours or longer.

The 20,000sq-foot (1,860sq m) **Orlando Museum of Art** displays the works of nationally and world-renowned artists and frequently presents exhibitions, tours and classes. On permanent display is an intriguing collection of primarily American work – 19th- and early 20th-century American Impressionists; a gallery showcasing three centuries of American portraits and landscapes from the Colonial era to the early 20th century; the popular Art of the Ancient Americas; and contemporary art. Occasionally the museum welcomes high-profile traveling exhibits such as "Of Cloth and Culture II," featuring African textiles from the Norma Canelas and William D Roth collection, and "Currents in Contemporary Art."

Shows at the **Orlando Science Center** are particularly educational and entertaining, and appeal to curious children and intrigued adults. The highlight of the plentiful hands-on exhibits and experiments may be a pulley-system display that allows a kid to hoist a Volkswagen single-handed. A tour of the human body will have you entering **BodyZone**℠ through a giant mouth – you'll have to go there to find out where the exit is. **TechWorks** offers a chance to create imaginary landscapes using models, simulation and computers, while **ShowBiz Science** puts you in the middle of movies so you can hang off the side of a building, set the mood with lighting and learn the secrets of special make-up effects. If you're under 4 feet (1.2m) tall, you will enjoy **KidsTown**℠, a giant science-related playground. The **Crosby Observatory** has Florida's largest publicly accessible refractor telescope.

For an additional fee, you can take in IMAX films on coral reefs, space and the Lewis and Clark expedition.
✠ 224 D5

Orlando Museum of Art
✉ 2416 N. Mills Avenue, I-4 to Exit 85, head east ☎ 407/896-4231; www.omart.org ⊙ Tue–Fri 10–4, Sat–Sun noon–4; closed Mon and major holidays ⊘ Inexpensive. Parking free

Orlando Science Center
✉ 777 E. Princeton Street, I-4 to Exit 85, head east ☎ 407/514-2000 or 888/OSC-4FUN; www.osc.org ⊙ Thu–Tue 10–5; closed most Weds ⊘ Inexpensive; parking inexpensive

Stained glass in the Museum of Art

Farther Afield

The impressive neo-Gothic and art deco bell tower at Bok Tower Gardens

22 Bok Tower Gardens

For a half day of sightseeing, pack up a picnic and travel 50 miles (80km) southwest of Orlando to Bok Tower, in the middle of one of Florida's true treasures, the citrus groves. The spiritual beauty of this sanctuary, a National Historic Landmark garden, has been welcoming visitors since 1929. The centerpiece of the gardens is one of the world's greatest carillon towers. Housed inside the pink and gray Georgia marble and Florida coquina of this 205-foot (62m) bell tower, the bells will soothe your soul as you lie on the lawn or stroll the garden paths. The park hosts special events and has a gift shop, visitor and education center and cafe. You can also tour Pinewood Estate, a 1930s-style Mediterranean Revival home with French, Italian and Spanish antique furnishings.

➕ 221 D3 ✉ 1151 Tower Boulevard, Lake Wales, I-4 west to Exit 55; travel 28 miles (45km) south to Lake Wales and turn left at CR 17A (Burns Avenue) ☎ 863/676-1408; www.boktower.org 🕐 Daily 8–6
🎫 Inexpensive; under 5 free

23 Legoland

Cypress Gardens in Winter Haven has undergone a change and is due to open in late 2011 as the world's largest Legoland, featuring a mix of rides, shows, restaurants, shopping and other family-oriented attractions. While the 150-acre (60ha) Florida park will include Lego signatures like giant brick models and kid-powered rides, it will also incorporate some of Cypress Garden's most revered original attractions, including the botanical gardens and one of the old wooden roller coasters, into the new design.

➕ 221 D3 ✉ 6000 Cypress Gardens Boulevard, Winter Haven ☎ 877/350-LEGO; http://florida.legoland.com

24 Seminole Lake Gliderport

Well away from the theme parks and in a peaceful country setting, the instructors at SLG can take you aloft as a passenger or potential pilot. For between $90 and $150, depending on how long (from 20 to 45 minutes), a tow plane will carry you and your instructor to about 3,000 feet (915m)

where you'll get a sharp thrill when you detach from the tow plane and set sail – sans engine – for a soaring, diving, climbing adventure that offers a definite buzz and a superb aerial view of Florida countryside. Just ask and chances are you'll be able to take the controls.

➕ 220 C3   ✉ Highways 33 and 561 Clermont
☎ 352/394-5450; www.soarfl.com 🕐 Tue–Sun
(call in advance) 💲 Very expensive

25 Wekiwa Springs State Park

Few places in Orlando rival this park's natural beauty. It's full of opportunities to hike, picnic, fish, camp and swim. The spring-fed water stays a frigid 72–74ºF (22–23ºC) year round, but diving 15 feet (4.5m) down to peer into the gushing mouth of the spring is worth the goose bumps. Canoeing is a must and rentals are available just beyond the bridge (tel: 407/880-4110, inexpensive first two hours).

➕ 221 D4   ✉ 1800 Wekiwa Circle, Apopka,
I-4 east to Exit 94, left to Wekiwa Springs
Road, turn right, drive 4 miles (6.5km) to
park entrance on right ☎ 407/884-2008;
www.floridastateparks.org/wekiwasprings/
🕐 Daily 8–dusk 💲 Per car: inexpensive

26 Mount Dora

About 30 miles (48km) northwest of Orlando is Mount Dora. The town was founded by Northern settlers in the 1870s on a low rise overlooking the waterfront. Thanks to a local resident who knew the governor, a new highway was routed around the small town in the late 1950s. Although it delayed downtown commercial growth for around three decades, it preserved the village and eventually outsiders rediscovered the untarnished town. Resting on the shores of a 4,500-acre (1,800ha) lake, the soft hills, quiet neighborhoods and thriving shopping village perfectly capture a slice of small-town America.

➕ 221 D4

Mount Dora Area Chamber of Commerce
✉ 341 Alexander Street, Mount Dora
☎ 352/383-2165; www.mountdora.com
🕐 Mon–Fri 9–5, Sat 10–4

27 Central Florida Zoo

If you would like to see a collection of native Florida creatures such as alligators and black bears, along with an arkful of zoo regulars, drive 20 miles (32km) north of Orlando to Sanford and spend a couple of hours strolling the boardwalk through different types of Florida habitats to see 400 varieties of native and exotic animals.

➕ 221 D4   ✉ 3755 US 17/92, Sanford, I-4
west from Orlando, Exit 104, follow signs
200 yards (180m) east ☎ 407/323-4450;
www.centralfloridazoo.org 🕐 Daily 9–5
💲 Inexpensive

Canoeing at Wekiwa Springs State Park is fun for all the family

Where to... Stay

Prices
Expect to pay per room per night:
$ under $125
$$ $125–$250
$$$ over $250

See page 36 for general information on hotels and resorts.

WALT DISNEY WORLD® RESORT

⚜️⚜️ Disney's All-Star Sports, Movie and Music Resorts $$

Choose from sports, movies or music motifs at this trilogy of theme resorts inside the Disney resort. All three provide good-value, family-friendly accommodations that include perks like in-room pizza delivery (handy after a long day in the park).

➕ 225 A2 ⊠ 1701–1991 W. Buena Vista Drive ☎ 407/934-7639

⚜️⚜️⚜️ Disney's BoardWalk Inn and ⚜️⚜️⚜️ Disney's BoardWalk Villas $$$

The Atlantic Coast boardwalks of the 1940s were the inspiration behind this whimsical resort, located on Crescent Lake. The hotel spills onto an actual boardwalk – complete with old-fashioned vending carts and midway games – and the result is one of the most enchanting places on Disney soil. The lobby is filled with amusement park memorabilia, such as a model roller coaster, vintage posters and a fun-park-themed mural. Most of the rooms contain two queen-size brass beds and comfortably cozy furnishings; many also have balconies overlooking the lake. The villas range in size from spacious studios to three bedrooms, and most are equipped with kitchen and laundry facilities. The two facilities share a swimming pool.

➕ 225 B2 ⊠ 2101 N. Epcot Resorts Boulevard ☎ 407/939-5100

⚜️⚜️⚜️ Disney's Coronado Springs Resort $$

Near Disney's Animal Kingdom Theme Park, the Coronado borrows inspiration from Mexico and the American Southwest. The huge complex has three categories of accommodations: ranchos, cabanas and casitas (modeled on ranch houses), beach clubs and Mexican-style dwellings. The lobby and all the rooms feature Mexican tiles, earth tones and original art. There is a lake in the middle of the resort, and the pool is designed like an Aztec ruin, with a waterfall tumbling down the side of a pyramid. The one full-service dining option is the Maya Grill, offering good quality Mexican food; there is also an extensive food court.

➕ 225 A2 ⊠ 1000 W. Buena Vista Drive ☎ 407/939-1000

⚜️⚜️⚜️ Disney's Grand Floridian Resort & Spa $$$

This hotel is modeled on the style of the grand resorts in Florida at the turn of the 19th century. The spacious rooms continue the theme with papered walls, wood trim and stately bathroom fixtures. Many of the rooms have their own balconies. This hotel is billed as Disney's premier spot, so they have made an effort to truly excellent service. The public spaces are very pretty with paths winding through well-tended lawns, foliage and a lovely pool. In 1995 the property opened a full-service spa, making this the most luxurious choice on Disney property.

➕ 225 A3 ⊠ 4401 Floridian Way (off World Drive) ☎ 407/824-3000

Disney's Port Orleans Resort $$

You can see a working cotton gin powered by a 32-foot (10m) water wheel at this mid-priced resort styled after an antebellum plantation. The lodgings are set amid such Southern foliage as azaleas and magnolia trees. There's a mansion area with 19th-century Southern architecture and a rustic bayou area with faux swamp houses. The rooms, though on the small side, are still comfortable. The swimming area is called "Ol' Man Island" and is located in the center of a creek.

⊞ 225 B2 ⊠ 1251 Dixie Drive, at Bonnet Creek Parkway ☎ 407/934-6000

Disney's Wilderness Lodge $$–$$$

Disney even seems to have recreated the chill mountain air at this magnificent replica of a grand, turn-of-the-20th-century Northwestern lodge, complete with flickering lanterns that light the pine tree-lined entryway. The vast lobby has two authentic totem poles, Native American artifacts, a huge fireplace and comfortable leather Adirondack chairs and couches. The property, which really looks as if it's nestled in the wilderness, smells of pine, and the swimming pool is built into an enormous, albeit fake, rock formation. The rooms are comfortable and furnished in the Mission style; most have two queen-size beds. There is a restaurant, Artist Point (▶ 94), that specializes in food and wine from the Pacific Northwest; the Territory Lounge, a lively bar that celebrates the Westward expansion of explorers Lewis and Clark; and a lobby restaurant, Whispering Canyon Café, where kids help to fight off hostile bandits during dinner.

⊞ 225 A2 ⊠ 901 W. Timberline Drive (off Cypress Point Drive) ☎ 407/824-3200

Disney's Yacht & Beach Club Resort $$$

These adjoining hotels evoke the feel of a grand Victorian coastal resort. Disney's Yacht Club is a spacious wooden structure with comfortable furniture and a huge wraparound veranda, complete with rocking chairs. Disney's Beach Club is more casual but also takes full advantage of the coastal motif. The shared pool area has a natural-looking body of water that even has a sandy bottom, as well as a pool with real fish. The rooms are light and airy with two queen-size beds or one king-size. Many have good views of the picturesque lake. The Yachtsman Steakhouse offers prime aged beef, grilled to perfection. There is also a health club and a video-game arcade that has an attached ice-cream parlor.

⊞ 225 A2 ⊠ 1700–1800 Epcot Resorts Boulevard (off Buena Vista Drive) ☎ 407/934-8000

OUTSIDE WALT DISNEY WORLD®

Hard Rock Hotel $$$

The rock-themed hotel and restaurant chain worked with Universal to create this huge complex in Orlando. Within walking distance from the two theme parks, it offers dining and entertainment options on-site, along with upscale rooms with rock 'n roll legend-inspired decor.

⊞ 224 C4 ⊠ 5800 Universal Boulevard ☎ 407/503-2000

Hyatt Regency-Grand Cypress Hotel $$$

Just over the Disney border, this luxury property offers many wonderful amenities in an indulgent setting. It boasts a top-rated 45-hole golf course designed by Jack Nicklaus, 12 tennis courts, an enormous pool with waterfalls, and a lakeside beach that stretches for almost quarter of a mile (400m). The lobby displays an impressive collection of Asian art and has a tropical feel, complete with wildlife and palm trees. The rooms are elegantly appointed and they all have terraces. There is entertainment on the weekends in

Where to...
Eat and Drink

Prices

Expect to pay per person for a meal, excluding drinks:

$ under $15 $$ $15–$30 $$$ over $30

As part of the general push to attract more adult travelers, Walt Disney World® Resort has made an admirable effort to add diverse restaurants of high quality that will appeal to discerning diners. Virtually all the restaurants, however, do encourage dining with children and offer children's menus. In general, prices tend to be high, so choosing wisely is especially important if you are on a budget. The following choices have been selected for the quality of the food and the fact that they offer pleasurable dining experiences for all ages.

Any restaurant that accepts reservations is a hot ticket. For information and reservations, tel: 407/939-3463; www.disneyworld disney.gocom/reservations/dining/. For those not staying on Disney property (or for those who just need a break), Orlando also has a wide variety of restaurants.

WALT DISNEY WORLD® RESORT

Artist Point $$$

The Frank Lloyd Wright-inspired decor, like all replicas at Disney, is extremely well done at this restaurant, which specializes in the food and wine of the Pacific Northwest. The wine list is impressive in that many of the well-chosen bottles come from Washington or Oregon. The menu features specialty items such as elk, buffalo and ostrich. Certain dishes are soulful and tasty, such as the cold-smoked roast chicken; others such as the elk and rabbit sausage sound good but are ultimately disappointing.

🏠 225 A2 ⊠ Disney's Wilderness Lodge

California Grill $$$

A fantastic view of the Magic Kingdom Park is one of the main draws at this California-style restaurant atop Disney's Contemporary Resort. The clientele is a mix of locals and tourists. The menu runs the gamut from brick oven-baked flatbreads to sushi and sashimi to fusion entrées such as tempura bonsai tuna or grilled beef filet with tamarind barbecue glaze. Unfortunately the food does not live up to the glowing reviews. Perhaps

🏠 225 A2 ⊠ Disney's Contemporary Resort

the lobby bar, several full-service restaurants, including the highly rated La Coquina and Hemingway's. There is a full health club with a sauna and steam room.

🏠 225 B2 ⊠ 1 Grand Cypress Boulevard (off Route 535) ☎ 407/ 239-1234 or 800/233-1234

Peabody Orlando $$$

This hotel is most famous for the ducks that parade through the lobby each day. It's a sophisticated hotel in the middle of Orlando's tourist area. Rooms are decorated in Southern style – the original Peabody is in Memphis, which is where the strange duck tradition began – and are light and airy with attractive pale wood furnishings. The top floors are the concierge level and extra amenities are offered. There is live entertainment in the lobby each night, and there are several full-service restaurants, including the elegant Dux.

🏠 225 C3 ⊠ 9801 International Drive ☎ 407/352-4000 or 800/PEABODY

it remains a favorite because it was the first serious restaurant in the park. It does, however, have a good wine list of mostly Californian bottles. The atmosphere can be hectic but it's great fun too.

🕇 225 A3 ☒ Disney's Contemporary Resort

〰〰 Citricos $$$

This sophisticated eatery at Disney's premier hotel property, Disney's Grand Floridian Resort & Spa (▲ 92), was conceived with a citrus theme in mind, which is reflected in the pleasing decor that makes full use of attractively bright orange and yellow tones. The French food is some of the best to be had in Disney – thankfully the original dreams of a citrus-based cuisine have been abandoned. Dishes such as zucchini (courgette) and shallot soup with oak-grilled shrimp, or six-hour braised veal shank with orzo, are expertly prepared. There is also an excellent wine list.

🕇 225 A3 ☒ Disney's Grand Floridian Resort & Spa

〰〰 Flying Fish Café $$$

Huge gold-scaled fish-tail sculptures act as columns at this trendy seafood restaurant. The open kitchen turns out full-flavored American food that borrows much of its inspiration from the Southwest. A good way to start is with the buttermilk fried oysters, followed by potato-wrapped red snapper or seared yellowfin tuna with shrimp-basmati rice and Peking sauce. In addition there are simple New York strip steaks, grilled pork chops and homemade pasta. You'll want to stroll along the boardwalk after indulging in the highly recommended Vahlrona chocolate lava cake.

🕇 225 B2 ☒ Disney's BoardWalk

〰〰 Narcoossee's $$$

Located in a boathouse just a short walk from the lobby, this bustling yet cozy spot offers pretty views of the twinkling water outside. The inventive, mostly seafood, menu is highlighted by Maine lobster,

Fanny Bay oysters and wild Alaskan salmon. They also serve filet mignon as well as toasted coconut, or sautéed wild salmon with couscous. The wine list offers some great selections to complement the eclectic menu. If you're dining late, stick around for Magic Kingdom's fireworks show, visible high over Cinderella Castle.

🕇 225 A3 ☒ Disney's Grand Floridian Resort & Spa

〰〰 Portobello Yacht Club $$–$$$

It is easy to have a very good and reasonably priced meal at this Tuscan eatery if you stick to the selection of hearty pasta dishes – rigatoni with Italian sausage, crimini mushrooms, black olives, escarole and several more – or the pizzas. There are other traditional Italian dishes such as veal marsala and chicken Milanese. The restaurant is attractively styled with earth tones and nautical paraphernalia.

🕇 225 B2 ☒ Downtown Disney

〰〰 Rainforest Café $$

This enormous restaurant is worth a visit for the sheer spectacle, as well as the refreshing smoothies and fruity cocktails. In addition to the lush tropical foliage overhead, complete with replicas of tropical birds and gregarious gorillas, there are huge tropical fish tanks, playful elephants, a giant volcano and a "real" rainstorm every few minutes. The dishes are all named to fit the theme, such as "rumble in the jungle." The restaurant serves only environmentally ethical food, such as line-caught fish. Also a good vegetarian selection.

🕇 225 B2/A2 ☒ Downtown Disney Marketplace and Animal Kingdom

〰〰 Restaurant Marrakesh $$

The winding approach to this vast Moroccan restaurant, through a simulated souk, transports you to the Magreb. The dining room is adorned with Islamic mosaic tiles, tapestries and slim columns. The menu is a collection of

🕇 225 B2 ☒ Downtown Disney

favorites from the North African country, somewhat toned down for American palates, and features different types of couscous, traditional roasted lamb and fragrant mint tea. Belly dancers and Moroccan music complete the illusion. There is a small selection of Moroccan wines.

✠ 225 B2 ⊠ Morocco Pavilion, Epcot

⊽⊽⊽ Spoodles $$–$$$

The casual trattoria-like feel and superb Italian-inspired fare at Spoodles are very popular, especially with families. The open kitchen, complete with a wood-burning oven, turns out truly impressive dishes – oak-fired quail with seeded wild rice and truffle honey, whole roasted *loup de mer* (a Mediterranean sea bass that is flown in specially for the restaurant), and seared dayboat scallops with warm root-vegetable salad and pistachio brown butter vinaigrette.

✠ 225 B2 ⊠ Disney's BoardWalk

---

where a variety of choices (pork, chicken, beef, fish) is served in an equally diverse variety of ways (jerked, wood-grilled, coconut-crusted, etc.). Casual island-style setting and a pleasing patio with live tropical music. Don't worry about your order – just point anywhere on the menu for good food.

✠ 225 B2 ⊠ 8735 Vineland Avenue, Lake Buena Vista ☎ 407/938-9010

⊽⊽⊽ Bice $$$

Authentic Italian cuisine from Liguria is integrated with seafood dishes from around the world and served on tableware designed by Versace at this swanky restaurant inside the Portofino Bay Hotel. Other perks include views over the bay of the same name and a charming Mediterranean ambiance.

✠ 224 C4 ⊠ Portofino Bay Hotel, 5601 Universal Boulevard ☎ 407/503-1415

⊽⊽ Black Tulip $$

The cuisines of France and Italy collide at this cozy, fine-dining

---

⊽⊽⊽⊽ Victoria & Albert's $$$

At this intimate, formal and very expensive restaurant, diners are greeted by servers in period dress and presented with personalized souvenir menus. It serves good, classic Continental fare. The menu changes nightly and diners can choose from the regular six-course menu or upgrade to a menu that can include such luxurious items as terrine of foie gras, Russian caviar, lobster in Newburg sauce, succulent baby lamb, plenty of truffles and elegantly sinful desserts. The dining room is somewhat staid and stuffy, but there is a "chef's table" in the kitchen where diners can enjoy dinner behind the scenes.

✠ 225 A3 ⊠ Disney's Grand Floridian Resort & Spa

OUTSIDE WALT DISNEY WORLD

⊽⊽⊽ Bahama Breeze $

From the folks who brought you Red Lobster and Olive Garden is this Caribbean-style restaurant

---

restaurant in historic Cocoa Village, off Cocoa Beach. Try the pasta dishes or the steak au poivre at dinner; if you're visiting for lunch, perhaps before or after a trip to the Kennedy Space Center, there are lighter salad and soup options, in addition to the dinner menu favorites. And don't miss the fresh-baked bread rolls – crispy on the outside, warm and gooey inside.

✠ 221 E3 ⊠ 207 Brevard Avenue, Cocoa Village ☎ 321/631-1133

⊽⊽⊽ The Boheme $$$

This is an elegant, artistic restaurant at the Grand Bohemian hotel whose tag line reads: Seafood, steak, art, music. Very true. The Bösendorfer Lounge (named after the Imperial Grand Bösendorfer piano) is a great place for sipping a martini.

✠ 224 D5 ⊠ 325 S. Orange Avenue ☎ 407/581-4700

⊽⊽⊽ Hue $–$$$

One of the trendiest restaurants in Thornton Park, the artsy district east of downtown, Hue was named one of the "Best New Restaurants in the World" by Condé Nast *Traveler* magazine and appeals to a growing number of trendy diners. Creative spins on traditional items lead to "progressive American" entrées such as tamari-roasted duck breast with sesame hoisin sauce. The setting is warm, active and inviting.

🚹 224 D5 ☒ 629 E. Central Boulevard
☎ 407/849-1800

🍷 K Restaurant and Wine Bar $$-$$$

This creatively decorated Orlando gem has exposed brick walls and giant windows paired with deep red walls. The menu, which focuses on seasonal, fresh and, if possible, local ingredients, changes daily and is equally artistic. There is a lengthy wine list. Call ahead if you are dining on Monday; the only option on this day is the $35 prix-fixe menu.

🚹 224 D6 ☒ 1710 Edgewater Drive
☎ 407/872-2332

🍷 Miller's Ale House $

Directly across from Universal Orlando is this popular restaurant. Casual fare ranges from wings and hamburgers to crab legs and filet mignon. It has a full liquor bar and more than 75 types of beer.

🚹 224 C4 ☒ 5573 Kirkman Road
☎ 407/248-0000

🍷 The Palm Restaurant $$$

Part of the well-known, family-oriented Palm steakhouse chain, this place delivers all chops and cuts of steak prepared exactly as you specify, plus a selection of chicken, seafood and salad entrées. Dinner is served in the upscale, family-friendly environs of the popular Hark Rock Hotel (▶ 93).

🚹 224 C4 ☒ Hard Rock Hotel, 5800 Universal Boulevard ☎ 407/503-7256

🍷 Sonny's Real Pit Bar-B-Que $

Hearty portions of big food, including ribs, chicken, beef, pulled or sliced pork, corn on the cob, baked beans, coleslaw, fried okra and sweet potatoes – all the dishes that make Southern food comfort food.

🚹 224 D4 ☒ 7423 S. Orange Blossom Trail
☎ 407/859-7197

🍷 Taverna Opa $$

It gets rowdy at this airy Greek eatery inside the Pointe Orlando complex come dark when a belly dancer shimmying between the tables sets the festive mood, and as it gets later, don't be surprised to find your fellow diners kicking off their shoes and dancing on the tables. Lunch is a more casual affair, but whenever you go, expect a solid selection of tasty Greek classics with plenty of vegetarian choices.

🚹 225 C3 ☒ 9101 International Drive, Suite 2240 ☎ 407/351-8660

THEMED RESTAURANTS AND DINNER SHOWS

With the emphasis more on entertainment than cuisine, people usually come for the shows rather than the food. They are usually great fun and the kids will enjoy themselves, though some may be unsuitable for younger children. Call in advance, since show times can change.

Arabian Nights

A Bedouin show that includes a three-course prime-rib dinner while you watch 25 feats of horsemanship, including a chariot race.

🚹 225 B1 ☒ 3081 Arabian Nights Boulevard ☎ 407/239-9223; www.arabian-nights.com ⏰ Daily 7:30pm 💲 $$$ adults, $$ children 3–11

Capone's Dinner & Show

This show takes you to Prohibition-era Chicago, where you say a secret password and are ushered into Al Capone's Underworld Cabaret and Speakeasy.

🚹 225 C1 ☒ 4740 W. US 192 ☎ 407/397-2378 or 800/220-8428; www.alcapones.com ⏰ Daily 7:30pm (call for showtimes) 💲 $$$ adults, $$ children 4–12

Medieval Times

This meal is held with lords and ladies, noblemen and knights. You dine in a magical venue, with enough room to accommodate dozens of serfs and knights. There are two shows in peak season.

🔒 225 C1 ⌖ 4510 W. US 192 ☎ 407/396-1518 or 800/229-8300; www.medievaltimes. com ⏰ Daily 6 and 8:15pm 💲 $$$ adults, $$ children 3–12

Pirate's Dinner Adventure

Partake in a swashbuckling adventure on the high seas at this pirate-themed show.

🔒 225 C3 ⌖ 6400 Carrier Drive ☎ 407/248-0590 ⏰ Show 7:30pm 💲 $$$

Sleuth's Mystery Dinner Show

In the tradition of popular murder mystery evenings, guests at Sleuth's dine on a four-course meal while working on one of seven mysteries in one of several theaters.

🔒 225 C3 ⌖ 8267 International Drive ☎ 407/363-1985; www.sleuths.com ⏰ Times vary 💲 $$$ adults, $$ children

Where to... Shop

WALT DISNEY WORLD® RESORT

Few people have ever left Walt Disney World® Resort without a souvenir. Each theme park has a primary gift shop and there are lots more boutiques, gift kiosks and strolling sales hosts anxious to get your money. For the widest selection check out the Emporium at the Magic Kingdom, the Centorium at Epcot, Disney Outfitters at Disney's Animal Kingdom and, at Disney's Hollywood Studios®, Mickey's of Hollywood (with a special visit to see the Tinseltown memorabilia at Sid Cahuenga's One-of-a-Kind).

The main shopping area, however, is Downtown Disney, a three-part collection of stores, restaurants, a theater, discos, sports bars, comedy clubs, blues bars, speakeasies and a Western saloon, divided into the Marketplace, West Side and Pleasure Island. Depending on your mood and your age, you will have to decide which of the three suits you. You can order anything at Walt Disney World® Resort through the mail (although you pay shipping costs); tel: 407/363-6200 for information. If you are a resort guest, most stores can deliver purchases back to your hotel.

Marketplace

The tamest of Downtown Disney's trio is Marketplace, a pleasantly casual shopping village that includes 20-plus stores and restaurants. The rambling World of Disney dwarfs other stores, with the largest selection of Disney merchandise anywhere, ranging from a $2 candy bar to a $13,500 diamond-encrusted Pooh pin. There is also a huge LEGO Imagination Center and other toy stores, as well as stores specializing in resort wear, a glass shop and a kitchen supply store. Smaller themed stores are hidden down quiet lanes, and larger ones include Ghirardelli Chocolates, Disney's Days of Christmas, Pooh Corner, Mickey's Mart and the Art of Disney. Don't miss Once Upon a Toy, a huge store filled with Hasbro toys marked with Disney logos and characters.

West Side

On the West Side (▶ 100–101) there is Celebrity Eyeworks, with fashion sunglasses and eyewear from designers such as DKNY, Ray Ban and Calvin Klein, and Hoypoloi, a unique gift shop with handmade Judaica, wind chimes, sculpture and Zen products. There is also the Sosa Family Cigar Store; Magnetron (which is good for anyone who owns a refrigerator or a piece of metal);

Starabilias, which sells overpriced collectibles; and other spots for unusual gifts.

Epcot's World Showcase

Shop the world through the eyes of Disney at this international marketplace (▶ 67–68). Head to Japan for Hello Kitty and cute toys, to Morocco for a belly-dancer kit or the UK for Mickey Mouse shortbread and tartan shawls.

OUTSIDE WALT DISNEY WORLD®

Because Orlando is so geared to tourists, the shopping areas are easy to navigate by foot. Unlike many other cities, Orlando has outdoor shopping areas where visitors can easily spend a pleasant afternoon. You can find just about everything, from souvenirs to high fashion.

International Drive

International Drive stretches from Orlando to South Orange County and is most notable for the abundance of neon that adorns the strip. There are several mini-malls on or near International Drive.

Festival Bay Mall (5250 International Drive, tel: 407/351-7718) is the rare shopping mall that can present a 20-screen movie theater, along with a massive (and incredibly themed) sporting goods store, glow-in-the-dark miniature golf, a surf shop, a pub, and a skate park, as well as around 40 specialty shops and 7 restaurants.

Premium Outlets (4951 International Drive, between International Drive and I-4, tel: 407/352-9600) offers savvy shoppers savings of 30 to 60 percent in 180 stores with premium merchandise such as **Calvin Klein, Nike, Timberland, Tommy Hilfiger, Lalique** and more (▶ 86).

The Florida Mall

The Florida Mall, the largest mall in the tourist area, has more than 250 specialty stores, including a huge Sears, and is about 5 miles (8km) from International Drive (8001 S. Orange Blossom Trail, at Sand Lake Road, tel: 407/851-7234).

Mall at Millenia

The three anchors at this huge upscale mall – Neiman Marcus, Bloomingdale's and Macy's – are exclusive to Orlando. Among the 170 stores are Gucci, Brookstone, Cartier, Tiffany & Co and Orlando's only Apple store. Mall services include a concierge selling area attraction tickets, a post office and valet parking (take I-4 to Exit 78, tel: 407/363-3555; www.mallatmillenia.com).

Winter Park Village Marketplace

In one of the success stories of urban renewal, an old mall was bulldozed and a village put up in its place. It has a good mix of stores, restaurants, sidewalk cafes and a 20-screen movie theater. Evenings are very active and there's a good vibe here (take I-4 to Exit 88, head east 2 miles/3km to Route 17/92, turn right [south] and it's a quarter of a mile on your left).

Winter Park

Winter Park (grid reference 224 E6. Take I-4 to Exit 45 east, then left on Park Avenue, tel: 407/644-8281; www.winterpark.org) is an affluent suburb of Orlando about 40 minutes from Disney. The main drag is **Park Avenue**. It offers adults the most sophisticated assortment of boutiques in the area.

There are big names, as well as more exclusive clothiers. There are also other upscale chain stores (**Williams-Sonoma and Pottery Barn**). Many galleries selling unusual jewelry, gifts and artwork have opened right on Park Avenue or just off it on one of the many quaint side streets.

Of note is **Timothy's Gallery**, on Park Avenue, which sells jewelry, handmade clothing, ceramics and art books. There are some good restaurants and cafes, including a Japanese sushi restaurant, a brunch cafe and a good Italian eatery, making Winter Park a very pleasant place to spend an afternoon.

Where to...
Be Entertained

Orlando is full of entertainment options, whether on or off Walt Disney World® Resort. There is also a lively nightlife, with most clubs and bars clustered together in the various entertainment complexes. Since Walt Disney World® Resort governs itself, its clubs can stay open later than other local bars. If you drive yourself, get here before 9pm as the parking lot fills quickly. Disney operators can provide a list of shows and cover charges. For information or reservations, tel: 407/939-3463; www.disneyworld.com/entertainment/.

WHAT'S ON

Several publications provide comprehensive listings of what's happening around town. One of the best is the *Orlando Weekly*, a free paper that tells you what's happening every day of the week from music, to clubs, to theater, to sporting events, to galleries. The paper lists happenings that will appeal to a wide audience. If you want to go out and do anything from dancing to reggae to strolling through an art exhibit, this is your definitive source.

Running a close second is the *Orlando Sentinel's* Calendar section, an insert that comes in Friday's newspaper. With movie listings, a concert calendar, restaurant reviews and announcements for a slew of free activities, it's worth getting.

Orlando Magazine is a monthly that runs articles about various activities in the city. There are often features that revolve around restaurants or bars that will tell you what's hot at the moment. In the back pages of the magazine is an About Town section that lists various happenings around Orlando. While the listings are not nearly as exhaustive as those in the *Orlando Weekly*, it is a good selection of what's out there.

The Orlando/Orange County Convention and Visitors Bureau (tel: 407/363-5872) puts out an official visitors guide, which is a good source for information about the many attractions in the area other than Walt Disney World® Resort. The guide also has restaurant and shopping listings, but it does not give information on specific happenings such as concerts, shows or museum exhibits.

ENTERTAINMENT COMPLEXES

Disney Dinner Theaters
The South Pacific-styled Spirit of Aloha at Disney's Polynesian Resort is one of three park dinner theaters. The show features enthusiastic drumming, lots of stomping, rowdy dancing and fire-stick play by men and women in traditional Polynesian garb. At the Fort Wilderness Resort, check out the very popular, western-themed **Hoop-Dee-Doo Revue**. It features three totally goofy nightly shows with corny jokes, cowboy decor and lots of dancing and singing of American classic folk and children's songs like "Hokey-Pokey." **Mickey's Backyard Barbeque**, also at the Fort Wilderness Resort, is one of Disney's character meet-and-greets. Besides the beloved mouse, the show entertains with a country-and-western song-and-dance medley on stage and a fried chicken feast.

Disney West Side
Without resorting to hyperbole, the **House of Blues** on Disney West Side is the greatest club in the world. Juke-joint decor, folk art, hot music and great Cajun food

are presented so well it would be easy to stay the night enjoying a Mississippi Delta meal, listening to a singer in the restaurant and blues bar, grooving to live reggae in the lakeside Voodoo Garden, and wrapping up the night in the Music Hall, watching acts that include Brian Setzer, David Byrne, Steve Miller and Los Lobos.

Just as enjoyable is Cirque du Soleil® La Nouba. A multimillion-dollar theater was built especially for this show. With the highest-priced ticket in town ($50 for kids and up to $112 for adults), the show – a fantastical circus extravaganza that combines breathtaking acrobatics with New Age music, contortionists and impressive production values – is worth every penny. Reserve early to get better seats. Call for tickets and show times (tel: 407/939-7600).

Across the walk, DisneyQuest is a five-floor video/virtual-reality arcade filled with cutting-edge computer games, team video sports and a virtual jungle cruise. It's fairly expensive (about $35 for all-day admission; $29 for children 3–9) so save it for a rainy day.

Disney's BoardWalk

This is another pleasant entertainment destination. There is an ESPN Club for sports fans, the Big River Grille & Brewing Works microbrewery, and a few stores and restaurants. Admission to the BoardWalk is free, but there may be cover charges for certain activities.

Universal Studios CityWalk

Constructed in 1999 as a bridge between Universal Orlando's two theme parks, CityWalk (grid reference 228 C4; 6000 Universal Boulevard, off I-4 or International Drive, Exit 74A Westbound, 75A Eastbound; tel: 407/224-2691; www.citywalkorlando.com; daily 11am–2am) is the place to be in the resort after dark. The entertainment complex features a mix of restaurants, bars, dance clubs, performing arts venues, movie theaters, shops, a carousel and even a fountain for kids to splash in, all clustered along a narrow, well-landscaped pedestrian mall. It is packed virtually every night with a crowd as diverse as its entertainment attractions – you'll find teenagers and adults on dates, families with kids and plenty of partying 20- to 40-somethings who have come specifically for the themed restaurants and clubs, many of which crank out live music.

Try Bob Marley – A Tribute to Freedom for Jamaican-inspired cooking and reggae music in a space modeled after Marley's Kingston home. Jimmy Buffett's Margaritaville is another fun option. Its three bars are done up to resemble the king of boat music's most popular balmy beach ballads. It serves a full menu and has live music after 10pm nightly.

If you've dreamed of being a rock star, or you just like singing your heart out in front of an audience, head to CityWalk's Rising Star for a dose of karaoke to live music on stage. It also runs talent contests. Inside a huge space designed to look like a retro dance hall is CityWalk's main dance club, The Groove. Come here to rock out to well-loved sounds from the 1970s and 1980s, and shake your hips to a backdrop of sleek blue neon walls.

If you only want to visit one club you can pay a cover charge (between $5 and $8) at the door. But if you plan to jump between any of the places mentioned above, buy a CityWalk Party Pass for $12, which offers unlimited access to all the bars and clubs.

For less alcohol-oriented entertainment, catch a performance by Blue Man Group (tel: 407-224-2691; tickets from $60). The show is a wacky, high-energy, multisensory experience. It stars three blue-painted, bald men performing crazy circus antics, dancing and playing percussion while hurling everything from paintballs to marshmallows off the stage at the audience. Beware of sitting in the "poncho section" up front or volunteering to participate.

The gigantic **Hard Rock Live Orlando** (tel: 407/351-5483; www.hardrocklive.com) is an alternative. It books some fairly big-name rock bands and comedy acts and shows cost between $25 and $50 depending on who is playing.

AMC Universal Cineplex offers 20 wall-to-wall screens playing the latest blockbusters and a concession stand that sells beer and wine along with popcorn, candy and soda. You can even arrange a movie-and-meal deal for $25.

Pointe Orlando

Pointe Orlando (grid reference 225 C3; tel: 407/248-2838; www.pointeorlando.com), near the

Convention, is a large shopping complex with more than 40 stores (jewelry, books, clothing, etc.) as well as an abundance of dining options (The Capital Grille, Tommy Bahama's Restaurant Bar) and entertainment venues (BB King's Blues Club, Improv Comedy Club). It had a welcome face-lift in 2006.

Florida has become a major destination for sports fans eager to see baseball players in spring training, basketball and ice hockey. While Orlando has lagged behind other cities such as Tampa and Miami in the sports department, it is finally catching up and offers the avid fan ample entertainment.

The Orlando Magic

The only professional sports franchise in Orlando, basketball team the **Orlando Magic** (grid reference 224 D5; Orlando Arena, 600 W. Amelia Street, between I-4 and

Parramore Avenue; tel: 407/849-2020; www.orlandomagic.com) continue to harbor high hopes for the playoffs.

Disney's Wide World of Sports™ Complex

Check out the events at Disney's Wide World of Sports™ Complex (grid reference 224 A1; tel: 407/828-3267) and you will find plenty to watch – everything from soccer and beach volleyball matches to tennis, cycling and rugby games. During spring training the facility is home to the Atlanta Braves. The team plays its spring training games before Disney spectators. There is also the interactive **NFL Experience**, which allows budding football stars to try passing, catching and kicking field goals.

Golf

Considering Florida is home to more golf courses than most other states, it should come as no surprise that Floridians take the game very

seriously. You are never far from a good golf course in Florida. Unfortunately, many of the best courses are associated or attached to exclusive resorts and access is granted only to registered guests.

There are 125 courses in and around Orlando. Disney maintains the largest number of top-quality golf courses (99 holes) in the area; to find out about them tel: 407/WDW-GOLF (939-4653) or 407/824-2270. The meticulously maintained, 18-hole championship courses on Disney property are the **Lake Buena Vista Course**, the **Osprey Ridge Course**, the **Eagle Pines Course**, the **Palm Course** and the **Magnolia Course**.

Every October, Disney hosts the **National Car Rental Golf Classic** tournament.

Fortunate guests at the **Hyatt Regency-Grand Cypress Hotel** (▶ 93–94) have access to 45 holes designed by Jack Nicklaus. For more courses, check www.orlandogolf.com.

Miami and the South

Getting Your Bearings

The only small thing about South Florida is the distance
between destinations. Everything else – from Miami's
ethically diverse, vivacious spirit to alligators in the
Everglades, glass-bottom boats under which zebra-
striped fish swim in the laidback Keys to the mansions
of Palm Beach – feels supersized.

If you only have time to explore one part of Florida, head
for the south, starting with Miami, the unofficial North
American capital of the Latin world. Swaying proudly
to its multilingual beat, this wonderful art deco city
is like no place on earth. In many neighborhoods
Spanish is spoken before English, in others French or
Portuguese. The city is a pan-Latin melting pot that's
more ethnically diverse than any Central or South
American city.

Miami is more than culturally intriguing,
it's also one of America's most beautiful urban
beach destinations – and not just because of its
architecture or the sparkle of the warm turquoise
sea. The people here are also known for their
model good looks. Whether you're sipping on
a café con leche (Cuban coffee with milk),
driving the A1A across Biscayne Bay at sunset
or checking out South Beach's after-dark
scene, Miami is a sizzling seductress. Don't
get lost in the magic for too long as there is
just so much more to see.

Head down to the laidback Keys – a
palm-fringed paradise. The water is as
clear as the silver rum the local's love,
and fish of all sizes, shapes and colors
can be spotted from glass-bottom
boats or while snorkeling or
diving on the continent's largest
coral reef system. Fishing
is another favorite local
pastime. This dreamy
string of tropical
islands is also home
to some of America's

**Page 103
(left to right):
Ocean Drive,
SoBe; the
Fontainebleau
hotel, Miami
Beach; SoBe
night scene**

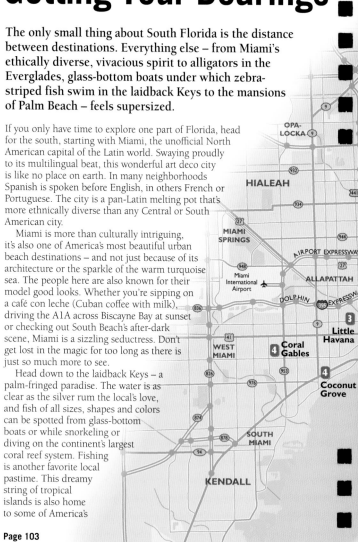

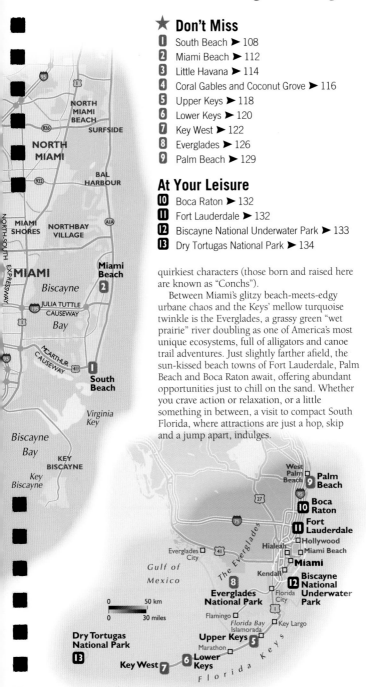

★ Don't Miss

At Your Leisure

quirkiest characters (those born and raised here are known as "Conchs").

Between Miami's glitzy beach-meets-edgy urbane chaos and the Keys' mellow turquoise twinkle is the Everglades, a grassy green "wet prairie" river doubling as one of America's most unique ecosystems, full of alligators and canoe trail adventures. Just slightly farther afield, the sun-kissed beach towns of Fort Lauderdale, Palm Beach and Boca Raton await, offering abundant opportunities just to chill on the sand. Whether you crave action or relaxation, or a little something in between, a visit to compact South Florida, where attractions are just a hop, skip and a jump apart, indulges.

In Five Days

If you're not quite sure where to begin your travels, this itinerary recommends a practical and enjoyable five days in Miami and the South, taking in some of the best places to see using the Getting Your Bearings map on the previous pages. For more information see the main entries.

Day 1

Morning
Begin in **1 South Beach** (➤ 108–111), with a leisurely breakfast at the News Cafe (➤ 138), a neighborhood institution with fabulous people-watching. Walk off breakfast strolling along the **Promenade** (➤ 108–109) and through the **Art Deco Historic District** (➤ 109–110).

Afternoon
In the afternoon, rest and enjoy some people-watching at South Beach's (SoBe's) **Lummus Park** (➤ 109). As SoBe forms the southern end of **2 Miami Beach** (➤ 112–113), which runs north through the city and beyond, it makes sense to explore this next. Head to the **Mid-Beach** boardwalk first and soak up the atmosphere before enjoying a cooling swim. As evening sets in, grab dinner back in SoBe, at one of the ultra-chic restaurants on Ocean Drive.

Day 2

Morning
Rise early and head straight for **3 Little Havana** (➤ 114–115), where you can wake up with a cup of strong Cuban coffee from one of the bustling sidewalk cafes. After exploring the epicenter of Cuban Miami, head south to the genteel, European-style planned villages of **4 Coral Gables and Coconut Grove** (➤ 116–117) to swim in the spring-fed waters of the **Venetian Pool** (above).

Evening
Return to **South Beach**, home to one of America's hottest après-dark club scenes (only Los Angeles and New York can compete) after sunset, and spend the night shaking your hips to a new style of Latin dance or chilling with a mojito and model pout at one of the ultra-swanky, red-rope lounges.

Day 3

Morning
Bid Miami goodbye and head south to the Keys. **John Pennekamp Coral Reef State Park** in the **5 Upper Keys** (left; ➤ 118–119) should be your first destination. Take a glass-bottom boat trip or, better still, jump into the turquoise sea and view the stunning fish and coral through a snorkel mask.

Afternoon
Back on shore, have a true Keys lunch of conch fritters and fries at Alabama Jack's (tel: 305/248-8741). After lunch keep driving south to the **6 Lower Keys** (➤ 120–121) and one of the only good beaches on this string of tropical islands: **Bahia Honda State Park** (➤ 121).

Evening
Try to arrive in the most playful and wacky isle of them all, **7 Key West** (➤ 122–125) before dark. Head straight for **Mallory Square** (➤ 123) for the famous nightly sunset celebration ritual – its quirky pageantry embodies Key West's one-of-a-kind spirit. Afterward, a cruise of the bars down **Duval Street** (➤ 124) is mandatory.

Day 4

Morning
It's a full day drive from Key West back to the Florida mainland, where your next destination, the Everglades, awaits.

Evening
Break up the trip with a night in **Key Largo** (➤ 118), sleeping beneath the sea at **Jules' Undersea Lodge** (➤ 118).

Day 5

Morning
Explore the dynamic ecosystem of the **8 Everglades** (right; ➤ 126–128) in the morning, paddling through the swamp in a canoe looking for alligators.

Afternoon
Drive north to **9 Palm Beach** (➤ 129–131) when you're finished. One of America's wealthiest communities, it's home to million-dollar mansions and a sun-kissed strip of sand. Window-shop for haute couture on swanky Worth Avenue, take a dip in the Atlantic, then have dinner at the Breakers (➤ 136). This enigmatic center of Palm Beach's social scene is the perfect spot to end a successful South Florida vacation.

⓪ South Beach

Miami's most seductive neighborhood, South Beach (SoBe) is a playful, sexy beauty queen, all turquoise-hued hair and pale sandy skin, wearing an art deco crown. With a taste for gourmet fusion food and creative fruit, herb and alcohol infusions served at swanky restaurants and designer bars, and legendary for its ultra-hot, after-dark club scene, its legion of beautiful residents and magnificent, one-of-a-kind architecture, SoBe makes falling in love all too easy.

It's so easy in fact, that it's not uncommon for tourists to arrive in South Beach with the idea of strolling along the beach, grabbing a meal and maybe staying the night, then falling so hard that a week later they're still checked in at the same hotel. It isn't that Miami Beach's southern end – between 5th and 21st Streets, and universally known as South Beach – is so large it warrants a week's exploration (although to hit every bar and club in SoBe could take months), it's simply everything about the destination is so exciting it's hard to see the point in leaving.

Ocean Drive is SoBe's main drag

The Promenade and Ocean Drive

Fashion photographers and Hollywood location scouts have been obsessed with this dazzling 10-block strip of sea, sand and promenade for decades now. This is the South Beach featured on the pages of *Vogue* and *Marie Claire*, as famous for stealing the scene in movies and magazines as it is for people-watching, celebrity-spotting and its Caribbean colored water. The beach running along here is known as **Lummus Park**, and this is where Miami's beautiful people make a beeline on the weekends for a spot of swimming in the turquoise sea, sunning on the china-white sand or playing beach volleyball. Running parallel to the beach for 10 blocks, between 5th and 15th streets, the **Promenade** is another iconic Miami image, filled with lithe, tanned rollerblading, jogging and dog-walking locals on weekends, and a favorite location for early-morning fashion shoots.

    Ocean Drive, on the promenade's opposite side, is America's most legendary cruising strip, an integral part of Miami's unique spirit. Here you can watch an endless, entertaining procession pass by – classic cars and convertibles driven by muscled young men in designer swimwear with leggy models riding shotgun, celebrities trying to go incognito by hiding behind oversized sunglasses, and celebrity wannabes, dressed to the nines to match the stars, hiding nothing. The experience is made even more surreal by the rainbow-colored, art deco skyline, which adds an extra layer beyond Ocean Drive to this multicolored scene photographers and filmmakers so love to memorialize.

Pastel-colored art deco buildings are a feature of this area

Art Deco Historic District

In the early 1980s, the vintage hotels along South Beach were run down, but dedicated preservationists rescued them from

demolition, and SoBe's Art Deco Historic District, between the Atlantic Ocean and Lenox Avenue on the east and west, and 6th Street and 23rd Street-Dade Boulevard on the south and north, became the first 20th-century district to be named on the National Register of Historic Places.

Today, more than 1,000 meticulously preserved, ice-cream-colored buildings with palm leaf motifs and opaque glass are on the roll. In the old beach patrol headquarters, one of the neighborhood's most impressive art deco buildings doubles as the **Art Deco District Welcome Center**. It sells postcards, posters and reproduction deco accessories. You can book guided walking tours ($20) here, which offer an excellent introduction to South Beach's layout and history.

SoBe's art deco buildings embrace a number of different styles, which have changed with the decades. The 1950s were known for MiMo, an acronym for "Miami Modern," which has a space-age, grandiose feel. Mediterranean revival is another popular style, and a good place to see it is on Espanola Way Promenade. Built as the entertainment complex for a long-gone hotel, this is where the young Desi Arnaz introduced the conga to America and Al Capone once ran a casino. Today the lovely, century-old, rose and cream, Spanish-style terra-cotta and cobbled arcade hosts galleries, boutiques and cafes galore. Try to visit on Friday through Sunday when it becomes a venue for a collection of flea-market merchants with a big open-air craft market.

Ocean Drive is lined with restaurants, cafes, bars and hotels

Lincoln Road Mall

An elongated pedestrian-only boulevard from Washington Avenue to Alton Road, Lincoln Road Mall is South Beach's cultural heart and center of Miami's see-and-be-seen beautiful people scene, filled with galleries, restaurants and cafes. The alfresco mall pays tribute to another famous kind of art deco architecture, the loopy, neo-baroque South Beach style, partially fathered by Morris Lapidus, who designed several buildings between the 5th and 11th blocks of the mall, including the strangely impressive Colony Theater.

The Sunday Flea Market at Lincoln Road Mall

In the middle of the mall, the creative **ArtCenter/South Florida** is worth visiting to visualize South Beach's artistic hub. Established by a small but forward-thinking group of artists in 1984, the compound is home to 52 artists' studios, many of which are open to the public, and it runs a variety of classes and lectures (check the website for details of fees). A farmers' market dominates the mall on Sundays, while an antiques and collectibles market joins in on the second and fourth Sunday of each month.

➕ 226 C3

Art Deco District Welcome Center
✉ 1001 Ocean Drive ☎ 305/531-3484; www.mdpl.org ⏰ Daily 11–6 🎟 Free

ArtCenter/South Florida
✉ 924 Lincoln Road ☎ 305/674-8278; www.artcentersf.org 🎟 Free

---

SOUTH BEACH: INSIDE INFO

Top tips Look for **parking garages** on Collins Avenue at 7th and 13th streets, on Washington Avenue at 12th Street, and west of Washington at 17th Street. If you park on the street, feed the meter or risk a ticket.
- Drop by Lincoln Road Mall's farmers' market on Sundays for **beach picnic fare** to go.
- Crimes against tourists have dropped significantly, but don't be careless. **Avoid back streets** and areas away from the central tourist areas.

Hidden gem Don't miss a visit to the **Delano** (1685 Collins Avenue). A weirder hotel you will never see. Walk back to the pool area, which is open to the public, and you'll feel you have traveled through a looking glass – not surprising considering the *Alice in Wonderland*-inspired surrealism.

2 Miami Beach

South Beach is just the beginning, the southern end of Miami Beach, that long stretch of pearly white sand and turquoise surf running the length of the city and beyond. Exclusive of SoBe, the northern end of Miami Beach is split into Mid-Beach and North Beach. From ethnic diversity to opulent luxury, this neighborhood epitomizes Miami's materialistic but multiracial soul that is altogether fascinating to explore.

Miami Beach is home to a truly eclectic, multicultural mix of residents. Where else on the planet can you grab a plate of *lox y arroz con moros* (salmon with rice and beans) at a restaurant catering equally to Orthodox Jews and South American Catholics, located just blocks away from Miami's most legendary exclusive hotel – the Fontainebleau?

Mid-Beach

Mid-Beach is where the city's large Jewish population sleeps, eats and plays. Arthur Godfrey Road (41st Street) is the heart of the scene, a long shopping drag where you can pop into a kosher sushi restaurant in true multicultural Miami fashion. Get a feel of the atmosphere by strolling down the boardwalk, where Orthodox Jews in yarmulkes and headscarves mingle with joggers and bikini-clad sunbathers. Here you can properly enjoy the beach and take a dip in the water. Unlike at South Beach, where the scene is all about looking, in Mid-Beach people actually swim.

North Beach

Just north of Mid-Beach's heart is Miami's most iconic hotel, the **Fontainebleau Miami Beach**. Created in 1954 by Morris Lapidus, a well-known Miami design master, it's a crowning example of Modern Miami (MiMo) architecture, the space-age design fad in 1950s Miami. This French provincial masterpiece on 44th Street, across from the beach, is a commanding place, with 1,200 over-the-top rooms, and has recently undergone an astonishing $1 billion face-lift. It's a celebrity favorite, as popular today as it was when director Brian De Palma used it as the setting for Al Pacino's infamous cocaine and killing spree scene in *Scarface*. From the masterful trompe l'oeil mural on the southern exterior, painted over an eight-week period by Edwin Abreu and designed by Richard Hass, to the lagoon-style water park out back and the massive

---

MIAMI BEACH OR SOUTH BEACH: WHAT'S THE DIFFERENCE?
Technically anything north of the 20s (numbered streets are referred to as decades here) is considered Miami Beach, and anything south is South Beach, although locals will often split northern Miami Beach into further subsections: Mid-Beach starts in the 40s, and North Beach begins in the 70s.

The iconic Fontainbleau hotel has appeared in many films over the years

lobby's dizzying stairway to nowhere, everything about the iconic hotel is a grand reflection of Miami's past.

Next door, the **Eden Roc** resort (► 135), Lapidus' second ground-breaking masterpiece, offers another fine example of MiMo architecture and celeb-spotting possibilities. The hangout for the 1960s Rat Pack, including Frank Sinatra, Dean Martin, Sammy Davis Jr and other lesser-known hangers-on, today the Eden Roc has reopened following extensive renovation and recently debuted in an episode of the hit American MTV series about this century's Rat Pack, *The Hills*. It's popular with the young Hollywood crowd for its sweet rooms and cabana pool scene.

➕ 226 C4

Fontainebleau Miami Beach
✉ 4441 Collins Avenue ☎ 305/538-2000, 800/548-8886;
www.fontainebleau.com

Eden Roc Renaissance Miami Beach
✉ 4525 Collins Avenue ☎ 305/531-0000;
www.edenrocmiami.com

MIAMI BEACH: INSIDE INFO

Top tip There is also a **city of North Miami Beach**, which is separate from the northern Miami Beach described here.

Hidden gem Drive the **A1A causeway** between Miami and South Beach over the turquoise sparkle of Biscayne Bay when the sun is setting. It's a beautiful experience. The sky turns orange and pink with dark fuchsia streaks, the palms sway gently in the early evening breeze and the cruise ships plowing the bay begin to twinkle as the sky fades to black. Put a Latin-themed soundtrack on your iPod to add an extra sensory element.

3 Little Havana

From tangy lime and mint mojitos to hip-shaking dances, hot buttery sandwiches to sweet cigars, Cubans have played an integral role in shaping Miami's character, not to mention its political, moral and even nutritional dynamics since the city was born. Nowhere is this contribution more evident than at its Cuban center, Little Havana, the pulsating heart of Miami's largest Latin-American population (➤ 28–30).

Until the 1959 revolution put a stop to formal trade, Little Havana was the epicenter of trade between Havana and Miami. Even after Castro's takeover, when America and Cuba's political relationship officially ended, immigrants continued to arrive and settle in Little Havana, keeping the legendary neighborhood alive. Many learned to cash in on the tourist appeal, and although there is no doubt that Little Havana is touristy, it still manages to feel authentic. Immigrant numbers dramatically increased in the 1980s after President Jimmy Carter granted amnesty to any and all Cubans wishing to come to America; and Castro responded by allowing any Cubans who wanted to leave to do so, but also simultaneously emptied out the country's prisons and psychiatric hospitals. In an incident dubbed the "Mariel Boat lift," a flotilla of some 125,000 people – including many of the freed criminals and mental patients – washed up on Miami's shores. Afterwards, Little Havana's population swelled and Miami's crime rate skyrocketed.

Cigars are still hand-rolled in Little Havana

A Slice of Life

The best way to experience this neighborhood is to grab a seat at one of the numerous sidewalk cafes lining **Calle Ocho** (S.W. 8th Street). This is Little Havana's main drag and vivacious heart. Cuban American superstar hip-hop artist Pitbull's highest grossing single, "I Know You Want Me (Calle Ocho)" is named after this famous road. Order a mojito and watch this Miami slice of life run by.

Despite being *the* public face of American Cuba, the street is reminiscent of any immigrant community's main drag, full of mom-and-pop shops selling cheap phone cards and Virgin Mary

Calle Ocho is the commercial and cultural heart of Little Havana

candles, and Spanish-named restaurants emitting smells so exotic, spicy and deliciously greasy they make your stomach grumble. A highlight on Calle Ocho is **El Credito Cigars**, popular with celebrity cigar enthusiasts like Robert DeNiro; get a dose of Cuban culture and a chance to watch the masters roll your fine smoke at the same time.

At the corner of Calle Ocho and S.W. 15th Street is **Maximo Gomez Park**, Little Havana's central gathering point and one of Miami's most memorable full-on sensory experiences. Spend a while watching the elderly, cigar-puffing gentleman play dominoes and gossip about Cuban politics in rapid fire Spanish to a backdrop of a 1993 Summit of Americas mural painted in vibrant rainbow colors, and you'll feel transported back to the romanticized Cuba of old.

🞡 226 B3

Maximo Gomez Park
✉ Calle Ocho and S.W. 15th Street ✋ Free

LITTLE HAVANA: INSIDE INFO

Top tips If you want a true Cuban sandwich, order a **sandwich mixto**, which comes with pickles, sliced roasted pork, ham and baby Swiss cheese individually layered between thick white buttered Cuban bread. After it is assembled, sandwiches are put in hot presses and toasted until the cheese melts. Order one, but skip the next meal and two days' worth of dessert – this is one calorie-loaded sandwich.

■ If you happen to be in Little Havana in early or mid-March, don't miss **Carnaval Miami** (tel: 305/644-8888; www.carnavalmiami.com), a nine-day-long citywide festival that includes a Calle Ocho cooking contest.

Hidden gem If you like your coffee thick and black and your sandwiches flat and hot, order up a **Cuban tinto** (a potent espresso) and a Cuban sandwich at any ramshackle sidewalk window in Little Havana.

④ Coral Gables and Coconut Grove

George Merrick designed Mediterranean-style Coral Gables in the early 1920s as an example of a model suburb. Nearby Coconut Grove began in the 1800s as a haven for artists, intellectuals and writers, and following World War I, more people in *Who's Who in America* listed this bayside paradise as their winter residence address than anywhere else. Today both remain genteel, offering respite from the SoBe crowds, and a little slice of European elegance in South Florida's heart.

Coral Gables

The Mediterranean-style village of Coral Gables, filled with shops, restaurants and bars, runs along a four-block section of Coral Way, between Douglas and LeJeune roads, called the Miracle Mile. The neighborhood's architectural crown jewel, the 1926 **Biltmore Hotel**, is the city's other luxury hotel (although sleeping here is more affordable than at the Fontainebleau). Once home to a speakeasy run by Al Capone, today this National Historic Landmark plays host to world leaders, movie stars and the largest hotel swimming pool in the country. The staff don't mind if you poke around the public areas. Gawking at the swimming pool is allowed, and there are even free hotel tours on Sunday. Or take afternoon tea in the magnificent lobby.

Just half a mile (0.8km) away is Coral Gables' other watery highlight, the spring-fed **Venetian Pool**, created from an old rock quarry. Don't miss the chance to swim amid waterfalls and grottoes in the opulent (but affordable) Italian Renaissance environs.

Coconut Grove

Nearby Coconut Grove is centered on upscale, chain-oriented malls, but a few reminders of the heady bohemian hangout days remain – check out the duck-egg blue Coconut Grove

The Biltmore Hotel, with its replica of Seville's Giralda Tower

Playhouse in the central village. The Grove bustles day and night, although most of the action takes place after dark. **CocoWalk**, a three-story entertainment complex with restaurants, bars, stores and a multiplex theater, is one of the two malls built around the central village. It usually buzzes around 8pm. The **Streets of Mayfair** is the second mall, with dozens

Vizcaya – a little bit of Italy in America

more shops, mostly boutiques, plus a few chain stores such as Ann Tayor Loft and Bath & Body Works.

While in Coconut Grove, visit the **Vizcaya Museum and Gardens**. Inside an Italian Renaissance-style villa, it has 70 rooms filled with centuries-old furniture and art. Afterward take a walk around the lovely formal gardens with grottoes and fountains; it is a popular place to get married.

✠ 226 B3

The Biltmore Hotel
✉ 1200 Anastasia Avenue ☎ 305/445-1926; www.biltmorehotel.com
🍴 Moderate

Venetian Pool
✉ 2701 DeSoto Boulevard ☎ 305/460-5306;
www.coralgablesvenetianpool.com ⏰ May–Sep Mon–Fri 11–7:30, Sat–Sun 10–4:30; Oct–Apr Tue–Fri 11–5:30, Sat–Sun 10–4:30 🍴 Inexpensive

CocoWalk
✉ 3015 Grand Avenue ☎ 305/444-0777

Streets of Mayfair
✉ 2911 Grand Avenue ☎ 305/448-1700; www.mayfairinthegrove.net

Vizcaya Museum and Gardens
✉ 3251 S. Miami Avenue ☎ 305/250-9133; www.vizcayamuseum.org
⏰ Daily 9:30–4:30 🍴 Moderate

CORAL CABLES AND COCONUT GROVE: INSIDE INFO

Top tip Skip the stressful parking space fight in the central village on weekends; instead **follow signs to parking lots** just a few blocks away (inexpensive).

Hidden gem About half a mile (0.8km) south on Main Highway, you will pass Devon Road and the **Plymouth Congregational Church** (tel: 305/444-6521; call ahead to arrange a tour). The coral rock church resembles a Mexican mission, set in a deep wooded hammock with beautiful grounds and gardens.

5 Upper Keys

Spend a little too long on this 100-plus-mile (160km) string of tropical islands floating in warm jade water south of Miami, where the attitude is decidedly mellow, and you'll be struck with a peculiar ailment they call "Keys Disease." Unfortunately it has only one known cure, but luckily it's not a bad one: book a return ticket to paradise.

The closest area to mainland Florida, the Upper Keys can appear cluttered with touristy shops and motels from the highway, but get out on the water and you'll discover some of the best snorkeling and diving around. The Keys first became accessible to tourists without boats with the birth of Henry Flagler's short-lived railroad in 1912. Although its destiny was ultimately doomed (a devastating hurricane blew much of it away 22-years-later), what remained ended up paving the way for the construction of a network of bridges, known as the Overseas Highway (US Highway 1), which linked the Keys and mainland with even easier access via a drivable ribbon of steel. You can get regional travel information from either the **Key Largo Chamber of Commerce** or the **Marathon Visitor Center**, both of which have maps and brochures.

Key Largo

Key Largo caught the world's attention after Bogart and Bacall romanticized it in the 1948 movie of the same name (which, with the exception of a couple of exterior shots, was filmed entirely on a Hollywood sound stage). The largest of the keys, and also the closest to the mainland, it offers visitors a delightful range of watery entertainment, including a hotel beneath the sea (see panel below).

The underwater **John Pennekamp Coral Reef State Park** is the country's first and finest underwater preserve, and offers the best access to the continent's largest coral reef system. View the stunning fish and coral from a glass-bottom boat or sign

---

SLEEP UNDER THE SEA

Key Largo's most unique sleeping experience is the **Jules' Undersea Lodge**, the world's only underwater hotel. The place is really tiny, with only two guestrooms (six guests maximum), but how can you beat sleeping 30 feet (9m) beneath the sea, watching fish swim past your window when you awake? The lodge, in a protected lagoon, was originally designed for scientists who lived onboard. Even if all the backup generators and system failed there would still be about 12 hours of breathing time inside the hotel. Telephones and an intercom connect guests with the surface; staff members are on duty 24 hours; guests must be at least 10 years old; no alcohol. To have a peek without staying, sign up for a three-hour mini adventure, which also gives access to its facilities and three breathing hookahs – 120-foot-long (36m) air hoses for an awesome no-tank diving experience!

✉ MM 103.2 Oceanside, 51 Shoreland Drive ☎ 305/451-2353; www.jul.com 🏷 Expensive

The "Christ of the Deep" statue at John Pennekamp Coral Reef State Park

up for a snorkeling or scuba charter to swim among them in the 75-square-mile (195sq km) park that serves as a refuge for 55 varieties of coral, more than 500 species of fish, and shipwrecks from the 1600s. **Island Ventures** is one of dozens of snorkeling and scuba outfitters taking visitors to the shallow reef. One of the most popular attractions here is the *Christ of the Deep* statue. Just 11 feet (3.4m) below the surface, it's easily accessible. For a do-it-yourself adventure, rent a canoe or kayak and set out on a journey along a 3-mile (5km) network of canoe trails.

Marathon

Halfway between Key Largo and Key West is Marathon, a hub for numerous commercial fishing and lobster boats, with some sizeable marinas. At the city's southwest limit, the graceful Seven Mile Bridge is the longest of the more than 40 bridges linking the chain of keys. On its north side stands remnants of the original Seven Mile Bridge, built in the early 20th century as a part of the railroad to Key West and billed as the 'world's longest fishing bridge'. While on Marathon, visit the **Turtle Hospital**, which rescues, rehabilitates and releases injured sea turtles, including Gulf oil-spill victims. Tours can be set up, but call ahead.

🕂 223 D1

Key Largo Chamber of Commerce
🕂 223 E2 ✉ MM 106, Key Largo ☎ 305/451-4747 or 800/822-1088; www.keylargo.org ⏲ Daily 9–6

Marathon Visitor Center
🕂 223 D1 ✉ MM 53.5 ☎ 305/743-5417 ⏲ Daily 9–5

John Pennekamp Coral Reef State Park
🕂 223 E2 ✉ MM 102.5 ☎ 305/451-6300; www.pennekamppark.com

Island Ventures
✉ MM 103.9 dock ☎ 305/451-4957; www.islandventure.com

Turtle Hospital
✉ 2396 Overseas Highway ☎ 305/743-2552; www.turtlehospital.org
⏲ Daily 9–6 🅙 Inexpensive

UPPER KEYS: INSIDE INFO

Top tip Many addresses in the Keys are noted by their **proximity to mile markers** (indicated as MM), showing distances between Key West (MM 0) and the mainland at Florida City (MM 126).

⑥ Lower Keys

If you visit the Lower Keys long enough you'll hear locals talking "Conch Republic" politics at some point. These are the islands that most emulate its breakaway republic-conscious culture – to be a "Conch" (pronounced "Conk") you must not only be born in the Keys, but also raised here.

The legendary breakaway Conch Republic story originated during a 1982 US border patrol lockdown in Key West. Customs agents erected a roadblock at the bridge onto the island to catch drug smugglers and illegal aliens, but as traffic jams mounted and tourists disappeared, residents became angry. To voice their outrage, a number of fired-up residents decided to secede from the USA. After forming the "Conch Republic," they made three declarations, in the following order: secede from America, declare war on America, then surrender and request $1 million in foreign aid. The roadblock was eventually dismantled, but every February Conchs celebrate its anniversary with nonstop parties and numerous signs bearing the slogan "We Seceded

Key Largo – the self-proclaimed "Diving Capital of the World"

WHAT'S A KEY, ANYWAY?
The Keys get their name from the Spanish *cayo*, shortened to cay (pronounced "key") in the Caribbean and nearby Bahamas. A key is defined as a low-lying island, usually no less than 10 acres (4ha) – anything smaller is a sandbar, shoal or reef. According to the US Geological Survey, there are 882 keys in Florida, but it's this 113-mile (181km) chain between Florida City on the mainland and Key West at the tip, that's the most romanticized string of islands in the Continental US.

Where Others Failed." The vibe here is more working-class rural and lived-in than fantasy resort. Another aspect of the Keys mentality is its open-door policy to all humans, with an emphasis on tolerance and mutual respect for gays, straights, blacks, whites, reds and, if you happen to be so, blues.

The farther south you travel in the Keys, the more the development – apart from in Key West – slips away. The sea's jade sparkle spreads out beyond the bridges linking the islands and the watery vistas open up dramatically.

Beachfront Property in Bahia Honda

Despite what you might expect, the Keys are not actually known for having many good beaches, despite the tropical swaying palm allure and crystalline water. One exception is at **Bahia Honda State Park**. The 524-acre (212ha) park on Big Pine Key is home to the most beautiful beach in the Keys, with a long stretch of sand and warm, clear, shallow water. Nature trails, ranger programs and water-sports equipment rentals are other highlights. You can camp or stay in a cabin in the park, and it makes a perfect overnight stop if you are traveling south to Key West. Camping under the stars by the sea is sublime, but book ahead as it fills quickly. There are also six waterfront cabins.

An aerial view of US Route 1, looking west to Bahia Honda State Park

🚩 222 C1

Bahia Honda State Park
🚩 223 D1 ✉ MM 37 ☎ 305/872-3210; www.bahiahondapark.com
🎫 Inexpensive; activities vary

LOWER KEYS: INSIDE INFO

Top tip If you're on Big Pine Key on Saturday or Sunday, stop by the flea market (MM 30.5, Oceanside; 8am–dusk). It's a great place to find some of the more eccentric Keys' souvenirs and memorabilia.

7 Key West

Key West is the USA's southernmost city, a legendary party town, home to almost 600 bars, and yes, there is a T-shirt you can buy to prove it, that's in a quirky class of its own. It's also famed for the artistic geniuses it produces. Both Jimmy Buffet, king of American beach ballads, and the author Ernest Hemingway were influenced by this off-the-grid tropical paradise's hedonistic craziness.

Sitting at the very end of the chain, Key West is the most playful isle of them all, a no-holds-barred destination that once was Florida's largest and wealthiest city. Over the decades it has played home to a motley crew of pirates, fishermen, dropouts, authors, artists and hippies.

When Jimmy Buffett began spreading the word about this remote island, wealthy escapees arrived en masse. Key West's lifers, called Conchs – residents who were born, raised and

still reside on the island – fought back, refusing to let their paradise become just another generic American beachfront community.

The Heart of the City

Key West is famous for being too weird for mainland Florida, and the best way to absorb this beautiful island's kitsch, quirk and downright craziness is to take a tour around it. You'll get a 90-minute overview with the **Conch Tour Train**, which covers all the basic local customs. (Note: Some visitors may find Key West a bit too wacky, irritating or downright rude for their taste, but go with the flow and understand it's all part of the experience and you'll have a good time.)

Duval Street is famous for its specialty shopping, art galleries, cafes and bars

Mallory Square is the epicenter of Key West's chaos. Take a stroll around the square and its surrounding blocks in daylight, but to really taste Key West's crazy subculture, return at sunset. As the sun sinks, turning the sky pink and purple and making the buildings glow golden, a giant street party – the Sunset Celebration – kicks off in the square. Arrive at least a half hour before sunset and you'll see the true side of Key West: street performers juggling fire, balancing kitchen ranges on their faces, walking tightropes and performing impossible tricks on bicycles. It's a scene of family-friendly madness (though slightly edgy). Grab a beer and a conch fritter, and wait for the sun to disappear beyond the darkening ocean, then the nightly carnival's vibe reaches a whole new level.

Unless the thought of belligerently drunk people vomiting on the streets and yelling makes you want to throw up yourself, don't miss walking down **Duval Street**, Key West's most famous road. Even if it does, you should at least try it for a block, as this bawdry strip of bars and restaurants, T-shirt shops, hometown theaters, boutiques and art studios is the material visualization of the island's soul. Following sunset, dinner and a clean-up, it's a Key West right of passage to return to the main shopping street for the nightly pub hop known as the "Duval Crawl."

The Hemingway Connection

Hemingway House, a gorgeous Spanish Colonial mansion where Ernest Hemingway lived between 1931 and the 1940s, is now a museum dedicated to the famous author. He moved here in his early 30s with his second wife, a *Vogue* fashion editor, who was also the former friend of his first wife, and lived here until running off with his third wife, nine years later. While on Key West he wrote *The Short Happy Life of Francis Macomber* and *The Green Hills of Africa*, and also installed Key West's first saltwater swimming pool in his home. The giant pool was so expensive to construct that Hemingway pressed his "last penny" into the pool deck's cement when it was sealed. It's still there today, and can be seen on a tour of the house and grounds. The author's old studio is also preserved here. The house is also famous for its bizarre six-toed cats – ask around for the story.

If you think the six-toed cats at the Hemingway House are weird, wait until you tour the gardens at **Casa Antigua**, Hemingway's first Key West home. You can get tickets for the self-guided garden walk inside the Pelican Poop Shoppe.

Key West Icons

The **Key West Cemetery**, not far from Casa Antigua, is a quirky attraction filled with gravestones bearing crazy epitaphs such as, "I told you I was sick." Admission to the cemetery on the aptly named Passover Lane is free and there are self-guided walking tour maps. For more structured fun, join one of the guided walking tours, which include freakish details about the graves you wander past.

Drinking is big in Key West, home to 582 different bars. Business, for visitors at least, centers around two watering holes. **Sloppy Joe's Bar** is legendary, while **Capt. Tony's Saloon**, around the corner, and actually the site of the original Sloppy Joe's Bar, is more authentic and less touristy.

Underwater Key West

Key West isn't known for its beaches, but you can experience the glory of the sea from below or its beauty skimming on top or even from high above. Try snorkeling, parasailing or a tall ship cruise aboard one of the charter boats that depart from the Harbor Walk at the end of William Street. The *Fury* catamaran is a safe bet. The huge, steady boat departs from the Hilton Marina, sails out a mile or so and serves free champagne, beer, wine and soda along the way. It also offers an earlier snorkeling/ sunset cruise combination.

No one is more associated with Key West than Ernest Hemingway, whose house is now a museum

222 C1

Key West Welcome Center
✉ 24746 Overseas
Highway ☎ 305/296-4444
or 800/284-4482; www.
keywestwelcomecenter.com

Conch Tour Train
✉ Mallory Square ☎ 305/294-
5161; www.historictours.com
🕐 Daily 9:30–4:30 💲 Moderate

Hemingway House museum
✉ 907 Whitehead Street
☎ 305/294-1136;
www.hemingwayhome.com;
🕐 Daily 9–5 💲 Inexpensive

Casa Antigua
✉ 314 Simonton Street, Pelican
Poop Shoppe ☎ 305/296-9955;
www.pelicanpoopshoppe.com
🕐 Daily 10–5 💲 Inexpensive

Capt. Tony's
Saloon – one
of Key West's
most popular
watering holes

Key West Cemetery
✉ 701 Passover Lane ☎ 305/292-8177, tours 305/292-6718;
www.keywest.com/cemetery.html 🕐 Daily 7–6
💲 Free. Tours: inexpensive

Sloppy Joe's Bar
✉ 201 Duval Street ☎ 305/294-5717; www.sloppyjoes.com

Capt. Tony's Saloon
✉ 428 Greene Street ☎ 305/294-1838; www.capttonyssaloon.com

Fury catamaran
☎ 305/294-8899 or 800/994-8898; www.furycat.com 🕐 Daily sailings
💲 Moderate

KEY WEST: INSIDE INFO

Top tips If you're not used to driving in America, **US 1 is not the place to learn**.
Narrow lanes and speeding drivers make the only highway in and out of the
Keys fairly nerve-racking. Drive defensively, and keep your headlights on
to be seen.

■ The peak season is from the beginning of February through May, and again
from October through December. It's **slow and very hot** in June and July.
Make reservations.

Hidden gem Far enough from the tourist strip to retain its authenticity is the
Green Parrot Bar (Southard and Whitehead streets, tel: 305/294-6133). A local
favorite and true Key West natural, the open-air bar has pinball machines,
pool tables and motorcycle collectibles, as well as drinks.

8 Everglades

There's no question that the Everglades doesn't share the grandiose majesty of other parks, such as Yosemite and Yellowstone. However, if you'd like to see a natural phenomenon and Florida at the microcosmic level, closer to its original native state, this is the place to be.

It may resemble a giant alligator-infested swamp, swarming with mosquitoes and filled with prickly grasses that make your legs itch, but at 1.5 million acres (6 million ha), it's one impressive swamp. But even that stereotype is wrong – this wildly unique ecosystem is actually a prairie wetland, a true river of grass (▶ 16–19). The Everglades National Park was not established as a park until 1947. For prior decades it was viewed as disposable property. Developers eager to turn land into cash spent years draining it to create room for farms and houses before environmentalists pointed out that this was, in fact, a river that filters water, prevents flooding and is a major habitat for wildlife and plant life.

The watery wilderness of the Everglades provides refuge for a wide variety of creatures

Visiting the "Glades"

Drop into the **Shark Valley Visitor Center** if you have only limited time to explore the park. One of five national park visitor centers, it's the most convenient for those traveling from Miami. It offers two-hour tram tours following a 15-mile (24km) asphalt trail, home to numerous grinning gators – especially in the winter months when they use the sun-heated black tar pavement as a personal sauna. Narrated by knowledgeable park rangers, these tours not only teach you about the endangered ecosystem and its wildlife residents, they allow you to experience the park's subtle beauty from the comfort of a breezy, open-air vehicle. Halfway along the trail, the tours stop at a 65-foot (20m) high concrete tower that gives a dramatic aerial view of the saw grass prairie's birds and alligators. Other guided ranger-led tours include bird walks, canoe trails and shoreline strolls, which you can arrange at the visitor center.

If you have more time on your hands, head to the **Ernest F Coe Visitor Center**, southwest of Miami, which is full of trail and activity information and boasts museum-worthy exhibits. Call ahead for a schedule of fun ranger-led excursions from here, including the not-to-be-missed, two-hour wet walk through a slow-moving grassy river, known as the "slough slog." To look for wildlife yourself, try walking the Anhinga Trail, Snake Bight, Chokoloskee Bay, Loop Road or Turner River Road. Wherever you roam in the Everglades, heed the advice of the rangers, who caution guests never to attempt to touch or feed the docile-looking manatees, turtles and raccoons. Many have lost their fear of people and see a snack instead of a finger.

Wilderness Waterway by Canoe

For a completely different take on the Everglades, visit the northwestern edge. The **Gulf Coast Visitor Center** is where to get your bearings before exploring the remote Ten Thousand Islands area, home to mangrove forests and numerous waterways offering amazing canoeing and kayaking adventures. If you're a thrill seeker, the 99-mile (160km) **Wilderness Waterway** is a canoe/kayak trail through mangrove islands with several shorter loops, including 5.2-mile (8.3km) Nine-Mile

AIRBOATS

Flat-bottom boats with giant fans on their backs – commonly known as airboats – are forbidden on waterways inside the national park (they disturb and disrupt the peace and environment), but to take a break from paddling and experience whooshing through the swamp on a boat propelled by air, visit the **Everglades Alligator Farm** in nearby Homestead. You can take a 30-minute airboat ride and also hold baby alligators.

The Everglades stretches to the horizon, criss-crossed by secretive waterways

Pond, and 2-mile (3km) sections on Noble Hammock, Mud Lake and Hells Bay. You'll need navigational charts for this, and permits from the visitor center if you decide to rough it and camp for the night on your own. You can also join a 90-minute boat tour or ranger-led canoe trip for a bit more direction and education.

➕ 223 D2

Shark Valley Visitor Center
✉ Tamiami Trial, 25 miles (40km) west of the Florida Turnpike, off Exit 25 (follow signs) ☎ 305/221-8776 🕐 Daily 8:30–6 ✋ Tram tours: moderate

Ernest F Coe Visitor Center
✉ 11 miles (18km) southwest of Homestead on Route 9336 ☎ 305/242-7700 🕐 Daily 8–5 ✋ Inexpensive

Everglades Alligator Farm
✉ 40351 S.W. 192 Avenue, Homestead ☎ 305/247-2628; www.everglades.com 🕐 Daily 9–6 ✋ Moderate

Gulf Coast Visitor Center
✉ 815 Oyster Bar Lane, off Highway 29, Everglades City ☎ 239/695-3311 🕐 Daily 9–4:30 ✋ Boat tours: moderate; canoe rentals: inexpensive

---

EVERGLADES NATIONAL PARK: INSIDE INFO

Top tips There are **five visitor centers** where you can sign up for tours and pick up maps and brochures.
- The park is **open year-round**, with the peak tourist season occurring between December and April when it's drier and cooler (summer is hot, wet and mosquito-plagued).
- **Give plenty of room** to the alligators and snakes you'll encounter, since venom and sharp teeth will win out over your jogging shoes.

Don't miss Guided, **full-moon bicycle tours** are offered from January to April; ask at the visitor centers.

9 Palm Beach

A favorite winter playground for America's wealthiest families for more than a century, Palm Beach was the focal point of Florida's Jewish society, the host of numerous charity balls and benefits during the snowbird season before the Bernie Madoff scandal cleaned out a number of the richest, and most philanthropic, residents.

Palm Beach has long been synonymous with swanky wealth. It's the kind of place that's famous for its "season," the winter circuit of parties thrown in the name of charity by Palm Beach society's most connected and wealthiest residents, all of whom head some type of charitable foundation helping the sick, the needy and the poor. Or at least they were helped before part-time Palm Beach resident Bernie Madoff swooped in and stole their fortunes.

The Bubble Bursts

Palm Beach has had a rough last couple years. The arrest of legendary money manager Bernie Madoff in December 2008 on charges of securities fraud, and his subsequent confession that his investment business was "all just one big lie," left many of Palm Beach's Jewish community, most of them members of the elite Palm Beach Country Club where Madoff recruited numerous investors, stunned. Many foundations were forced to close or restructure after the incident. One investor, Carl Shapiro, who considered Bernie like a son, lost more money than any other individual: a whopping $1 billion dollars. Madoff pleaded guilty to the charges and was sentenced to 150 years in federal prison in 2009; today he is behind bars in North Carolina.

Henry Flagler's Whitehall served as a hotel until 1959, when it became the Flagler Museum

Today's Reality

Less than a year before Madoff confessed, real-estate tycoon Donald Trump signed a contract to sell a Palm Beach mansion for $100 million, just $3 million shy of the most expensive home ever sold. That's the kind of place Palm Beach was before the 2009 global recession and Madoff fallout.

Today, from the exterior, it has hardly changed. The rich-and-famous' playground still revolves around society benefit balls and bashes, second houses (think huge mansions on the beach), haute couture shopping on an avenue called Worth and dining at The Breakers, the flagship to-be-seen hotel. Drive the back roads, however, past those sprawling ocean-facing mansions, and you'll see a number of small, unobtrusive "for sale" signs on the manicured lawns leading up to the pastel-colored dwellings, signaling Palm Beach hasn't completely escaped the downturn.

Strolling Worth Avenue

To see the opulence for yourself, and really appreciate the town, stroll along the gold spun sand beach, dipping into the warm blue hues of the Atlantic Ocean for a swim or take a bike ride around the side streets, past those gilded, pastel mansions with beautiful lawns and technicolor bushes and flower gardens that Palm Beach is famous for. Of course, if you need a new pair of Dior sunglasses or Louis Vuitton luggage, Worth Avenue, Palm Beach's most famous glittery shopping strip, is happy to indulge.

Enduring Legacy

There's no better example of Palm Beach's legacy of over-the-top luxury than **The Breakers** (► 136), modeled on Rome's Villa Medici and still the center of Palm Beach's social scene. It is worth a visit even if you can't afford to stay there. The hotel dates back to 1926, when 75 Italian artisans arrived to complete the magnificent paintings on the ceilings of the 200-foot-long (61m) main lobby and first-floor public rooms. Today's rates may be daunting, but you can walk around the lobby and public area for free and get a sense of the size, style and elegance.

The Breakers, like much of Palm Beach, is largely the creation of railroad pioneer Henry M Flagler, who first saw the future of Florida tourism in the late 1800s. Flagler was in

Worth Avenue is one of the world's most exclusive shopping streets

The dining room at The Breakers, a fabulously ornate Italian-style hotel

his 50s when he opened up the state to tourism by building the Florida East Coast Railway, which delivered travelers to the doors of resorts in St Augustine, Daytona, Miami, Key West and, of course, the grand dame resort city of them all, Palm Beach.

✚ 223 F4
Palm Beach County Convention & Visitors Bureau
✉ 1555 Palm Beach Lakes Boulevard, Suite 800, West Palm Beach 33401
☎ 800/554-7256; www.palmbeachfl.com

PALM BEACH: INSIDE INFO

Top tip Don't confuse Palm Beach with the working-class mainland city of **West Palm Beach,** located across Lake Worth.

Hidden gem The area north of Palm Beach is dubbed the **Treasure Coast**. Here you can explore Jupiter Island (65 miles/105km north of Fort Lauderdale) by canoe – paddle down the Loxahatchee River, past mangrove forests, looking for alligators.

At Your Leisure

🔟 Boca Raton

When their town was incorporated in 1925 at the height of the Florida land boom, Boca Raton's city fathers commissioned famed society architect Addison Mizner to plan a world-class resort community. Although the end of the boom squelched most of his plans, one of Mizner's projects – City Hall – was completed in 1927. It still bears the original footprint of the Mizner design, and was constructed using ironwork, tile and woodwork supplied by Mizner Industries. Restored to its former elegance, today it serves as home of the **Boca Raton Historical Society**, which doubles as a tourist office. Boca remains an affluent city anxious to show off its wealth, and it does so at places like **Mizner Park**, a shopping and residential district where upscale boutiques, art galleries, jewelers and cafes set the scene for concerts by top-name performers. Relax in the amphitheater, or on the grass and enjoy. Pick up information on the town from the Boca Raton Historical Society.

✚ 223 E4

Boca Raton Historical Society
✉ 71 North Federal Highway ☎ 561/395-6766; www.bocahistory.org

Mizner Park
✉ 500 S.E. Mizner Boulevard ☎ 561/362-0606; www.miznerpark.org

🔟 Fort Lauderdale

Once a legendary wild child, Fort Lauderdale has matured a lot since its 1980s spring-break party heyday. Today it's known for a long and stunning sun-kissed beach, canals reminiscent of Venice and swanky hotels. Fort Lauderdale still knows how to party – it has just swapped cheap beer for Grey Goose martinis in its A-list-only clubs.

Take the hop-on hop-off **Water Bus** to get acquainted with Fort Lauderdale. It stops at different points around town (check the website for exact locations) and educates and entertains passengers in the process – the drivers are famed for their endless stream of knowledgeable chatter, including info on passing sights and local history and lore.

The **Fort Lauderdale Beach Promenade** is the star attraction. Spend some time strolling its wide, palm-lined brick walkway running parallel to the white sand beach that starts right downtown. More hours should be devoted to worshiping Florida's sun and swimming in the sky-blue Atlantic Ocean on this 7-mile long beach stretching north from the city centre.

With 300 miles (480km) of navigable inland waterways criss-crossing the city, Fort Lauderdale is often called "America's Venice" – not to be confused with Venice on the Gulf Coast side of the state (► 165).

The Intracoastal Waterway at Boca Raton, part of a coastal boating route

Sailing at Fort Lauderdale Beach

Explore Fort Lauderdale's canals on a romantic **Gondola Tour**, replete with an authentically dressed gondolier. It's a lovely way to take in the stylish and sophisticated city.

In the heart of downtown, check out the collection at the **Museum of Art**. It is one of Florida's best, and includes works by Picasso, Matisse, Dalí and Warhol. True art lovers will appreciate the large William Glackens collection.

➕ 223 E3

Greater Fort Lauderdale Convention & Visitors Bureau
✉ 100 East Broward Boulevard, Suite 200
☎ 954/765-4466; www.sunny.org

Water Bus
☎ 954/467-6677; www.watertaxi.com
🕐 Daily 10:30am–midnight 💰 Moderate

Gondola Tour
☎ 877/926-2467; www.gondolaman.com

Museum of Art
✉ 1 E. Las Olas Boulevard ☎ 954/525-5500; www.moafl.com 🕐 Tue–Wed, Fri–Sat 11–5, Thu 11–8, Sun 12–5 💰 Inexpensive; university/college students admitted free with valid student ID

🄓 Biscayne National Underwater Park

Southeast of Miami, off the road that leads to the Keys, is Biscayne National Underwater Park. About 95 percent of this magnificent 181,500-acre (62,600ha) park, home to a portion of the world's third-largest coral reef, is actually located beneath the surface of the Atlantic Ocean.

Stop off at the **Dante Fascell Visitor Center** where you can sign up for guided snorkeling and dive trips to the reefs, perhaps the best way to experience the park, and see a great film about it.

Three-hour snorkeling trips depart daily at 1:15pm, and allow for around 1 to 1.5 hours in the water. Dive trips only take off Friday through Sunday, departing at 8:30am. The two-tank dives are very affordable. All trips require a minimum of six people; scuba dives require proof of certification and equipment rental.

If you don't feel comfortable in the water but want to experience the underwater world, try a three-hour glass-bottom boat tour, which can also be arranged at the visitor center. Skimming above the clear jade water you'll be able to scan down and see sea turtles, dolphins, tropical fish, coral reef and, if you're lucky, even manatees.

➕ 223 E2

Dante Fascell Visitor Center
✉ 9700 S.W. 328th Street, Homestead
☎ 305/230-7275; www.nps.gov/bisc 🕐 Daily 8:30–5 💰 Scuba and snorkel trips: moderate

NIGHT DIVING

For an extra-special experience, plan your trip to Biscayne National Underwater Park around the single-tank night dives, which are offered once a month. You'll see a totally different variety of underwater creatures that stay hidden in daylight hours, such as black, red and gag groupers. It is a truly great way of experiencing this hidden world beneath the waves.

13 Dry Tortugas National Park

Spanish explorer Ponce de León christened this tiny archipelago, about 70 miles (112km) west of Key West, the Tortugas ("the turtles") in honor of the abundant green, leatherback, hawksbill and loggerhead sea turtles who also call this group of seven islands home. Today the islands reward visitors who take the effort to reach them with a romantic back-to-nature retreat, boasting amazing snorkeling, diving, birding and after-dark stargazing. Spending a night here is a special experience, as long as you don't mind roughing it. Camping is the only accommodation, and while the national park (under the control of the **National Park Service**) has toilets, no freshwater showers or drinking water are available (bring everything you need with you).

Garden Key is the park's hub. Check out the imposing, but unfinished **Fort Jefferson**, which once served as a Union prison during the Civil War. Today the decaying military fort is a strange hexagonal, red-brick centerpiece rising up from Garden Key's mottled greenish-blue water. You can pitch a tent at the park's **campground**, which has 13 sites. These fill quickly, so book ahead. If you're camping out, bring extra food, water and other drinks from the mainland to barter with the Cuban-American fishing boats trawling the water around Garden Key. You can swap these with the crews for fresh-caught lobster, shrimp and crab, which taste delicious when cooked with butter and salt on a campfire. Just paddle right up to the fishing boats to make your trade, but don't swim after dark when the fishing attracts a lot of sharks.

To reach the Dry Tortugas, take the **Sunny Days Catamaran**, which runs between Key West and Garden Key, leaving Key West at 8am and arriving on Garden Key around 10am. If you don't want to spend the night, the company does day trips that allow around five hours to enjoy Garden Key, including time for snorkeling and a fort tour. A picnic lunch and on-board breakfast is provided. To camp, let the crew know in advance that you are booked to stay; there will be an extra $30 overnight fee.

✚ 222 A1

National Park Service
☎ 305/242-7700; www.nps.gov/drto

Garden Key Campground
☎ 305/242-7700; www.nps.gov/drto
🛏 Inexpensive

Sunny Days Catamarans
☎ 305/296-5556; www.sunnydays
keywest.com 🛏 Expensive

Fort Jefferson's moat was once patrolled by sharks and barracudas

Where to...
Stay

Prices

Expect to pay per room per night:

$ under $125 $$ $125–$250 $$$ over $250

MIAMI

▽▽▽ Cadet Hotel $$$

With hotel rates making a great leap forward, it's nice to find this plain, quite unassuming hotel a few blocks from the fabled Delano. Nothing too fancy (parking's scarce but available), except a cute little porch cafe/garden, and 38 rooms done in art deco style with bamboo floors and Egyptian linens. Clark Gable stayed here while completing flight training in World War II.

✛ **226 C3** ☒ **1701 James Avenue, Miami Beach** ☎ **305/672-6688;** www.cadethotel.com

▽▽▽ Eden Roc Renaissance Miami Beach $$$

On a par with its next-door neighbor, the Fontainebleau, Eden Roc is a celebrity hot spot overlooking Miami Beach. It reopened after a $200 million overhaul and has been a staple on the beautiful people scene ever since, with a cabana pool scene and glamorous modern rooms, many of which feature jeted tubs. Book one with a terrace for fabulous ocean views.

✛ **226 C3** ☒ **4525 Collins Avenue, Miami Beach** ☎ **305/531-0000;** www.edenrocmiami.com

▽▽▽ The Hotel $$–$$$

This hotel is a fashion statement in its own right. Designed by Todd Oldham, the four-story, 52-room boutique property is a fantasy of cloud patterns, mosaic tiles, hand-blown glass and an overall casual beauty. The comfortable rooms feature modern amenities, and even the unusual robes were designed by Oldham. There's an impressive rooftop pool overlooking the ocean, complete with changing areas, a juice bar and a fitness facility. It's a perfect spot for solitude.

✛ **226 C3** ☒ **801 Collins Avenue, Miami Beach** ☎ **305/531-2222 or 877/843-4683;** www.thehotelofsouthbeach.com

▽▽▽ Loews Miami Beach Hotel $$$

Located right on the beach, this is one of the largest hotels in South Beach. It offers modern services such as valet parking that are hard to find in the smaller art deco hotels of the area. The comfortably furnished rooms are relatively large.

The pool area, however, is one of the most impressive in town. There are plenty of palm trees and chaise longues, a kidney-shaped pool and a hot tub. The best part is that its deck connects directly to the beach. There are several restaurants, including the stylish Emerils and the more casual Preston's Brasserie.

✛ **226 C3** ☒ **1601 Collins Avenue, Miami Beach** ☎ **305/604-1601 or 800/235-6397;** www.loewshotels.com

▽▽▽ ▽▽▽ Mandarin Oriental $$–$$$

The Mandarin Oriental is in one of Miami's most prestigious commercial and residential locations. The exterior is shaped like the company's fan logo and every room has a water view. Rooms and suites are crisp, clean and exotic, displaying a gentle Asian touch with earth tones and bamboo. A martini bar, pool area, private beach and restaurant make this a serious consideration. It's like a private sanctuary in the city's heart.

with refrigerators, are twice the size of standard rooms.

✚ 226 B3 ⊠ 500 Brickell Key Drive ☎ 305/913–8288; www.mandarinoriental.com

▼▼ The Setai $$$

Cambodian temple architecture meets Chinese interior decorating at the most expensive and eclectic hotel in Miami. Although you will pay a king's ransom to stay here, at least the service is superb (think 24-hour butler teams on every floor), and the clean-line, contemporary rooms are luxurious without being ostentatious, decorated with traditional Khmer and Chinese furnishings and lots of velvety chocolate teak.

✚ 226 C3 ⊠ 2001 Collins Avenue, Miami Beach ☎ 305/520–6000; www.setai.com

KEY LARGO

▼▼ Key Largo Grande Hilton $$–$$$

This four-story resort has all the usual modern amenities, plus charter fishing, windsurfing, parasailing and a boat dock. Suites,

a hotel of this kind, this is a first-class place, conveniently located and easily accessible. The 256 well-appointed guest rooms are large, spacious and feature modern furnishings and contemporary decor. The hotel boasts an outdoor swimming pool (with poolside bar and grill) with whirlpool, and a fitness facility.

✚ 223 E4 ⊠ 5150 Town Center Circle ☎ 561/392–4600; www.marriott.com

FORT LAUDERDALE

▼▼▼ Lago Mar Resort and Club $$

This family-owned, luxury beachfront resort has been renovated to update the rooms (most of which are spacious, stylish suites) and public areas. Located on the water, with a spectacular private beach, it is ideal for people traveling with children.

✚ 223 E3 ⊠ 1700 S. Ocean Lane ☎ 954/523–6511 or 800/255–5246; www.lagomar.com

KEY WEST

▼▼ Pier House Resort and Caribbean Spa $$$

This elegant resort offers a sophisticated respite from the frenzied main strip in Key West. Rooms vary in design – some have balconies, others have views over the water. Spa rooms feature large whirlpool bathtubs, and massage and other spa treatments are first-class.

✚ 222 C1 ⊠ 1 Duval Street ☎ 305/296-4600; www.pierhouse.com

PALM BEACH

▼▼▼ The Breakers $$$

If you intend to travel in style and jet-set luxury, this distinguished oceanfront hotel is the place to do it. In keeping with the town's

character, The Breakers is an elegant resort with outstanding service that caters to your every need. After a fire in 1925 destroyed much of the building, 75 Italian artisans were employed to rebuild the hotel in the style of Rome's Villa Medici. In less than a year, and at a cost of around $7 million, the work was complete. This is one of America's grand hotels, a showcase comparable to the finest hotels – or castles – of Europe. Opulence is the key here – marble staircases and bathrooms, crystal chandeliers and big closets. The hotel is close to the main shopping attractions of Palm Beach and has nine onsite restaurants.

✚ 223 F4 ⊠ 1 S. Country Road ☎ 561/655-6611 or 800/833-3141; www.thebreakers.com

BOCA RATON

▼▼▼ Boca Raton Marriott at Boca Center $$–$$$

With all the modern amenities and luxuries that you would expect of

Where to...
Eat and Drink

Prices

Expect to pay per person for a meal, excluding drinks:

$ under $15 $$ $15–$30 $$$ over $30

MIAMI

▽▽▽ Balans $–$$

This popular Lincoln Road Mall restaurant offers terrific value for money and consistently good-quality food. It has a wide-ranging menu, including American, Asian and international cuisines. Try the Indonesian noodles with chicken or shrimp, or the the pumpkin and mascarpone tortellini, followed by blueberry and pear granola crumble or a flourless pecan brownie. It's open daily from 8am for breakfast.

🚻 226 C3 ⊠ 1022 Lincoln Road, Miami Beach ☎ 305/534-9191

▽▽▽ Chef Allen's $$$

Allen Susser has been producing some of Miami's most exciting food for more than a decade. The restaurant is modern, filled with clean lines and features a glass-encased kitchen. The menu makes full use of the bountiful array of ingredients available in southern Florida, and thus the seafood dishes are particularly inspired. As a whole the New World food is excellent, if at times overly creative. Save room for one of the delicious soufflés.

🚻 226 C5 ⊠ 19088 N.E. 29th Avenue (between 191st Street and Biscayne Boulevard), Aventura ☎ 305/935-2900

▽▽▽ China Grill $$$

The New York branch of China Grill practically invented pan-Asian cooking more than a decade ago, and the more recent Miami outpost does the cuisine proud. The huge restaurant is located on an otherwise quiet corner that oozes colorful South Beach glitz. Try the incredible faux-Chinese fare such as dumplings filled with broccoli rabe or grilled Australian lamb with mandarin orange sauce. There is always a wait for a table, but the bar area is a great place to people-watch. For the more literary minded, there are passages from Marco Polo's travel diaries inlaid in a colorful mosaic to read while you're waiting. China Grill is popular with the in-crowd, so you should dress to impress.

🚻 226 C3 ⊠ 404 Washington Avenue, Miami Beach ☎ 305/534-2211

▽▽▽ Islas Canarias $

There is always a crowd at this cheery family-run Cuban restaurant in Little Havana. On Sunday afternoons (after church), entire families savor home-style cooking that includes rich stews, fried plantains, fried pork, and rice and beans. A cup of *café con leche* or a fresh fruit shake helps wash it all down delightfully. If you don't speak Spanish, just look around the room and point to the dishes you want to order.

🚻 226 B3 ⊠ 285 N.W. 27th Avenue, at 3rd Street ☎ 305/649-0440

▽▽▽ Joe's Stone Crab Restaurant $$$

Customers are happy to wait for an hour, or sometimes two, to get into this legendary South Beach eatery. Since it opened back in 1913, the restaurant has been serving its legendary stone crabs, with the fresh briny taste of having been just plucked from the water, which has become almost as famous as the crabs. The claws are served cold with a tangy mustard sauce and the meat is sweet and delicious; pure pleasure. The stone crab claws are very expensive, but don't try to save by ordering one of the other entrees. If you've waited for a table, you might as well splurge. The Key lime pie is the best dessert available. The restaurant closes from mid-May to October, when the crabs are out of season. It is also closed for lunch on Mondays during the season, but you can order from the take-out store and eat on the outdoor patio. The restaurant even ships its famous crabs all over the world, at a price.

226 C3 ⊠ **11 Washington Avenue, Miami Beach** ☎ **305/673-0365**

▽▽▽ Nemo Restaurant $$-$$$

The scene at Nemo's is white hot – which is usually an indicator of overpriced, inedible food and spacey service. Luckily Nemo's seems to be the exception that proves the rule! The Asian-accented food is light and often zestily spiced. Salmon comes wok-charred and served with a salad of sprouts

and pumpkin seeds, the steamed mussels with tomato-harissa broth, the pan-seared fillet of snapper with lobster hash brows and the hearty country bread with a delicious bean dip. The outdoor patio is lovely with graceful arching trees – only beware of hard seed pods that can sometimes fall on you while you dine.

226 C3 ⊠ **100 Collins Avenue, at 1st Street, Miami Beach** ☎ **305/532-4550**

▽▽▽ News Cafe $$

At the corner of 8th and Ocean, the News Cafe is a South Beach landmark eating spot. Serving world diner cuisine, sandwiches and breakfast all day and night (the best choice), the food is nothing spectacular, but the people-watching and sidewalk cafe location, reminiscent of the Riviera, certainly are. It also has a kiosk selling newspapers, magazines and cigars. It's open 24 hours a day.

226 C3 ⊠ **800 Ocean Drive, South Beach** ☎ **305/538-6397**

▽▽▽ Smith & Wollensky $$$

Once it was difficult finding a great piece of meat in South Beach. But it is all about the steak at this haven for carnivores. Beef is available in various cuts and styles – filet mignon, sirloin, prime rib, au poivre – and all are prepared exactly as ordered (beware, though, rare here means "still mooing"). All items are à la carte, so the bill can add up when you order tempting side dishes such as creamed spinach, hash browns and fried onions. As if great steak wasn't enough, the restaurant also has a magnificent view of South Beach and cruise ships on their way out to sea.

226 C3 ⊠ **1 Washington Avenue, at Collins Avenue, Miami Beach** ☎ **305/673-2800**

▽▽▽ Spiga Ristorante Italian $$$

Traditional Italian food is served in an intimate, candlelit atmosphere as this romantic restaurant, located

at the front of the Impala Hotel in the heart of SoBe's Art Deco district. The hearty, homemade breads (for which Spiga is famous) and delicious pasta dishes are what set it apart from its top-end South Beach peers. The focus here is on serving well-known Italian comfort food rather than eclectic, oddball fusion creations.

226 C3 ⊠ **1228 Collins Avenue, Miami Beach** ☎ **305/534-0079**

▽▽▽ Van Dyke Cafe $$

This Lincoln Road institution is where to come for sidewalk eating and prime people-watching, served with a side of Italian American classics like eggplant Parmigianino and juicy cheeseburgers, plus salads, sandwiches and meat and fish dishes. Exemplary service belies the casual ambience, and despite being popular with models and celebrities, prices are reasonable.

226 C3 ⊠ **846 Lincoln Road, Miami Beach** ☎ **305/534-3600; www.thevandykecafe.com**

Versailles $$

A legend in its own lifetime, this long-revered Little Havana hotspot feels like stepping into a live Latin-American soap opera, complete with gossip, revelry and big crowds of Cubans and tourists dressed to the nines and dining on delicious food. The party continues late into the night.

➕ 226 B3 ☒ 3555 S.W. 8th Street, Little Havana ☎ 305/444-0240

✿✿✿ Wish $$–$$$

Designed by Todd Oldham, Wish is pretty, sexy and tasteful all at the same time. The open-air patio, covered by big white umbrellas, is a particularly pleasant spot to dine. The indoor dining room is smaller but equally fun, with velvet banquettes and hand-blown glass ceiling fixtures. The food is well prepared and borrows elements from around the globe. There are duck and ginger spring rolls, tortilla soup, risotto, and beluga caviar for those who are willing to splurge.

➕ 226 C3 ☒ 801 Collins Avenue, Miami Beach, in The Hotel ☎ 305/674-9474

KEY LARGO

✿✿ The Fish House Restaurant $

Another nautical theme, but with an impressive ability to create seafood in a variety of ways. Spice up your life with fish prepared charbroiled, fried, Creole-style, pan-seared or Jamaican jerked. The spices and choices make it worth the wait for a table, although outdoor seating helps ease the anxiety of waiting – as does the homemade Key lime pie. All is served in a fun, friendly, and casual "Keys style" atmosphere.

➕ 223 E2 ☒ MM 102.4 102401 Overseas Highway ☎ 305/451-4665; www.fishhouse.com

KEY WEST

✿✿ Blue Heaven $$–$$$

The motto at this laid-back Key West staple is just like Jimmy Buffett sings

it: "No shoes, no shirt, no problem." Grab an ice-cold beer from the bathtub on the bar, then sit back, sip and order generous-sized portions of Caribbean barbecue shrimp, chicken jerk and fresh snapper.

➕ 222 C1 ☒ 729 Thomas Street ☎ 305/296-8666

✿✿ Jimmy Buffett's Margaritaville Cafe $

There's a difference between real Key West dining and a chain restaurant run by a multi-millionaire, but if you're a Buffett fan you may want to drop in and try the fish sandwiches, yellowfin tuna, Key West pink shrimp, ribs, beers... and the margaritas. Just kick back, have fun and enjoy some local food and listen to live bands.

➕ 222 C1 ☒ 500 Duval Street ☎ 305/292-1435; www.margaritaville.com

✿✿ Mangoes $$

Although most restaurants in the Keys highlight fish and seafood, some of the freshest, most creative and the best prepared is offered at this bustling eatery. Mangoes is known for "Floribbean" cuisine that blends Caribbean influences, local seafood and a touch of the Mediterranean. Conch chowder with lobster dumplings, fire and ice shrimp with cucumber-tomatillo relish, and local snapper are among the best choices. Also worth trying are the delicious pizzas.

➕ 222 C1 ☒ 700 Duval Street ☎ 305/292-4606

PALM BEACH

✿✿ Bice Ristorante $$–$$$

Although most outposts of this trendy Italian chain offer excellent food, at the Palm Beach location it's the clientele that makes dining exciting. The area's wealthiest residents seem to treat this like their own private dining room, hopping from table to table to say hello and chat with their friends. Many of them prefer the outside patio dining. The food is contemporary

Italian, with specialties from ultra-chic Milan such as saffron risotto, grilled dishes and roasted game in season among the best offerings.

➕ 223 F4 ⊠ 313½ Worth Avenue
☎ 561/835-1600

☜☞ The Leopard Lounge Restaurant $$$

Leopard print features in the carpeting of this elegant supper club's interior, which also boasts a hand-painted ceiling. A continental menu tempts with delicious entrées, and excellent service, potent cocktails and one of Palm Beach's hottest nightly entertainment scenes provide further sensual invigoration – think old Hollywood glamour at its most sexy.

➕ 223 F4 ⊠ The Chesterfield Hotel, 363 Coconut Row ☎ 561/659-5800

BOCA RATON

☞ Mississippi Sweets BBQ $

For delicious BBQ ribs and chicken drenched in a sweet house sauce

pay this tiny, incredibly popular restaurant a visit. It also does all the classic American southern sides, like deep-fried sweet potatoes and hush puppies.

➕ 223 E4 ⊠ 2399 N. Federal Highway
☎ 561/394-6779

FORT LAUDERDALE

☞☜ Casablanca Cafe $$

Although Sam isn't on the piano, this oceanside restaurant with excellent views features live music on Wednesdays, Fridays and Saturdays. There is an interesting eclectic "new Floridian" menu that mingles Continental and Mediterranean-inspired dishes, including warm macadamia nut and goat cheese salad. The service is warm and friendly and the atmosphere a good deal less pretentious than in other South Florida spots.

➕ 223 E3 ⊠ Corner of FLA A1A and Alhambra Street ☎ 954/764-3500

Where to...
Shop

South Beach

Looking frumpy in the Art Deco District is not the done thing. This is a land of beautiful people with perfect bodies dressed in the latest styles. Some who arrive with a suitcase full of clothing that would be perfectly acceptable in their home town feel the need to revamp their wardrobe, especially if they have any inclination to explore the club scene. Head to Collins and Washington avenues and you will find everything from haute couture and youthful clubwear to outlandish accessories and retro vintage styles.

Also in South Beach is the pedestrian promenade **Lincoln Road**. The redeveloped strip hosts occasional outdoor concerts and farmers' markets and is home

to a wide variety of restaurants, cafes and galleries, as well as a plethora of stores selling everything imaginable. Strolling and window-shopping up and down the road is a pleasurable experience.

Crimson Carbon (524 Washington Avenue, Suite 101, tel: 305/538-8262) has a range of ecofriendly, organic and chemical-free clothing. This hip boutique, two blocks west of Collins Avenue, is where to come for chic, California-inspired styles that not only look good, they are also good for the planet. It features Carilyn Vaile's line of raw bamboo clothing.

For a pure Miami glam shopping experience – or at least to try on the same clothes the stars wear – head for **En Avance** (734 Lincoln Road, tel: 305/534-0337). Inside are the season's latest collections by mid-range to high-end designers. The service is refreshingly unpretentious and you don't have to be a celebrity to shop here.

Bal Harbour

One of the premier shopping malls in the country is located just north of Miami Beach in the exclusive neighborhood of **Bal Harbour.** Visit the **Bal Harbour Shops** (9700 Collins Avenue, tel: 305/866-0311; www.balharbourshops.com) to bask in the opulence and moneyed splendor that is exuded from the dozens of premier boutiques.

Throughout the three-floor mall you can purchase serious jewels and watches at Bulgari, Georg Jensen, Cartier, Tiffany & Co., Van Cleef & Arpels and Tourneau, or spend thousands on top designer fashions at Neiman Marcus, Saks Fifth Avenue, Giorgio Armani, Prada, Chanel and Versace. There are also shops for children's wear, such as Bonpoint and Mini Oxygene.

Opening hours for the malls are generally Mon–Fri 10–9, Sat 10–7, Sun noon–6, but there are exceptions.

Biscayne Boulevard

Design your own wax-and-dyed artwork, known as batik, to go on a T-shirt at **Hiho Batik** (6925 Biscayne Boulevard, tel: 305/754-8890; www.hihobatik.com), a cool little store whose friendly staff have a love of art. If you just want to shop, you will find all sorts of funky little fun gifts, like pop-up books, magnets, journals and cards with priceless quotes at the attached **Sprocket Gift Shop.**

Loehmann's, the famous discount women's clothing store that originated in Brooklyn, New York, is the centerpiece of **Loehmann's Fashion Island Mall** (18701 Biscayne Boulevard, tel: 305/932-4207; Mon–Sat 10–9, Sun noon–6). The Loehmann's here also sells men's clothing, shoes and home furnishings, all at discounted

prices. The mall also boasts other stores selling designer fashions and shoes, a jewelry exchange, home furnishing stores, a 16-screen movie theater and a choice of restaurants.

Little Havana

Buy your stogies at **El Credito Cigars** (1106 S.W. 8th Street, tel: 305/858-4162; daily 10–6), one of the Miami's most popular cigar stores, in the heart of Little Havana.

From CDs to old vinyl records and even cassette tapes, **Do Re Mi Music Center** (1829 S.W. 8th Street, tel: 305/541-3374; daily 10–6) sells Latin music, as well as instruments. The staff are extremely helpful and will take time to explain the different rhythms and styles from salsa to samba to tango.

Cuban ride T-shirts, posters, flags, photo books and business card cases are all for sale at **Little Havana-To-Go,** the area's official souvenir store (1442 S.W. 8th Street, tel: 305/857-9720). Many of the

gifts make great stocking fillers at Christmas, and there's also a good range of authentic Cuban clothing.

Coconut Grove

In addition to Bal Harbour, there are lots of other malls in the area that house mostly chain stores. **CocoWalk** (3015 Grand Avenue at Virginia Street, tel: 305/444-0777; www.cocowalk.net) is a three-level, outdoor mall with a tropical feel and plenty of lively restaurants and bars, as well as a movie theater. There are more than 40 stores ranging from expensive clothiers, shoe stores and jewelers to T-shirt shops and kiosks that sell funky jewelry, gifts and the like. CocoWalk was conceived as much more than just a shopping mall; there's a strong cultural and entertainment component here too.

South Miami

The Falls (8888 S.W. 136th Street, off US 1/S. Dixie Highway, tel: 305/255-4571; www.shopthefalls.com) is a huge, outdoor mall with a Macy's and Bloomingdale's, in addition to Coach, which sells beautiful leather goods; Abercrombie & Fitch, a legendary name in fashion; Pottery Barn, for home furnishings; The Disney Store, with enough stuff to please kids of all tastes; Brooks Brothers, with clothing for the well-dressed man; and many more.

Festivals and Markets

There are several outdoor flea markets and festivals in Miami that run at different times of the year. They are great fun to stroll through to find unusual merchandise and see colorful people and join in the party atmosphere.

The Art Deco Weekend (Ocean Drive from 5th to 15th streets, tel: 305/672-2014) is a street festival that happens for four days each January, and is one of the liveliest events of the year. The street is crammed full of vendors selling all types of vintage merchandise, as well as food kiosks and clothing booths. The festival stays open until midnight and the atmosphere is happy and eclectic, and sometimes feels more like a party than a place to shop.

The Outdoor Antique and Collectible Market (800–1100 blocks near Alton Road/Lincoln Road, tel: 305/673-4991; www.antiquecollectiblemarket.com) runs the first and third Sunday from October to May. Here serious antiques tempt collectors.

For handmade international crafts and funky used clothing, the Espanola Way Flea Market (Espanola Way, between Drexel and Washington avenues) is the place. The market is open Friday through Sunday and is always lots of fun.

Down in Key West, the prices are high and the selection ranges from tacky souvenirs to stuffed toy manatees. If you really must use your credit card to feel as if you've had a vacation, look for cigars or local crafts (kites and glasswork) in the stores along Duval Street.

Where to...
Be Entertained

Nightlife is supreme in Miami, where the club scene is seriously hot and the people are super cool. Ask at your hotel or pick up a copy of Miami New Times, a free alternative newspaper that has the latest information on the best clubs in town. You'll find it in kiosks around SoBe.

If you are staying in one of South Beach's cool hotels, ask the staff what's on. Otherwise consult one of the many publications that devote pages and pages to the club scene, such as Channel and Ocean Drive, both available free in most hotels. A lot of clubs cater to a thriving gay culture, and have a plethora of colorful drag shows. Many clubs set up velvet ropes and have huge bouncers and stylish door people who monitor the guest list and decide which people will get to go inside. While this can seem very intimidating, it is rare to be turned away completely; simply wait your turn and try to look like you belong. Be sure to call ahead to check cover charges; they can be quite expensive at some places.

NIGHTCLUBS AND LOUNGES

For celebrity DJs and a hip mix of house, trance and progressive music, walk around Espanola Way, along the Lincoln Road Mall, and between the 1200 and 1500 blocks of Washington Avenue. Where you spy a line of fashionable young people trying their best to look hip and unaffected, you know you've arrived at the nightclub du jour.

Miami is America's gateway to South America, and appropriately the Latin music scene is one of the most happening in the country. **Yuca** (501 Lincoln Road, at Drexel Avenue, tel: 305/532-9822) is a popular Latin-influenced restaurant.

Miami's ultra-hot nightlife scene is constantly in flux, but a few places remain perennially cool with staying power. Start with a visit to **Skybar** (1901 Collins Avenue, tel: 305/695-3900) in the Shore Club. This is where to go for a cocktail with the beautiful people and dizzying city views. Or dress to seriously impress and try to gain entry into the all-crimson, totally A-list **Red Room** (where the celebrities hang out).

Also in South Beach, **BED** (929 Washington Avenue, tel: 305/532-9070) is Miami's happening club. Featuring a DJ booth and plenty of beds for lounging (although to lay down you'll need to order bottle service, so bring cash for the experience), it is where mere mortals come to dance and get crazy to the throbbing house vibes. You can also get into the groove at **Nikki Beach Miami** (1 Ocean Drive, tel: 305/538-1111), which offers alfresco dancing between swanky gossamer beach cabanas. .

Power Studios (3791 N.E. 2nd Avenue, at N.E. 37th Street, tel: 305/576-1336) is a lively entertainment complex, with a jazz and blues room, a rock and dance floor and an art gallery.

CINEMA

Several movie theaters show foreign and independent movies exclusively, with the occasional revivals thrown in for good measure. Check local newspapers for locations and the latest listings.

THEATER, MUSIC AND DANCE

Miami is a vibrant and changing city, and as such venues and performances come and go with amazing frequency. For perhaps the most up-to-date account of what's in and what's out in the performing arts community, check online (www.miamidadearts.org).

For theater lovers there are several good venues that put on quality productions.

For glitzy musicals with show-stopping numbers, check out the **Actors Playhouse** (280 Miracle Mile, between Ponce de León Boulevard and Salzedo Street, Coral Gables, tel: 305/444-9293; www.actorsplayhouse.org).

For excellent thought-provoking and sometimes avant-garde plays, head to **New Theatre** (4120 Laguna Street, Coral Gables, tel: 305/443-5909; www.new-theatre.org).

Miami is a wonderful city for dance, and aficionados can enjoy performances that range from classical ballet to unusual modern ensembles. The best way to find out what's happening is to contact the **Florida Dance Association** (tel: 305/310-8080; www.floridadance association.org) and ask for a copy of its Florida Dance Calendar.

From October to May, **New World Symphony** (Lincoln Theater, 541 Lincoln Road, at Pennsylvania Road, tel: 305/673-3331 or 800/597-3331; www.nws.org) puts on a grand array of concerts to showcase its immense talent.

The **Florida Grand Opera** (www.fgo.org) performs classics such as *La Bohème* at the Miami-Dade County Auditorium (2901 W. Flagler Street, at S.W. 29th Avenue, tel: 305/854-1643).

The **Florida Philharmonic Orchestra** performs at the Gusman Center for the Performing Arts (tel: 800/226-1812 – box office; www.floridaphilharmonic.org).

KEY WEST

In the spirit of the island's most famous resident, Ernest Hemingway, drinking and beachcombing are the two major pastimes in this resort town.

As a gay mecca, Key West has a number of fun dance clubs that fill up on weekend nights and provide entertainment for a mixed crowd. Key West is informal, so don't hesitate to venture out in your shorts and flip-flops.

SPORTS

Miami has always been proud of its thriving football culture – the Dolphins are the only NFL team to ever have an undefeated season, and the University of Miami Hurricanes dominated college football in the 1980s and 1990s.

Each year the city hosts the Orange Bowl for college teams, and the city's Dolphin Stadium was the site of the 2007 Super Bowl XLI. Football aside, Miami has never been as much of a sports city as Chicago or New York. In recent years, however, the city has flourished in this department with the addition of ice hockey, basketball and baseball teams.

Tickets for all Miami sports events can be bought over the phone with a major credit card, by calling Ticketmaster on tel: 305/350-5050.

Football

If you attend one American sport, make it football. It's the modern-day equivalent of a gladiator battle. The **Dolphins'** 1972 undefeated season is legendary. However, in recent years the team has not been much of a dominating force. Nonetheless it is always great fun to attend a pro football game (Pro Player Stadium, 2269 NW. 199th Street, North Dade; tel: 1-888/FINS-TIX; 888/346-7849; www.miamidolphins.com) – season-ticket holders throw elaborate tailgate (car-boot) parties and go all out.

The University of Miami's football team, the **Hurricanes,** may be even more popular than the Dolphins. They play in the renowned Orange Bowl (1501 NW. 3rd Street, between NW.

14th and 16th avenues; tel: 305/643-7100 or 800/462-2637; www.hurricanesports.com) and have racked up an impressive championship record during the past two decades.

College sports are often more intense than professional sports, with revved-up fans, marching bands, cheerleading squads and athletes who are still young enough to really care about the game. A Hurricanes game is no exception.

Basketball

Under former New York Knicks coach Pat Riley, the **Miami Heat** (www.nba.com/heat) was transformed into a dominating force in the game of basketball. Superstar center Alonzo Mourning, one of the league's top scorers, led the Heat to the playoffs for three consecutive seasons. Today, the team plays home games at the new Bayside American Airlines Arena (601 Biscayne Boulevard; tel: 786/777-1000; www.aaarena.com).

Golf and Polo

Many of the best golf courses in Miami are attached to resorts and limited to registered guests. Among them, the famous **Blue Monster** course at the top-ranked Doral Golf Resort and Spa (4400 NW. 87th Avenue, at NW. 41st Street, tel: 305/592-2000; www.doralresort. com) ranks the highest.

If you are staying at the **Fairmont Turnberry Isle Resort and Club** (19999 W. Country Club Drive, tel: 305/932-6200; www. fairmont.com/turnberry), you can play on two Robert Trent Jones courses.

The **Biltmore Hotel** in Coral Gables (1200 Anastasia Avenue, tel: 305/460-5364) has a challenging course that is open to the public.

Catch a match at the **Palm Beach Polo & Country Club** (11199 Polo Club Road, Wellington, tel: 561/798-7000; www. palmbeachpolo.com). In addition, it has the Equestrian Club, which hosts the Winter Equestrian Festival.

Tampa Bay Area

Getting Your Bearings

Although Tampa's preservationists have faced an uphill battle (as witnessed by empty lots where historic homes once stood), they have managed to save enough of their city to reveal a coastal town that isn't driven solely by tourism.

At the turn of the 20th century, however, the troika of tourism, shipping and cigars made Tampa a cultural and commercial center. Yet as the decades passed, the bloom came off the rose as Miami and Palm Beach became the state's favored winter playgrounds, Walt Disney chose Orlando as his new kingdom, and Tampa and neighboring St. Petersburg shifted to a haven for retirees. In the last decade, both cities have been busy polishing their images. Professional sports teams attract national attention, once-blighted neighborhoods are being transformed into attractive walking villages, and beaches continue to be a top attraction (➤ 14–15).

Clearly, the pace here is significantly quieter than in Orlando or Miami. Options for entertainment range from the lone theme park (Busch Gardens) to abundant museums, antiques districts and some of the best beaches in the state.

From Tampa south, the Gulf Coast waters become ever more beautiful and the towns equally picturesque. While there's traffic to contend with along the highway that skirts the coast, it's worth the effort to visit towns such as Sarasota and the twin paradises of Sanibel and Captiva.

Opposite: Sarasota Beach
Page 145 (left to right): Henry B Plant Museum, Tampa; Clearwater Beach; Museum of Science and Technology, Tampa

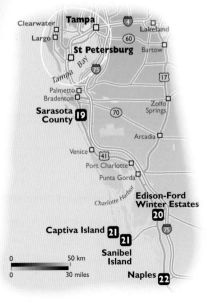

★ **Don't Miss**

In Three Days

If you're not quite sure where to begin your travels, this itinerary recommends a practical and enjoyable three days in the Tampa Bay area, taking in some of the best places to see using the Getting Your Bearings map on the previous pages. For more information see the main entries.

Day 1

Morning
Drive I-275 to Busch Boulevard and follow signs to ❶ **Busch Gardens** (➤ 150–153). An early arrival ensures no waiting on "don't-miss" rides. Beat the lunch crowd and take a long break at the Crown Colony Restaurant at the entrance to the **Edge of Africa**.

Afternoon
If you leave Busch Gardens early, take the afternoon to have a leisurely beachside drive up the Gulf Coast. If you stay till Busch closes, chill out at your hotel and get ready for the evening.

Evening
Drive up Bayshore Boulevard, then west on Swann Avenue to enter **Old Hyde Park Village** (➤ 172) for dinner at an outdoor cafe. Walk around the surrounding 1920s Arts and Crafts community.

Day 2

Morning
The Gulf Coast has hundreds of miles of beaches. Southern beaches are fine, but if you head north on Highway 699 to ❸ **Clearwater Beach** (below; ➤ 156), the powdery sands will crunch beneath your feet. If you've settled down at Clearwater, grab lunch at Pier 60, then return to tanning.

Afternoon

If you want extra time in Tampa, head east. Take 60–90 minutes to hit the **9 Henry B Plant Museum** (left; ► 159; Victorian), the **6 Tampa Museum of Art** (► 158; pop to abstract to classical) or the **8 Florida Aquarium** (► 159).

Evening

Have a very exclusive dinner at Bern's Steak House (► 170), the restaurant with the largest wine list in the world and steaks to die for. Alternatively, drive back to downtown and head to the **7 Tampa Theatre** (► 158). One of the most beautiful movie palaces in the world, this time machine will take you back 70 years. Then it's an evening in **2 Ybor City** (► 154–155). By the time you arrive, the madding crowd will be there to energize you into overdrive.

Day 3

Morning

Take I-275 south to St Petersburg and arrive at the **14 Salvador Dalí Museum** (right; ► 161–162) when they open their doors. Beating the crowds allows you to appreciate the works of this madman/genius without interruption. The **13 Florida Holocaust Museum** (► 161) presents this horrifying episode with quiet dignity.

Afternoon

Take a break and have lunch at the waterfront Renaissance Vinoy (501 5th Avenue N.E., tel: 727/894-1000). The hotel opened in 1925, was completely renovated in 1992 and looks better than it ever did. Don't ask why the **12 Florida International Museum** (► 160) is in St Petersburg – just be thankful that it is. Exhibits are world class and presented with an eye on creativity. For a change of pace take a walk down to the end of **15 The Pier** (► 162). Less touristy are the abundant antiques shops on 4th Avenue. Catch a Tampa Bay Devil Rays baseball game if possible (played at St Petersburg's Tropicana Field, April to October; www.devilrays.com).

Evening

If you're feeling energetic, head over to BayWalk, the downtown entertainment complex with a 20-screen movie theater, stores, cafes and restaurants.

❶Busch Gardens

Busch Gardens, a slice of Africa thrust into the heart of urban American sprawl, has enthralled travelers from around the world for nearly half a century.

Busch Gardens brings together an unrivaled combination of incredible rides and amazing animals. When you walk through the African arches, hear the syncopated drumbeats, and see tribal masks and brass goods stacked high in the bazaar, you'll swear you've left Florida. If you're on a schedule, you may be tempted to breeze through the park hitting only highlights and getting back to the beach. Resist the temptation. This is worth a full eight hours.

Giraffes roaming the central Serengeti Plain

The parking lots open half an hour before the park, so arriving early is a smart option that allows time to reach the entrance, review the park map and beat the crowds. After parking, you'll take a tram to the ticket booth/entrance. If you know what tickets you need – or if you've purchased them in advance – you'll be ahead of the game. Once you're inside, pick up a park map and entertainment schedule and set off.

Morning

Busch Gardens' regions have been given African names. The majority of guests tend to move to their right to reach Egypt and its popular roller coaster, Montu, as well as the safari-like Edge of Africa. It's tempting, but you'll save time and avoid lines by starting at the far left side of the park.

Once through the turnstiles (lavatories on your left), you'll pass through the Moroccan village. Turn to your right and bypass the Myombe Reserve. Don't panic and think you're missing everything – you'll have your turn later.

By starting at the **Skyride**, you can ride above the 65-acre (26ha) **Serengeti Plain**, catching a glimpse of giraffes, zebras, lions, gazelles, impalas, lemurs, buffaloes, rhinos, ostriches, hippos, baboons and wildebeests – while obtaining aerial reconnaissance of the park's layout.

This gives you a lift above the increasing crowds and saves your feet on a one-way trip to the **Congo** region of the park. Since this is the far left corner of Busch Gardens, you'll have reached the park's farthest point in less than an hour. Leave the Skyride and head to your right to reach Montu's roller-coaster counterpart, **Kumba**. The highlight of this ride is three seconds of weightlessness courtesy of a spiraling 108-foot (33m) vertical loop. Height restrictions may prevent smaller kids from riding Kumba, but smaller and slower coasters such as Timbuktu's **Scorpion** provide equal opportunity to thrill them. Try to hit Congo early in the day to avoid the high-noon crowds that flock here to cool off on the water-based attractions. At the **Congo River Rapids** you sit in a circular, 12-person raft. Hang on tight as you fly through the whitewater. This must-see attraction is accompanied by neighboring **Stanleyville's** slower **Stanley Falls** (a log-flume ride) and the **Tanganyika Tidal Wave**. The biggest thrill of all is **SheiKra**, Florida's tallest roller coaster. In addition to a series of pitches and rolls, you'll experience an extra-serious 200-foot (60m), 70mph (112km), 90-degree drop.

Continue your clockwise walk through the park to **Timbuktu**, filled with exotic, carnival-style rides and arcade games geared toward younger teenagers. Inside the mammoth Timbuktu Theater you can watch two 4D movies (3D with special sensory effects). The newest show called Sesame Street Presents Lights, Camera, Imagination! is shown during the morning and is suitable for children under the age of 6. The more adult Pirates 4D, written by Monty Python's Eric Idle, takes over in the afternoon, using great gags like rumbling chairs and squirting water.

Midmorning

Nairobi, the next region, has no rides, but you'll feel compelled to stop when you see the elephants and tortoises. It should be around noon now and you'll have reached the Skyride Station where you began the day.

GWAZI

Bolt together 236 miles (380km) of lumber, add two tracks, six fly-bys and speeds up to 50mph (80kph) and you've got Gwazi. Like most rides in Florida, this has a theme – here it's the mythological animal with a lion's body and a tiger's head battling it out between two roller coasters that come perilously close to one another. Gwazi is one of Busch Gardens' quartet of roller coasters (Kumba, Montu and SheiKra are the other three). Near the entrance, it is Florida's first dueling wooden roller coaster and the Southeast's largest and fastest wooden roller coaster.

Afternoon

After lunch you'll run into the flood of guests who began their day on the right side of the park. You've already covered more than half of the park with little interruption. The Crown Colony Restaurant is at the entrance to the circular **Edge of Africa**, a walk-through attraction. At the entrance, walk to your left and you'll reach an area where you're only a pane of glass away from baboons, hippos, crocodiles and most of the other animals you saw earlier from the Skyride. If your timing is right, you may catch the lions wolfing down chunks of chicken or the hippos swallowing a vegetarian platter. If this is the closest you'll get to Africa, you may want to go on the half-hour jeep safari across the **Serengeti Plain** (expensive).

Spring 2011 sees the opening of a sensational new high-speed mega-attraction, combining man-made thrills through a new launch coaster – **Cheetah Hunt** – with nature's fastest land animal, the cheetah.

The walking path boomerangs back past flamingos, and within a few seconds you'll encounter a massive wall that seems to have come from the Valley of the Kings. This is **Egypt**, home of **Montu**, the largest inverted roller coaster in the Southeast. If you can ignore the screams of terrified

SheiKra sends riders on a breathtaking, three-minute journey 200ft (60m) up, then 90 degrees straight down

passengers, work your way into the line. Unlike traditional sit-up-and-yell roller coasters, this one will have you spinning upside down, plunging into tunnels and shrieking as you fly through the steel maze at up to 60mph (97kph). If you doubt it's fast, check out the warning sign: "If you wear a prosthetic limb, make sure that it is firmly secure."

After this, you've done nearly every must-see ride – but you still haven't experienced the **Myombe Reserve**. This is home to chimps and gorillas – animals that command your attention even when they're doing nothing more than sleeping. Very close to Myombe Reserve and next to the Bird Gardens is the newly opened **Walkabout Way**, where guests can hand-feed kangaroos and wallabies, laugh along with a kookaburra and encounter magpie geese, Australian black swans and other Australian animals.

Now the only things left to see are performances ranging from ice shows and 1950s musicals to bird and dolphin shows. They're fun shows to watch, but only if your schedule allows. Near the front of the park, **Bird Gardens' Lory Landing** is a walk-through aviary where you can pay $1 to feed nectar to birds.

If you're traveling with kids, chances are they'll be dragging by now. They may come back to life when you take them to **Sesame Street's Safari of Fun**. It's another new Busch Gardens attraction, aimed at the park's youngest visitors, and features Air Grover, a kid-friendly roller coaster with "mini-drives," and Elmo's Tree House, as well as water rides named for favorite Sesame Street characters, like Oscar's Swamp Stomp and Bert & Ernie's Water Hole. You can even dine with the characters.

You should just about have reached the end of the road by now – time to go home and take a rest before deciding how to spend the evening.

➕ 220 B3 ✉ 10165 N. McKinley Drive ☎ 888/800-5447;
www.buschgardens.com 🕐 Daily 9:30–6, extended hours summer, holidays
and weekends 💲 Very expensive; combined ticket available ➤ 76

BUSCH GARDENS: INSIDE INFO

Top tips If you plan to visit Universal Orlando, SeaWorld Orlando and Wet 'n Wild Orlando, see page 76 for details of the **Orlando FlexTicket and Value Ticket.**

■ Most of the rides (especially Congo River Rapids) **promise significant drenching,** so wear something that will dry quickly or take a change of clothes with you.

■ Even though the food here can be inexpensive, you can bring in your own provisions – just not in a cooler. **Backpacks and water bottles are allowed.**

■ The Visitor Information Center (3601 E. Busch Boulevard, tel: 813/985-3601; Mon–Sat 10–5:30, Sun 10–2), across from the park, **sells discounted admission tickets.** Also check the park's website.

Getting there Busch Gardens is 7 miles (11km) north of downtown Tampa and can be reached from either I-75 or I-275. Both highways have well-marked signs (the exit is Busch Boulevard).

2 Ybor City

From cigars to nightlife, restaurants to cobblestones, Ybor City is the coolest neighborhood in Tampa. Revitalized but not rebuilt, this once downtrodden area is now a dignified, preserved 19th-century historic district where Tampa's party scene and Cuban cultural connection meet.

A few years ago, Ybor City was just another run-down neighborhood. Then, people with money saw a gold mine, bought the buildings, raised the rents and brought in new businesses to reap the rewards. That said, you won't find the spectrum of stores that were here a few years ago, but there are still plentiful reasons to visit Ybor City. Ybor is a National Historic Landmark District, and Barrio Latino, the area's watchdog group, makes sure buildings remain true to their Spanish/Cuban heritage. And a fairly impressive heritage it is. Before the turn of the 20th century, when others saw only a heavily wooded and mosquito-infested clump of nothing, Key West cigar-maker and entrepreneur Don Vicente Martinez Ybor visualized the Cigar Capital of the World. Spaniards and Cubans, Italians, Jews and Germans began arriving for the steady work and wages that were offered.

The Old Cigar District

Although it was primarily known to smokers, Ybor City's profile was raised when Teddy Roosevelt and his Rough Riders used Tampa as their point of embarkation to Cuba in the Spanish-American War. As soldiers and the press descended on Tampa, they discovered a thriving ethnic community in the heart of Central Florida. Shopkeepers lived above their stores on La Septima (7th Avenue) and the citizens gathered at casinos and their mutual aid societies.

If you arrive during daylight, a good place to get started is the **Ybor City State Museum**, housed in the old La Ferlita Bakery. Here you will get an interesting introduction to Ybor's beginnings, heyday, decline and resurrection. Presentations include artifacts from the cigar factories, pictures and a

Enjoy a movie and your favorite cocktail at Muvico

Channelside entertainment and shopping complex, near Ybor City

10-minute video on the history of the district. A restored cigar worker's home, La Casita, has been furnished in period style and can be viewed (Tue–Sat 10–3).

Try dinner at the **Columbia Restaurant**, founded in 1905 and still in business (► 170–171). Ornate, handpainted tiles, several dining rooms, a courtyard and good service reflect the best of Spain. When Ybor City was a stop on the Havana–New York–Tampa entertainment circuit, the Columbia would feature flamenco dancers and classical guitarists – and it still does. There are floor shows Monday through Saturday.

Centro Ybor

If you're around after dark, by 10pm the streets become home to a wide selection of people, from bikers and bikers' chicks to punks and Rastafarians. To cater to the cross-section of culture, Ybor has opened clubs for just about every taste. Most of these are found along E. 7th Avenue. **Centro Ybor**, is a typical entertainment complex with trendy stores, a comedy club, a cigar museum, restaurants and a 20-screen movie theater. There is also a large number of soul clubs, R&B dives, country saloons, gay bars and techno-pop dance halls.

✚ 220 B3 🚹 1514 1/2 8th Avenue ☎ 813/248-3712; www.ybor.org

Ybor City State Museum
✉ 1818 E. 9th Avenue ☎ 813/247-6323; www.ybormuseum.org 🕓 Daily 9–5 💲 Inexpensive

Centro Ybor
✉ 1600 E. 8th Avenue ☎ 813/242-4660; www.centroybor.com

YBOR CITY: INSIDE INFO

Top tips HARTLine runs the **2.4-mile (4km) TECO Line streetcar** system between downtown, the Channel District and Ybor City from 10am to midnight on weekdays and until 3am on weekends. The fare is $2 for a single trip, $4 for an all-day pass.

■ On weekend nights, **7th Avenue becomes a pedestrian mall.** Park outside that area if you plan to arrive early and stay late. Meters are enforced from 8am–3am Mon–Sat. Unmetered parking is available on side streets.

■ Don't travel too far off 7th Avenue; **it's not particularly safe.**

■ Want to walk on Cuban soil in the US? Ybor City's El Parque Amigos de Marti Park **belongs to Cuba.**

3 Tampa Bay Area Beaches

The Gulf stays pretty calm most of the time. With that peace of mind, you can relax on sands that, for the most part, are soft and sugary and will persuade you to extend your leisure time on the beach.

There are 7 miles (11km) of undeveloped beaches southwest of downtown St Petersburg at **Fort DeSoto Park**, and North Beach is a consistent favorite with locals. There are facilities here, the fort, a fishing pier and other activities to keep you occupied when you get tired of tanning. Most visitors think they'll have better luck on St Pete Beach. Perhaps, but when you reach the beaches along Highway 699 (also known as Gulf Boulevard), stingrays often skim in the shallows. Hotels here suggest you do the "stingray shuffle" (carefully shuffling your feet on the surface of the sand) to scare them away – which is not a pleasing thought if you just want to dive in and splash around like a maniac.

Playing beach volleyball at Clearwater Beach

Several miles north you'll find a beach that's not rocky or stingray-plagued. **Treasure Island** is a typical Florida beach town with everything you need for a good day of sunning and swimming. There's plenty of parking, facilities and a snack bar, and if you need more supplies there are several grocery stores within a short walk. You can rest here, or keep exploring.

North past John's Pass Village and Boardwalk in Madeira Beach, communities such as **Redington Shores**, **Indian Rocks Beach** and **Belleair Shores** have hidden entrances to beaches that provide more privacy – all good choices if your motivation is to experience seaside serenity.

The mother of all beaches is **Clearwater Beach**, and bright blue cabanas suggest a scene from the French Riviera. The beach is wide and wonderful. You're never too far from essentials, and there are fishing charters and parasailing boats departing from the marina. At the end of the day, you can walk down to Pier 60 to take part in the daily sunset celebration.

At Your Leisure

4 Adventure Island

Gulf waters are smooth and salty, which makes this high-energy freshwater water park more popular with some folks. Aquatic thrills include Riptide, Adventure Island's most wicked flume tube race, shooting the flume at Runaway Rapids, and rocketing twisty tubes at Calypso Coaster and Key West Rapids. The 30-acre (12ha) water park has nearly two dozen slides, heated pools, a wave pool, volleyball courts and snack bars. It takes about five hours to make the rounds, and although there are places to snack you may want to pack your own food and drinks.

🚹 220 B3 🖂 10001 N. McKinley Drive, adjacent to Busch Gardens, Tampa Bay (► 150–153) ☎ 813/ 987-5600; www.adventureisland.com 🕐 Mar–Oct, hours vary 🎟 Moderate. Parking inexpensive

You can see some of nature's finest wildlife at Safari Africa, Lowry Park Zoo

5 Lowry Park Zoo

You could travel the world over to see four continents of wildlife, or you can just come here. From the Asian Domain to Primate World, roughly 1,600 animals call these natural surroundings home. There are baboons, lemurs, chimps and tigers. The Florida Wildlife Center showcases natives such as alligators, panthers and black bears. The Manatee and Aquatic Center is one of only three rehabilitation centers in Florida. Plump, cute-as-a-button sea cows spend their days swimming in a huge aquarium. At the interactive Lorikeet Landing you can invite birds to feed out of your hand, while the 6-acre (2.5ha) Safari Africa exhibit features zebras, elephants, giraffes and warthogs.

🚹 220 B3 🖂 1101 W. Sligh Avenue, Tampa, I-4 west to I-275 North to Exit 48; go west on Sligh Avenue to N. Boulevard ☎ 813/935-8552; www.lowryparkzoo.com 🕐 Daily 9:30–5 🎟 Inexpensive

6 Tampa Museum of Art

Art lovers who like eclectic collections of classical and contemporary art will enjoy pottery and busts from the classical period of Greece and Rome, and the traveling shows ranging from pop art, abstract oils and sculptures to the traditional images of Ansel Adams. The tour takes an hour or so, with a few minutes in the gift shop and the gallery that overlooks the Hillsborough River and the University of Tampa.

➕ 220 B3 ✉ 120 W. Gasparilla Plaza (entrance on Twiggs off Ashley), Tampa ☎ 813/274-8130 🕐 Mon–Wed, Fri 11–7, Thu 11–9, Sat–Sun 11–5 💲 Inexpensive; 5 and under free

Tampa Museum of Art contains a diverse collection of work

7 Tampa Theatre

Built in 1926, this restored architectural masterpiece is one of the most picturesque movie palaces in Florida. Once facing extinction, the faltering theater was bought by the city in 1973 for $1. Through grants and fund-raisers, it was restored to its original splendor and is now listed on the National Register of Historical Places.

Unlike today's run-of-the-mill multiplexes, the interior theme of this atmospheric theater is a Florida Mediterranean courtyard on a moonlit night. Stars sparkle overhead, Roman statues frame flowering balconies, vintage sconces and decorative columns accent elaborate mosaic tilework (244,185 floor tiles to be exact, says a staff

member). With so much beauty surrounding you, it may be hard to watch the screen. Showing are first-run foreign films or, on weekends, classics such as *Casablanca*, *Gone With the Wind* or *The Princess Bride*. Like many old buildings, this one has a friendly ghost. Foster "Fink" Finley, the projectionist, died in the booth after 35 years on the job and is occasionally said to come back to check on things.

➕ 220 B3 ✉ 711 Franklin Street, Tampa
☎ 813/274-8981; www.tampatheatre.org
🕐 Daily 7:30pm; Sat–Sun, matinée times vary
💲 Inexpensive

🔟 Florida Aquarium

Your 90-minute tour of Florida's ecosystems begins here. With more than 10,000 oceanic and freshwater animals, plus plants and the Caribbean-themed family-friendly outdoor exhibit "Explore-A-Shore," it offers an instant education on the diverse ecosystems existing outside the theme parks. Exhibit placards give only limited information, so fish fanciers may want to take the taped tour for more details and flexibility, or catch up with staff members, who host various presentations throughout the attraction. The parking lot is about quarter of a mile (400m) away, so drop your group off first.

➕ 22 0 B3 ✉ 701 Channelside Drive, Tampa ☎ 813/273-4000; www.flaquarium.org
🕐 Daily 9:30–5 💲 Moderate

Florida Aquarium's impressive tanks

The Henry B Plant Museum, with its distinctive onion-domed minarets

🔟 Henry B Plant Museum and University of Tampa

Built in 1891 as a labor of love by railroad magnate Henry B Plant, the Tampa Bay Hotel was Florida's first all-electric, steam-heated, fireproofed, elevator-equipped hotel. Its quixotic and exotic blend of Moorish revival architecture, accented by cupolas, domes, keyhole arches, broad verandas and onion-domed minarets, each crowned with a crescent moon, makes this Tampa's most visible vintage landmark and a National Historic Landmark. After Plant's death in 1899, the resort was purchased by the city in 1904 for $125,000. Tours of the museum, in one of the old hotel's wings, begin with a short video, "The Tampa Bay Hotel: Florida's First Magic Kingdom," and rooms are themed to reflect popular Victorian pastimes.

Next door, the University of Tampa houses the hotel's grand rotunda, salon, and music and dining rooms.

➕ 220 B3 ✉ 401 W. Kennedy Boulevard, Tampa ☎ 813/254-1891; www.plantmuseum. com 🕐 Tue–Sat 10–5, Sun noon–5
💲 Inexpensive

The Museum of History in St Petersburg displays local and state history

🔟 St Petersburg Museum of History

If you want to see what happened here in the 500 years before you arrived, you might find the blend of history and culture at this museum interesting. Located at the entrance to the Pier (➤ 162), the small history center is highlighted by a display of the *Benoist* Airboat, the first scheduled commercial airline in the world. In 1914, one passenger could pay $5 and catch a 23-minute lift from St. Petersburg to Tampa and save six hours of driving muddy roads that encircled the bay. More recent displays show St Pete during its 1950s heyday through bathing-beauty shots, archive photographs and postcards.

🚸 220 B2 ⊠ 335 2nd Avenue N.E., St Petersburg ☎ 727/894-1052; www.spmoh.com ⏰ Mon–Sat 10–5, Sun noon–5 💲 Inexpensive; under 6 free

🔟 Museum of Fine Arts

This is the sort of aesthetically appealing museum preferred by traditional art enthusiasts. Its library-quiet formality complements the permanent high-end fine art selections such as Monet's *Houses of Parliament*, O'Keeffe's *Poppy*, Renoir's *Girl Reading* and Berthe Morisot's *La Lecture*, which are prominently displayed alongside works by Rodin, Cézanne and Gauguin. There are also oil landscapes reflecting the Hudson River School style, French furniture, a smattering of contemporary works and visiting shows. Give yourself an hour or so, and if you need a break, step outside to the open-air courtyard or into the gift shop.

🚸 220 B2 ⊠ 255 Beach Drive N.E., St Petersburg ☎ 727/896-2667; www.fine-arts.org ⏰ Tue–Sat 10–5, Sun 1–5 💲 Inexpensive; under 6 free

🔟 Florida International Museum

One of the most energetic museums in the state, the FIM has hosted impressive (and sometimes record-breaking) exhibits on the *Titanic*, JFK, Alexander the Great and Ancient Egypt. As an affiliate of the Smithsonian Institution, it houses artifacts from "America's Attic" and presents an assortment of traveling exhibitions.

🚸 220 B2 ⊠ 244 Second Avenue N., St Petersburg ☎ 727/341-7900; www.floridamuseum.org ⏰ Tue–Sat 10–5, Sun noon–5 💲 Inexpensive

🔳 Florida Holocaust Museum

Ordinarily, museums are places of beauty evoking pleasant emotions. Holocaust museums aren't. They are usually unsettling, sometimes disturbing. The Florida Holocaust Museum is no different. One subtle change in presentation, however, is a message of hope that permeates the displays. The first floor takes you through the Holocaust with personal tales told by survivors – some of whom are now local residents.

In the nation's third-largest Holocaust museum, an audio tour allows you to roam between exhibits and listen to a well-written and superbly narrated chronicle of events. From the Beer Hall Putsch through Kristallnacht and to the overdue Nuremberg Trials, the presentations are well-balanced for young and old visitors. Visual exhibits include a chilling display of Josef Mengele's medical instruments and two-year-old Doris Mathis's shoes – the only pair from millions that are traceable to their owner.

The second-floor art gallery showcases traveling exhibits and art of the Holocaust, while one floor above is an education center. The focal point of the museum, however, is a powerful reminder of the Holocaust: Auschwitz Boxcar No. 113-0695-5, used to transport Jewish people to the concentration camps. In the process of moving the boxcar to this location, a child's ring from the 1940s fell from the cracks and is now on display. Be prepared for some emotional moments.

🔲 220 B2 ✉ 55 5th Street S., at 1st Avenue S., St Petersburg ☎ 727/820-0100 or 800/960-7448; www.flholocaustmuseum.org 🕐 Fri–Wed 10–5 (last entry 3:30), Thu 10–8 (last entry 7) 💵 Inexpensive. Parking free

🔳 Salvador Dalí Museum

Dalí's dreamlike, surrealistic paintings continue to intrigue even casual observers, and the museum, which has now moved to a new location, contains the most comprehensive collection of the renowned artist's works in the world. There are 96 oil paintings, over 100 watercolors and drawings, and some 1,300 graphics, photographs, sculptures and objets d'art. Masterpieces include *The Hallucinogenic Toreador* and *The Discovery of America by Christopher Columbus*. Check out *The Disintegration of the Persistence of Memory* and *Oeufs sur le Plat sans le Plat* (which translates as *Eggs on a Plate Without the Plate*).

The Florida Holocaust Museum has a very moving account of this period in history

Try to come early, before busloads of people arrive, and then browse the delightful gift shop which offers a selection of Daliesque books, DVDs, postcards, T-shirts and jewelry.

➕ 220 B2 ✉ One Dali Boulevard, St Petersburg. Take I-275 South. Take Exit 22 (I-175) toward Tropicana Field. Follow I-175 to the end, which turns into Dali Boulevard (5th Avenue S.) The museum is on the left after the 4th light ☎ 727/823-3767; www.thedali.org ⏰ Mon–Sat 10–5:30 (also Thu 5:30–8), Sun noon–5:30 💷 Adult: moderate; child (6–12): inexpensive; under 5 free

🔟 The Pier

The Pier is one of the most recognized landmarks on Florida's west coast. It is a complex of specialty stores, an aquarium, restaurants and various attractions, housed in a five-story inverted pyramid, with fine views from its observation platform. In winter, HMS *Bounty* docks here.

While major league baseball games are played about a mile (1.6km) away at Tropicana Field, during Spring Training – which takes place each March – the Devil Rays play at **Progress Energy Park**, a few blocks from the Pier. Tickets to watch the team cost between $9 and $15, less than for a major league game.

➕ 220 B2 ✉ 800 2nd Avenue N.E., St Petersburg ☎ 727/821-6164 ⏰ Mon–Thu 10–8, Fri–Sat 10–9, Sun 11–7

Progress Energy Park
✉ 180 2nd Avenue S.E., St Petersburg ☎ 727/825-3250

🔟 Tarpon Springs

It's as if Poseidon had plucked this village from the Greek islands, placed it on Florida's west coast, then added a host of tacky T-shirt, shell and sponge stores. Greek divers came to Tarpon Springs around the turn of the 19th century to harvest a natural bounty of sponges. Today, the city boasts of having the largest natural sponge market in the world, with annual revenues of more than $5 million, despite a disastrous blight that wiped out most of the sponge beds in the 1940s. A sightseeing cruise from the sponge docks includes a live sponge-diving exhibition.

For another look at the city, drive over to Tarpon Avenue and visit the

Tarpon Springs is known as "America's Sponge Capital"

High-quality sponges make ideal gifts and won't take up too much space

downtown area, which is brimming with antiques and craft shops, jewelers and artists who work with stained glass.

🗲 220 B3 🟦 11 E. Orange Street (corner of Alternate Highway 19 and Orange), Tarpon Springs ☎ 727/937-6109; www.tarponsprings.com

🔢 John's Pass Village and Boardwalk

You'll see this either as a tacky tourist trap or a neat, Cape Cod-like waterfront fishing village with a Key West twist. This is a haven for seafood restaurants, gambling cruises, gift shops and an armada of wave-runner concessions clustered along the north bank. The pseudo village includes ice-cream parlors, T-shirt emporiums, nature-themed art galleries and the requisite bait and tackle stores. Boats set sail for sightseeing tours along the Intracoastal and romantic sunset cruises, but if you want to do it yourself rent a wave-runner, jet ski, three-passenger jet boat or another cutting-edge water toy. Hint: with so much competition, try striking a bargain (and watch for come-on prices that exclude additional charges). If you have time to fish, charter captains will take you out for snapper, kingfish, barracuda and amberjack, which you can take to the Friendly Fisherman restaurant to be cleaned, filleted and cooked for a nominal fee (provided you caught it from one of their boats).

🗲 220 B2 ✉ 12901 Gulf Boulevard E., Madeira Beach 🕐 Daily

Enjoying a meal and the view on the harborfront of John's Pass Village

Beach at Fort DeSoto Park, a welcome respite from the high-rise hotels along the Gulf

🔞 Fort DeSoto Park

This is one of Florida's best beach and camping bargains. More than 1,100 acres (445ha) on five interconnected islands provide the perfect blend of activities and relaxation, from the shaded 238-site waterfront campground to the magnificent beaches on the southern tip of the peninsula. Camping sites, if you can get one, include grills and picnic tables with nearby showers and lavatories. Day-trippers can forget the tents and set up a picnic near East Beach only a few miles away, or head east for an incredible view of the towering Sunshine Skyway Bridge. There are no swimming opportunities at this location, but bring your fishing pole, wade out and drop a line.

From a 1,000-foot (305m) pier on the road to the fort, you can watch the comings and goings of barges and sizeable ships as they exit the Gulf and pull into Tampa Bay. Up the road, the remains of Fort DeSoto provide a glimpse into history. The fort overlooks Egmont Key's historic lighthouse. If you save the best for last, North Beach is *the* beach to hit.

✚ 220 B2 ✉ 3500 Pinellas Bayway S., Tierra Verde ☎ 727/582-2267; www.pinellascounty. org/park 🎫 Moderate (cash only). Camping reservations must be made in advance; call 727/582-2267 (moderate); cash only

Fort DeSoto Canoe Outpost

☎ 727/864-1991; www.canoeoutpost.com
🕐 Mon–Sun 9–5 🎫 Moderate per canoe/ kayak per day

Farther Afield

⑲ Sarasota County

Once recognized primarily as the winter home of the Ringling Brothers Circus, **Sarasota** is now known as home to a lot of retirees. Add to the mix students from the Ringling School of Art and Design and you have an impressive degree of diversity. The two factions meet at the area's most visited attraction, the **John and Mable Ringling Museum of Art**.

The museum, located at the intersection of University Parkway and US 41, was part of the Ringlings' legacy, a supplement to their winter home, **Ca' d'Zan**. Upon his death in 1936, John Ringling bequeathed the entire estate and his impressive art collection to the people of the state of Florida. There are more than 500 years of art here, with bronze replicas of ancient Greek and Roman sculptures as well as paintings by Rubens, Bonheur, Alfred Stevens and other artists. If you like art, you'll love this; if not, you may want to skip it and head over to the Circus Museum or the mansion. Three architects worked on this project and the result is a Venetian-style, eclectic, $1.5 million masterpiece.

After recovering from your art attack, drive south down US 41 to the John Ringling Causeway, turn right and you're heading to the beaches and **St Armands Key**, the best place to get a feel for the area. In addition to restaurants, sidewalk cafes and courtyards with antique statuary, St Armands Circle is a world-renowned center of chic stores (tel: 941/388-1554). The best part of St Armands Circle is that it's only a few blocks from one of the nicest stretches of beach in Florida. The sunsets here are fantastic – perhaps the best in Florida – and if you can't get enough of the free show, then drive north on Highway 789, where there are small motels and beachside cottages. If you check with the tourist center, they'll tell you about opera, ballet, plays and golf tournaments, but it's far more pleasing just to lie on the beach and watch the sun.

The next town of any size is **Venice**, to the south of Sarasota. Although the name conjures images of a cultural Italian city, this is actually urban sprawl separated by a series of canals and bordered by nice beachfront at Nokomis and North Jetty Park. The draw here is shark's teeth, which wash ashore with great frequency (minus the shark).

Caspersen Beach, further south is the longest beach in Sarasota County and is relatively unscathed by modernization.

🔲 220 B2 ⚊ 1945 Fruitville Road, Sarasota
☎ 941/955-2508; www.sarasotachamber.org

John and Mable Ringling Museum of Art
✉ 5401 Bay Shore Road, Sarasota
☎ 941/359-5700; www.ringling.org ⚙ Daily 10–5 ⚙ Adult: moderate; child (6–17): inexpensive; under 6 free. Free for all on Mon

The Venetian-style Ca' d'Zan in Sarasota

🔟 Edison-Ford Winter Estates

The Edison-Ford Winter Estates in Fort Myers is where Thomas Alva Edison spent his winters working on the phonograph and teletype, and growing new plants in an effort to create a new source for rubber. The nice thing is that his laboratory is exactly as he left it, right down to the beakers and bottles. His home across the street is a great example of what an Old Florida house was like, nice and airy with wide windows and a broad veranda where he could sit and enjoy the Caloosahatchee River flowing at the end of his yard. After a hard day's work he could splash around in his swimming pool, one of the first modern pools in Florida, built in 1910.

It's all low key, but his home (and Henry Ford's house next door), plus the laboratory and sprawling banyan tree, make it worth the stop.

➕ 222 C4 ✉ 2350 McGregor Boulevard, Fort Myers ☎ 239/334-7419; www.efwefla.org ⏲ Daily 9–5:30 💲 Inexpensive

🔟 Sanibel and Captiva

Off the coast of Fort Myers are two of Florida's loveliest islands. **Sanibel**, on the south, is the larger of the two, but there is scant commercial development here since nearly two-thirds of the island is protected from future development.

That said, don't miss the **J.N. "Ding" Darling National Wildlife Refuge**, where you can take a guided tour among the 6,000-acre (2,430ha) habitat of roseate spoonbills, ospreys, pelicans and alligators. Rent a canoe or kayak and paddle beside mangrove trees and estuaries that are also explained in fascinating detail. There are several public beaches on the island, and the calm waters, white sands and shady trees make sunbathing a must.

Certain Gulf currents make this one of the world's best destinations for shell collectors, so when you're not filling up souvenir buckets for yourself, visit the **Bailey-Matthews Shell Museum**. Exhibits show the

Thomas Edison's house with its delightful porch – reminiscent of a bygone age

Blind Pass on Captiva – a favorite spot for doing the "Sanibel Stoop" or shelling

role seashells have played in ecology, medicine, literature, religion, art and as a food source. Sounds boring, but it's not. Not at all.

A few miles north, the island of **Captiva** is more laid-back and luxurious than Sanibel. Take a beach break at Blind Pass (the small river that separates the islands), and work your way up the lone road to the village, where there's a small grocery store, several nice art, clothing and gift galleries, and two popular top-drawer restaurants. The waterfront **Mucky Duck** (tel: 239/472-3434) is renowned for its Key lime pie and sunset views, and the **Bubble Room** (tel: 239/472-5558) is equally famous for its food as for a fun and colorful interior that looks like an exploded toy chest.

From **South Seas Resort**, a grand resort on the north end of the island, charter boats leave for neighboring islands such as Cabbage Key, the inspiration for Jimmy Buffett's anthem, "Cheeseburger in Paradise." If you can only see two islands in Florida, Sanibel and Captiva are sure to captivate you.

🞡 222 B4 🞣 1159 Causeway Road, Sanibel, tel: 239/472-1080; www.sanibel-captiva.org

J.N. "Ding" Darling National Wildlife Refuge
☎ 239/472-1100; www.fws.gov/dingdarling/
🞕 Inexpensive

Bailey-Matthews Shell Museum
✉ 3075 Sanibel-Captiva Road, Sanibel
☎ 239/395-2233; www.shellmuseum.org
🕐 Daily 10–5 🞕 Inexpensive; under 4 free

22 Naples

Yet another wealthy Florida community, Naples (about 165 miles/265km south of Tampa) has several points of interest for travelers. First, perhaps, is downtown itself. The **Fifth Avenue South** shopping district is a broad, tree-lined avenue of fashionable shops, art galleries and European bistros. You can get a good overview of this and the town's historic districts on a two-hour sightseeing tour with **Naples Trolley Tours** (tel: 239/262-7300) that rolls around town in a replica of a 1907 Cincinnati trolley. **Caribbean Gardens** began in 1919 as a 52-acre (21ha) botanical park. The gardens remain and, since the late 1960s, they've added the Naples Zoo, with exotic animals, boat rides, lectures, live shows and a petting farm.

Fifteen miles (24km) east of I-75, the **Corkscrew Swamp Audubon Sanctuary** is an 11,000-acre (4,500ha) preserve that's considered the crown jewel of the National Audubon Society's sanctuary system. One of the world's most popular destination for birders, photographers and wildlife watchers, the park is home to hundreds of alligators and almost 200 bird species. A 2.25-mile (3.5km) boardwalk passes through the nation's largest old-growth cypress forest and a tropical jungle of ferns, orchids and wildflowers.

Since Naples was established as a port town (note the tribute to Napoli, Italy), its greatest claim to fame is beaches that form mile after mile of the Gulf Coast. Ask locals about their favorites, or call the beaches directly for information. Among your choices are **Naples Beach**, which features the popular 1,000-foot (305m) fishing pier, **Lowdermilk Park** (tel: 239/434-4698), **Vanderbilt Beach** (tel: 239/597-6196), **Delnor–Wiggins Pass State Recreation Area** (tel: 239/597-6196), **Clam Pass Park/ Beach** and **Lely Barefoot Beach**. Most beaches have facilities that include showers, lifeguards, grills, picnic tables and pavilions, boat ramps, observation towers, restrooms, bath house, public parking, snack bars, boardwalks, fishing and gear rental, and beach chairs. When making your choice, also consider that some are quite remote while others may offer convenient access to nearby hotels.

🚌 222 C3 🏠 895 Fifth Avenue S., Naples; tel: 239/262-6141; www.napleschamber.org; www.naples-florida.com

Caribbean Gardens
✉ 1590 Goodlette–Frank Road ☎ 239/262-5409; www.caribbeangardens.com

Corkscrew Swamp Audubon Sanctuary
✉ 375 Sanctuary Road W. ☎ 239/348-9151
💲 Inexpensive; under 6 free

The colorful marina and Bayfront dining and shopping complex in Naples

Where to...
Stay

TAMPA

🛏🛏🛏 Grand Hyatt Tampa Bay $$$

The most upscale hotel in town is just a stone's throw from Tampa Airport. The service is attentive and friendly, and amenities – such as Armani's restaurant (▶170), the pool, fitness center and nature walk – are first rate. The rooms are comfortable and spacious, if a little dated. In keeping with the hotel's urban feel, the business and meeting facilities are carefully thought out.
➕ 220 B3   ✉ 2900 Bayport Drive, Tampa
☎ 813/874-1234 or 800/233-1234

🛏🛏🛏 Hilton Garden Inn/Tampa Ybor Historic District $$

In the heart of Tampa's most hip neighborhood, Ybor City, this hotel delivers Hilton-quality comfort in a buzzing city-center locale. On-site perks include a swimming pool and WiFi internet access. The rooms are upscale decorated but are value priced.
➕ 220 B3   ✉ 1700 E. 9th Avenue, Tampa
☎ 813/769-9267

🛏🛏🛏 Westin Tampa Harbour Island $$$

Located on its own 177-acre (72ha) island (Harbour Island), a small

development just off the mainland, this hotel is convenient to the convention center and downtown Tampa. The rooms are spacious, many with waterfront views, and the service is friendly and helpful. The hotel is also attached to a small mall with restaurants and shops, and a business complex. It provides easy access to the fitness trail and recreational walk along Bayshore Boulevard.
➕ 220 B3   ✉ 725 S. Harbour Island Boulevard, Harbour Island   ☎ 813/229-5000

ST PETERSBURG

🛏🛏🛏 Don CeSar Beach Resort & Spa $$$

Known as the "Pink Palace," this grand resort and spa is one of the best on the Gulf Coast. It boasts two swimming pools (one with an underwater sound system), a beautiful beach for relaxing or strolling with a variety of watersports equipment rentals and a spa where you can have your cares

massaged and wrapped away. Camp CeSar is ideal for young guests, as well as their parents.
➕ 220 B2   ✉ 3400 Gulf Boulevard, St Pete Beach   ☎ 727/360-1881

🛏🛏🛏 Renaissance Vinoy Resort $$$

About half an hour southwest of Tampa, this impressive hotel maintains the feel of the 1920s when St Petersburg was a premier tourist destination. The hotel went through a major restoration in the early 1990s, and now all of the rooms, many overlooking the bay, are equipped with every modern convenience, including TVs in the bathrooms. There is a wonderful waterfall on the property that spills into one of the hotel's pools, as well as tennis, golf, a marina, a fully equipped workout facility, day spa and salon. There are also three restaurants and outdoor dining.
➕ 220 B2   ✉ 501 5th Avenue N.E. (Beach Street), St Petersburg   ☎ 727/894-1000 or 800/HOTELS-1

Where to...
Eat and Drink

Prices
Expect to pay per person for a meal, excluding drinks:

$ under $15 $$ $15–$30 $$$ over $30

TAMPA

Tampa's location right on the water made it a booming port town, open to influences from all over the world. As with the rest of Florida, Tampa maintains strong ties with the Spanish and Cuban roots of many of its inhabitants. This is evident in much of the food, especially in Ybor City, where you will be spoiled for choice. There is a wide variety of restaurants well worth trying and the food is usually excellent. Prices tend to be fairly reasonable, even in some of the trendier places.

▽▽▽ Armani's $$$
Perched atop the Grand Hyatt Tampa Bay (▶ 169), Armani's offers stunning, panoramic views of Tampa. The setting is serene, with taupe and black accents. The fare is traditional Italian – think *osso buco, cioppino* and homemade pastas – with several creative dishes including bresaola with black truffles, veal topped with crab and lobster, and pepper-crusted, seared tuna. Opposing the view, the focal point of the room is an extensive antipasto bar. There is also a comfortable outdoor terrace, which lets you take even better advantage of the view. Jacket required for men. No jeans or tennis shoes (trainers).

✚ 220 B3 ⊠ Hyatt Regency Westshore, 2900 Bayport Drive ☎ 813/207-6800

▽▽▽ Bernini $$–$$$
Low-key, romantic dining with superb, artfully presented dishes. The menu features traditional Italian cuisine with an edge, including a mouthwatering braised lamb shank with redcurrant and marsala sauce, and an amazing fillet of beef with Gorgonzola and sun-dried tomato demiglace. The menu changes daily. This place is popular with locals. Ask for an upstairs table and look down on the dining area.

✚ 220 B3 ⊠ 1702 E. 7th Avenue, Ybor City ☎ 813/248-0099; www.berniniofybor.com

▽▽▽ Bern's Steak House $$$
Bern's is a restaurant that defies description. The decor is somewhere between a museum and a bordello, and there's a series of rooms with red walls, gold accents, 12-foot-high plaster sculptures, (3.5m) mirrors and mediocre artwork. The menu is a lesson in beef; the various cuts of steak and the aging process are described in minute detail. The wine list is held to be the most extensive in the world (really) with more than 6,000 different labels, the prices of which offer surprisingly good value. Guests get a tour of the kitchen after dinner before being escorted to the private dessert rooms upstairs. This restaurant is more than worth it for the sheer spectacle; as for the food, stick to steak (the rib eye is a favorite) and you will have a memorable meal. Be careful of the locale: Take a cab here and stay on the premises.

✚ 220 B3 ⊠ 1208 S. Howard Avenue ☎ 813/251-2421; www.bernssteakhouse.com

▽▽▽ Columbia Restaurant $$
Opened in 1905, this family-owned Spanish restaurant is a Tampa legend. The original corner cafe has expanded to a huge space that seats more than 1,500 people. One of

the nicest dining rooms is located in the center of the restaurant and has been designed to look like the courtyard of a Spanish hacienda, complete with palm trees and a fountain. Other rooms are darker and decorated with Spanish tiles. On some nights there is live entertainment and dancing. The menu offers Spanish and South American favorites – passable tapas, good *caldo gallego* (a bean soup with chorizo and greens), paella and traditional *arroz con pollo* (chicken with rice). Heavy on the garlic and the tourists, dinner is nevertheless satisfying.

➕ 220 B3 🗺 2117 E. 7th Avenue, Ybor City
☎ 813/248-4961

🍴 Kojak's House of Ribs $

A good place for an inexpensive BBQ, as well as a place to hang out with locals in a casual setting, Kojak's has tables inside and outside, and the mood is always festive. Not only is the food a draw, but the prices are reasonable and

the drive up Bayshore Drive offers a nice glimpse of downtown Tampa.

➕ 220 B3 🗺 2808 Gandy Boulevard
☎ 813/837-3774

🍴 Lonni's Cafe $

Part of a chain of take-out shops/cafes, Lonni's is a favorite among locals for interesting, healthy sandwiches on homemade bread – the wild-rice bread is known across the state. The staff is friendly and helpful and will gladly describe the nuances of Ron's Sunny Bird (turkey with cream cheese, sunflower seeds, sprouts, mayonnaise and honey dressing) or any of the other tasty concoctions on offer. Also available are soups and salads, healthy muffins and low-fat baked goods.

➕ 220 B3 🗺 513 E. Jackson Street
☎ 813/223-2333

🍴 Mise en Place $$

Dozens of votive candles light the way through this dark, sophisticated New American restaurant. The large

space is divided into several smaller rooms. Chef Marty Blitz serves up creative cuisine from a huge menu that has no fewer than 20 appetizers and 15 entrées. The food is fairly priced, if sometimes overwrought, and there is a five-course tasting menu that offers good value.

➕ 220 B3 🗺 442 W. Kennedy Boulevard
☎ 813/254-5373

🍴 P.F. Chang's China Bistro $

When you're accustomed to Asian dishes served in cardboard cartons, it's a treat to enter this contemporary restaurant where the soft lighting and the warm wood tones strike an elegant ambiance to complement the superlative dishes. Lettuce wraps, orange peel chicken, and mongolian beef are among the standards, and their "hot fish" (crispy slices of fish in a Sichuan sauce with stir-fried vegetables) is a standout.

➕ 220 B3 🗺 219 Westshore Plaza
☎ 813/289-8400

🍴 Samurai Blue Sushi and Sake Bar $$

In the Centro Ybor mall in Ybor City, this popular Japanese restaurant boasts a 30-foot-long (9m) sushi bar, a long list of sake wines and for those not in the mood for raw fish, seaweed and rice, there is an Asian fusion menu that includes some really delicious noodle dishes. Add in a funky architectural design angle and you are in for a dining experience as visually appealing as it tastes.

➕ 220 B3 🗺 1600 E. 8th Avenue, #C208, Ybor City ☎ 813/242-6688

ST PETERSBURG

🍴 Hurricane Seafood Restaurant $$

A popular seafood restaurant serving the usual lineup of crispy fried crustaceans and buckets of shrimp, the Hurricane is located across from the town's best beach Pass-a-Grille, about 20 minutes from downtown St Petersburg. Visit later in the day, when you can grab a table on the porch overlooking the sea and catch a view of the fabulous Gulf sunset. There is live entertainment on the rooftop deck bar after dark.

+ 220 B2 ⊠ 809 Gulf Way ☎ 727/360-9558

〰 〰 The Moon Under Water $

This is one of the best. A short walk from The Pier (▲ 162), museums and nightlife is this tribute to the glory days of the British Empire; a combination pub and restaurant that serves hand-drawn beers and ales as well as Indian curries, shepherd's pies and fish and chips. Absolute attention is paid to detail in both the atmosphere and in the menu. It's a rare restaurant that can take you back in time – and you'll love the trip. This cozy sidewalk cafe is the perfect place to dine out and gaze past the park to the bay beyond.

+ 220 B2 ⊠ 332 Beach Drive N.E. ☎ 727/896-6160

Where to...
Shop

Malls have been springing up around Tampa, including The Shops at Channelside, a downtown waterfront dining and shopping spot that is easily explored on foot, and Westfield Shoppingtown Citrus Park, north of downtown Tampa. International Plaza, near the airport, has Lord & Taylor, Neiman Marcus and Nordstrom as anchors. Other popular yet charming places include Old Hyde Park Village, a redeveloped area in the center of one of Tampa's historic neighborhoods, and the lively Centro Ybor in Ybor City (▲ 155).

Malls and Shopping Centers

Ybor City's most popular gathering spot, **Centro Ybor**, is a family-friendly shopping, dining and entertainment complex (1600 E. 8th Street; tel: 813/242-4600; www.centroybor.com). Highlights include GameTime, featuring interactive games and a nightclub/restaurant, the Improv Comedy Club, and a 20-screen Muvico Theater (where you can enjoy martinis, beer, wine and a light cafe menu). Don't miss the Ferdie Pacheco Gallery.

Old Hyde Park Village (Swann and Dakota avenues, off Bayshore Boulevard; tel: 813/251-3500), an outdoor shopping area, is located in the middle of Hyde Park, a quaint residential area that dates back to the late 1700s. The pretty streets of this village are home to a wide variety of stores, restaurants and cafes. Notable among the chain stores are Brooks Brothers, Ann Taylor, Williams-Sonoma, Anthropologie, Tommy Bahama, Pottery Barn Kids and even a canine boutique, Downtown Dogs. There are also many privately run boutiques that sell an eclectic array of goods – jewelry, hand-blown glass, Mexican pottery, toys and original clothing.

The Shops at Channelside (615 Channelside Drive; tel: 813/223-4250), located next to the Florida Aquarium along the downtown waterfront, is a shopping and entertainment complex, offering a mix of specialty stores and restaurants.

Other Shops

The Big Top Flea Market (9250 E. Fowler Avenue, Thonotosassa, tel: 813/986-4004; www.bigtopfleamarket.com; Sat–Sun 9–4:30) is just 7 miles (11km) north of Tampa via I-75 (Exit 265) and is a thrifty shopper's dream. With around 1,000 different stalls selling everything from clothes to electronics to cooking wares at below store prices, it is where to come to buy or simply to observe a local weekend flea-market feeding frenzy.

At the other end of the shopping experience is **Penelope T** (1413 S. Howard Avenue, Tampa, tel: 813/254-5740). This women's designer boutique features the hottest mid-range designers of the moment, plus a lot of currently unknown but up-and-coming (and sometimes local) names, with some very funky styles.

ST PETERSBURG

On Beach Drive, trendy shops offer clothing, tableware and art. Antiques can be found on Central Avenue between 12th and 13th streets at the **Gas Plant Antique Arcade** (1246 Central Avenue, tel: 727/895-0368), where dealers peddle their wares at what is considered the largest antiques and collectibles show on the west coast of Florida.

Where to...
Be Entertained

TAMPA

Some of the more happening spots in downtown Tampa can be a little hard to find because, other than 7th Avenue in Ybor City, there is not really a central neighborhood with visible nightlife. If you look, however, there is something for everyone on Tampa's night scene, and several free publications will give you all the inside information you need.

Inside Tampa is a free paper concerned mostly with covering news in the downtown area, but the second page is devoted to "doing downtown," a weekly listing of events, concerts, theater, movies, sports and museum exhibits. These listings are more geared toward popular high culture than down-and-dirty venues. At the other end of the spectrum is *Ink19*, an off-beat monthly devoted to West Florida's music scene. The center spread is a calendar of the month's concerts, mostly alternative music.

Lying between the philosophies of these two papers is the *Weekly Planet* with a calendar that describes many of the weeks more cultural entertainments, from Native American dance performances to the city's best Super Bowl party.

In the past few years Tampa has been making a great effort to upgrade the image of Ybor City and attract more people. The result is a proliferation of bars and restaurants that line 7th Avenue. During the week, the strip is relatively quiet, but on weekend nights it teems with people and the atmosphere is not unlike a large college fraternity party.

Downtown Tampa has its share of friendly bars and hot spots. **Four Green Fields** (205 West Platt, tel: 813/254-4444) is a neighborhoody Irish pub with a welcoming crowd, live Irish folk music and a great selection of beers. **Newk's Café** (514 Channelside Drive, tel: 813/307-6395), a seafood restaurant and bar, has a post-business crowd.

Perhaps the most reliable nightlife is at **Centro Ybor** (1600 E. 8th Avenue, tel: 813/242-4660). Anchored by the **Muvico Centro Ybor 20 Theater**, showing all the latest American blockbuster movies, it is also home to several nightspots, including the **Improv Comedy Club**.

ST PETERSBURG

For helpful up-to-the-minute information about what's happening in St Petersburg, look for the Friday "Weekend" section of the

St Petersburg Times or the free weekly *Daily Planet* tabloid.

In addition to live music concerts and nightclubs, you might want to take in a movie at **Muvico Baywalk 20** (151 2nd Avenue North, tel: 727/502-0965), which has stadium seats and digital sound. Or try cutting the rug at the **Coliseum** (535 4th Avenue North, tel: 727/892-5202), a 75-year-old ballroom with weekly Big Band Tea Dances.

Given the climate, it is something of an anomaly that Tampa, and Florida in general, has become so enamored of the game of ice hockey. The popularity of the sport, it seems, is due to the many Northerners who have relocated to Florida. Tampa is also home to the spring training camp for the New York Yankees baseball team, and exhibition games are always sellouts. Tickets for all of Tampa's sports events are

available by calling **Ticketmaster** on 813/287-8844.

Ice Hockey

The plush St Pete Times Forum is home to the **Tampa Bay Lightning**, and the arena (The Ice Palace, 401 Channelside Drive, Tampa; tel: 813/301-6500) is equipped with every amenity, including a full restaurant and bar. The ever-improving Lightning won the coveted Stanley Cup in the 2003–2004 season.

Football

The **Tampa Bay Buccaneers** won Super Bowl XXXVII in January 2003. The residents of Tampa are fiercely loyal and games are always lively and well-attended. The faithful fill the Raymond James Stadium (tel: 813/879-BUCS; www.buccaneers.com) for every home game. The stadium also plays host to the US college football bowl game known as the Outback Bowl.

Baseball

Home to the legendary **New York Yankees** during their mid-February to March preseason, George M Steinbrenner Field (1 Steinbrenner Drive, Tampa; tel: 813/875-7753; tickets tel: 727/287-8844; www.steinbrennerfield.com) is the largest of all the spring training facilities in Florida. It is actually a miniature replica of Yankee Stadium in New York. During the real baseball season, from April to September, the Yankees' minor league team, the Tampa Yankees, plays at George M Steinbrenner Field, providing spectators with a good opportunity to see some big talent before players get scooped up by the majors.

The **Tampa Bay Devil Rays** have earned quite a following after their impressive initial seasons. The indoor Tropicana Field stadium (Tropicana Field, 1 Stadium Drive, St Petersburg; tel: 727/825-3137; www.devilrays.com), with its impressive dome, is a great place to see a game.

Golf

Florida has more golf courses than any other state, and dozens of them are found in the Tampa Bay area. About a 90-minute drive from Tampa is the **World Woods Pine Barrens Golf Course** (17590 Ponce de Leon Boulevard, Brooksville, tel: 352/796-5500; www.worldwoods.com), which has been rated as the best course in the state.

Pine Barrens' sister course, **Rolling Oaks** (tel: 352/796-5500), closer to the city and with lower green fees, isn't bad either. You can drive and putt your way along several municipal courses, including **Babe Zaharias Municipal Course** (11412 Forest Hills Drive, tel: 813/631-4374) and the **Rogers Park Municipal Golf Course** (7910 N. 30th Street, tel: 813/356-1670). Or sign up for some lessons at the **Arnold Palmer Golf Academy World Headquarters**, at Saddlebrook Resort (5700 Saddlebrook Way, Wesley Chapel, tel: 813/973-1111).

The Panhandle and the North

Getting Your Bearings

The Panhandle stretches from Jacksonville, on the Atlantic Ocean, to Pensacola, near the Alabama border, encompassing nearly one-third of the state and, some think, its most beautiful region. Yet few tourists take time to explore it.

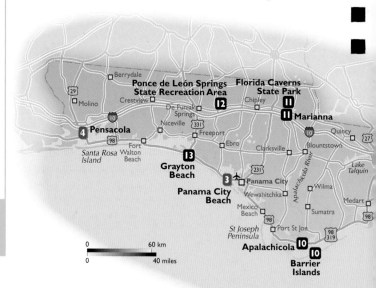

What they're missing, however, is Florida in its close-to-natural state. In the Panhandle, there are wonderful back roads such as Highways 20 and 90 and coastal road 98. There are small antebellum towns like Quincy, Havana, Monticello and DeFuniak Springs. There are hundreds of square miles of forests as well as hundreds of miles of Gulf of Mexico shoreline. Crystal-clear natural springs and the famous Suwannee River are here, as is Tallahassee, the state's capital, St Augustine (America's oldest city) and Daytona Beach.

If you have time, see this region. What you will discover is how Florida used to live, look and work. Back then, hospitality wasn't an industry – it was actually the fabled Southern hospitality that residents shared with their guests. What's more, the Panhandle places you within a short drive of Georgia and Alabama, and you'll seldom be more than an hour's drive from a great beach.

More akin to America's Deep South than the cosmopolitan pace of Miami, the Panhandle is less populated and more rural. It runs at a slower pace that, once you get accustomed to it, means you can take your time and still enjoy a great vacation.

Opposite: Amelia Island Plantation (top); Florida Caverns State Park (bottom)
Page 175 (left to right): Micanopy; hot-air balloons; a great egret

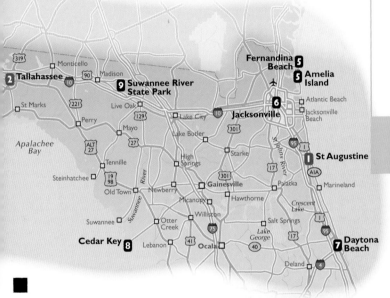

In Five Days

If you're not quite sure where to begin your travels, this itinerary recommends a practical and enjoyable five days exploring the Panhandle and the North, taking in some of the best places to see using the Getting Your Bearings map on the previous pages. For more information see the main entries.

Day 1

Morning
Wake up in St Augustine (right; ➤ 180–181). Walk along the promenade to the **Castillo de San Marcos**, the never-defeated fortress on Matanzas Bay. Step inside and, from the parapets, imagine what it was like here 400 years ago awaiting the arrival of the dreaded French fleets.

Afternoon
Take a trolley tour for a guided ride through the **Historic District**. Long after the Spanish left, wealthy tycoon Henry M Flagler made this one of his way stations on an East Coast railroad en route to Miami. The grand hotels and churches he built are still here. Stop for lunch at the 95 Cordova, a restaurant in one of these hotels – the 1888 Casa Monica (➤ 190).

Evening
A casual and romantic cruise on the bay would be the perfect way to wrap up the evening.

Day 2

Morning
The choice is yours: an hour's drive down the coast to **7 Daytona Beach** (➤ 187) or an hour's drive up the coast to **5 Amelia Island** (➤ 187). Or, better yet, skip both for now and head west via I-95 and I-10 to the state capital, **2 Tallahassee** (➤ 182–183).

Afternoon
The **Museum of Florida History** in Tallahassee (➤ 182) is a good place to learn what shaped Florida. Across the street is the **Capitol** building (left) and its observation deck.

Evening
Tallahassee is a college town. Find a bar near the university and drop in.

Day 3

Morning/Afternoon
Head out for **4 Pensacola** (right; ➤ 185–186) via Highway 90, a quiet back road that takes you through some charming small towns: Quincy (➤ 182), **11 Marianna** (➤ 189), DeFuniak Springs and Crestview.

Evening
Get settled at your Pensacola hotel. If you have the stamina, go out for the evening to the **Seville Historic District**.

Day 4

Morning
Start the day at the **Seville Historic District**, touring some of the old homes, many of which were part of a settlement built in the late 1500s.

Afternoon
Drive a few miles to see the restored flyers and IMAX film at the **National Museum of Naval Aviation** (➤ 185, 186) at the home of the Blue Angels, the Pensacola Naval Air Station.

Evening
If you're not too exhausted, a visit to the **Seville Square Historic District** or a ride out to the beaches for a sunset meal will be fun.

Day 5

Morning
Give yourself a break. Head straight to one of the many beaches on **Perdido Key** and **Santa Rosa Island** and laze on the powder-soft sands.

Afternoon
If you can pick yourself up and dust yourself off, start all over again by heading east along Highway 98 and ending your tour in Destin, Seaside, **8 Panama City Beach** (➤ 184) or **10 Apalachicola** (➤ 188).

Evening
Spend a real Old Florida evening in at your favorite Gulf Coast community, dining on fresh seafood, watching the sunset, and figuring out how to extend your stay.

⓪ St Augustine

Nearly half a millennium after it was settled, you would think that America's oldest city had settled into a routine. On the contrary, St Augustine's multiple personalities are displayed throughout this quiet town of hidden courtyards, antiques shops, cobblestone streets and horse-drawn carriages.

Located just two hours from Orlando, it was popularized as a turn-of-the-19th-century oceanfront resort and was once known as the Newport of Florida. Now history is repeating itself as elegant and seductive inns rise beside rustic attractions.

The Historic District

Anchored on the north by the sturdy **Castillo de San Marcos**, and on the south by a fleet of yachts moored at the small and lovely marina, the historic district is where most travelers begin their voyage into the past – and most start at the *castillo*. Built by the Spanish between 1672 and 1695, the never-defeated fort and its 24-foot-thick (7m) walls are steeped in history. You can tag along on a free guided tour. Outside the fort, sightseeing trains and trolleys circle the town in about an hour and you can hop on and off along the way. Too far to reach by foot, the **Fountain of Youth** suggests that it's the landing site of Ponce de León (it's not) and that the fountain here was the subject of his journey (it wasn't).

Still, beyond the fountain, the grounds are covered with soft grass and shady oaks and a cemetery built for Spanish settlers and Timucua Native Americans. Just south of the fountain is the tranquil **Mission de Nombre de Dios**, highlighted by the 208-foot-tall (85m) Cross of Christianity, which marks the site of the first Mass celebrated in America.

The Spanish/
Moorish
Revival-style
Flagler College

From Castle to College

Back on the waterfront, to the west of the bridge and marina, lies the **Plaza de la Constitución**. If you arrive on a Thursday evening in summer, spread out a blanket and enjoy a free concert. From here, walk two blocks west on Cathedral Place to Cordova Street and before you is the old **Ponce de León Hotel**. As part of his plan to build an empire of railroads and resorts along Florida's East Coast, Henry M Flagler created this castle in 1888. Today the hotel is **Flagler College**, arguably the most elaborate campus in America and open to visitors who join a tour. Across the street, Flagler's second effort was the stunning Hotel Alcazar, which now houses **City Hall** and the well-stocked **Lightner Museum**. Whether you visit the museum or not, you shouldn't leave town without going in this building.

Diverse Architecture

Across the street at the corner of Cordova and King is the **Casa Monica Hotel** (➤ 190). It was built by YMCA founder Franklyn Smith, and bought by Flagler three months after its grand opening in 1888. Recycled as the county courthouse in the 1960s, in 1997 it was restored as a hotel with an eclectic mix of Moorish and Victorian accents. Turn and walk north past the Casa Monica, through the campus of Flagler College, and then east through the historic district. Stop at patio bars like **Scarlett O'Hara's** (70 Hypolita Street, tel: 904/824-6535), then walk over to **St George Street**, a buzzing pedestrian mall during the day, but a quiet promenade for couples each evening.

A few blocks away beside the bay, carriages await, their lanterns casting a soft glow on the smooth coats of the horses. Step aboard and retrace the first leg of the Old Spanish Trail, which begins a few blocks north and tapers to a close 3,000 miles (4,800km) away in San Diego. As you roll over the old brick streets and listen as the driver shares centuries of secrets, you'll realize that Ponce de León was on the right track. You can recapture your youth in St Augustine.

🔆 219 F2 🛈 St Augustine/St Johns County Visitor Center, 10 Castillo Drive; tel: 904/825-1000; www.oldcity.com; daily 8:30–6:30

Castillo de San Marcos
✉ 1 S. Castillo Drive ☎ 904/829-6506; www.nps.gov/casa 🕐 Daily 8:45–5:15; grounds closed midnight–5:30am 💲 Inexpensive

Fountain of Youth
✉ 11 Magnolia Avenue 🕐 Daily 9–5; tours every 15–20 mins ☎ 904/829-3168 or 800/356-8222; www.fountainofyouthflorida.com 💲 Inexpensive

Flagler College
✉ 74 King Street ☎ 904/829-6481 🕐 Tours 10–3 every hour

Lightner Museum
✉ 75 King Street ☎ 904/824-2874; www.lightner museum.org 🕐 Daily 9–5 💲 Inexpensive

---

ST AUGUSTINE: INSIDE INFO

Top tip Leading back to the historic district, San Marco Avenue has several blocks of antiques shops, gift shops, clothing consigners, collectibles stores, and a superb antiquarian bookseller, **Wolf's Head Books** (67 San Marco Avenue, tel: 904/824-9357; www.wolfsheadbooks.com).

2 Tallahassee

Not only is Tallahassee the state's capital (it received that honor in 1824, as the midway point between the prime cities of Pensacola and St Augustine), it's also the one and only Southern capital spared in the Civil War.

Today, Tallahassee still seems to live in a slower, easier time that makes it a pleasure to visit. It is a cityscape of canopy roads and shady lanes surrounded by country stores, Southern plantations and gracious hospitality. A great starting point is the **Old Capitol**, located at the intersection of US 27 and Monroe Street (tel: 850/487-1902). Built in 1842, it houses a museum of Florida's political history as well as the old Supreme Court chambers and Senate Gallery.

Behind the Old Capitol is the city's focal point, the 22-story **Capitol** (tel: 850/488-6167). The governor's office is on the first floor, and House and Senate chambers on the fifth floor have viewer galleries for the legislative sessions (March through May). The top-floor observatory has outstanding views of Florida State University, City Hall, the León County Courthouse and other landmarks. The Florida Artist Hall of Fame is here, honoring citizens such as Ray Charles, Burt Reynolds, Marjorie Kinan Rawlings and Zora Neale Hurston.

Downtown Tallahassee

A few blocks away, the must-see **Museum of Florida History** is free and informative and covers 12,000 years of history. Exhibits include the remains of a giant mastodon found in nearby Wakulla Springs and a dugout canoe that once carried Native Americans into Florida's backwaters. One floor up is the **Florida State Archives and Library** (tel: 850/487-2073), where documents and photographs form a treasure trove of government records, manuscripts, genealogical records and other research materials.

After visiting the historic district, head for the **Tallahassee Museum of History and Natural Science**. Actually a combination museum and zoo, it's a little difficult to find, but worth the effort. Animals, many of which have been injured

EVEN MORE PANHANDLE PASTIMES

Antiques buffs make it a point to check out three communities. **Havana**, about 20 miles (32km) north of Tallahassee on Highway 27, has the greatest amount of antiques and adds a few sidewalk cafés and tearooms. **Monticello**, 20 miles (32km) east on Highway 90, is centered on a town square. Although the shops are not as plentiful, the preserved Victorian homes give this ride a pleasing payoff. The most intriguing community is **Quincy**, about 10 miles (16km) west of Tallahassee on Highway 90. Although it may look rough, it's claimed that there are more millionaires here per capita than any area in the nation. Why? About 100 years ago, a local banker suggested that his customers invest in a little-known soft drink. Coca Cola.

or orphaned, are given relatively free rein within an expansive 52-acre (21ha) natural habitat. You can see the endangered Florida panther from the safety of an elevated walkway. There's also the Big Bend Farm, an 1880s-era homestead.

Beyond the City

One of Tallahassee's biggest selling points is as a jumping-off point, making it a good place to stay while exploring the region. Within a 30-mile (50km) radius are intriguing and interesting sites such as the **Mission San Luís Archeological and Historic Site**, where explorer Hernando de Soto celebrated the New World's first Christmas.

In half an hour you can be sunbathing on Gulf beaches; a little farther and you can order a platter of oysters in Apalachicola or watch dolphins leap off undeveloped shores at the **St George Island State Park** (tel: 850/927-2111). Other sites within an hour's drive of the capital city include **Wakulla Springs State Park** (tel: 850/922-3633), a natural retreat highlighted by a 1920s Spanish-Mediterranean lodge, which may not be four-star, but the grounds are quiet and restful, and walking among the oaks is a completely peaceful experience. With a population of 125,000, somehow this metropolitan city has managed to preserve the gentility of the Old South. It's Florida – with a Southern accent.

The Westcott Building is the architectural centerpiece of Florida State University's campus

🔢 218 A3 🚹 Tallahassee Convention and Visitors Bureau
☎ 800/626-2866;
www.visittallahassee.com

Museum of Florida History
✉ 500 South Bronough Street
☎ 850/245-6400; www.museumof
floridahistory.com 🕐 Mon–Fri 9–4:30, Sat 10–4:30, Sun noon–4:30 🎫 Free

Tallahassee Museum of History and Natural Science
✉ 3945 Museum Drive ☎ 850/576-1636; www.tallahasseemuseum.org
🕐 Mon–Sat 9–5, Sun 12:30–5pm
🎫 Inexpensive

Mission San Luís Archeological and Historic Site
✉ 22100 W. Tennessee Street
☎ 850/245-6406 🕐 Tue–Sun 10–4
🎫 Inexpensive; under 6 free

TALLAHASSEE: INSIDE INFO

Top tip To see how important football is to America, on a Saturday in autumn, try to get a ticket for the **Florida State University Seminoles** (tel: 850/644-1830), who play at the Doak Campbell Stadium.

3 Panama City Beach

Be sure to visit the seaside community of Panama City Beach. As in Pensacola, wide white beaches and cloud-soft sands make it a popular resort area. It's so popular that the natural setting is rapidly being overshadowed by growth that peaks each spring and between June and August, when college students on break and families on vacation descend from the neighboring states of Georgia, Alabama and Mississippi.

They – and you – are here because Panama City Beach still has a natural beauty that showcases the incredible white sands, navigable waterways and popular watersports. You can rent cabanas, umbrellas, sailboats, wave runners and floats or, for a thrilling aerial view of the coast, you can strap yourself beneath a parachute and go parasailing behind a speedboat offshore. Snorkeling and scuba diving are extremely popular in the clear waters here. You can also dive among dozens of ships sunk by the city to create artificial reefs.

Off the Beach

Another option is staying at the **Gulf World Marine Park**. Although it pales in comparison to Orlando's SeaWorld, the park features sea lions, parrots, tropical gardens and a dolphin show. Interactive programs such as Trainer for a Day allow you to tag along with handlers to see how the animals are cared for.

Located at the eastern tip of Panama City Beach, the **St Andrews State Recreation Area** includes 1,260 acres (510ha) of beaches, pinewoods and marshes, as well as campgrounds, swimming areas, fishing piers and hiking along nature trails. From here you can board a ferry to **Shell Island**, a 700-acre (280ha) barrier island in the Gulf of Mexico.

➕ 217 D3   🛈 Panama City Beach Convention and Visitors Bureau
✉ 17001 Panama City Beach Parkway   ☎ 850/233-6503 or 800/722-3224;
www.visitpanamacitybeach.com   🕐 Daily 8–5

Aerial view
of Panama
City Beach

**Gulf World
Marine Park**
✉ 15412 Front
Beach Road
☎ 850/234-5271;
www.gulfworld
marinepark.com

**St Andrews State
Recreation Area**
✉ 4607 State
Park Lane
☎ 850/233-5140
🎟 Inexpensive

4 Pensacola

Far removed from the crowded tourist corridor of Orlando and the high-density cities of South Florida, residents of the state's westernmost city have the time and the space to appreciate their beautiful rivers, quiet lagoons, sparkling beaches, well-preserved historic district and thriving cultural calendar. In Pensacola, each worthwhile district abuts the next, so exploring can be done fairly easily by car or on foot.

The Big Lagoon State Recreation Area, southwest of Pensacola

One logical place to begin a tour is near downtown at the Seville Square Historic District (www.historicpensacola.org) that actually was downtown when it was first settled in 1565. Avenues with names like Barracks, Government and Church reveal the original purpose of the area, and guided tours are offered in this park-like setting, where rows of historic houses are lined up amid oak trees and gazebos.

Exploring Pensacola
A few blocks from Seville is the **Palafox Historic District**, a surprisingly active cultural conglomeration of music stores, theaters, stores and museums, including the **T.T. Wentworth Museum**), which is filled with artwork, antique photographs, a discovery center for kids and an exhibition on 2004's Hurricane Ivan and the unnamed hurricane of 1926 which both put Pensacola in the middle of the bull's-eye. If you're fascinated by the city's rich history, the **Pensacola Historical Museum** rotates exhibits on geology, maritime history, Native Americans and the city's multicultural heritage.

The **Pensacola Naval Air Station,** the home base for the US Navy's aerobatic team, the Blue Angels is another top attraction in town. A must-see on the base is the **National Museum of Naval Aviation**, one of the three largest aviation museums in the world.

Around the Town

In the community of Gulf Breeze, halfway between Fort Walton and Pensacola, is **Gulf Breeze Zoo**, a 50-acre (20ha) zoo where around 700 animals roam (relatively) free in their (artificially) natural habitats. The zoo is home to African wild dogs, one of only 18 zoos in the country to have them. You can see them up close and ride the Safari Line train that travels around the perimeter. There are also botanical gardens.

Sugar-white sands cover 52 miles (84km) of the shoreline, and much of the seaside activities are found on a pleasing barrier island south of the city. Santa Rosa Island's Pensacola Beach is part of the **Gulf Islands National Seashore** and is home to **Fort Pickens** (tel: 850/934-2600), a pre-Civil War brick fortress held by Union forces during the conflict.

Quieter and less populated are the top-rated beaches of **Perdido Key**, located about 15 miles (24km) southwest of Pensacola. For privacy as well as services, try the **Perdido Key State Recreation Area**, a 247-acre (100ha) recreation area with plenty of beach access.

✚ 216 B3 ⓘ Pensacola Area Conventiona and Visitors Bureau ✉ 1401 E. Gregory Street ☎ 800/874-1234; www.visitpensacola.com

T.T. Wentworth Museum
✉ 330 S. Jefferson Street ☎ 850/595-5990 🕐 Mon–Sat 10–4 🎟 Free

Pensacola Historical Museum
✉ 115 E. Zaragoza Street ☎ 850/433-1559; www.pensacolahistory.org 🕐 Mon–Sat 10–4:30 🎟 Free

National Museum of Naval Aviation
✉ 1750 Radford Boulevard ☎ 850/453-3604 or 800/327-5002; www.navalaviationmuseum.org 🕐 Daily 9–5

Gulf Breeze Zoo
✉ 5701 Gulf Breeze Parkway ☎ 850/932-2229; www.gulfbreezezoo.org 🕐 Daily 9–6 (last entry 5pm) 🎟 Inexpensive

Gulf Islands National Seashore
☎ 850/934-2600; www.nps.gov/guis 🎟 Inexpensive

Perdido Key
☎ 850/492-4660 or 800/328-0107; www.perdidochamber.com

Perdido Key State Recreation Area
☎ 850/492-1595; www.floridastateparks.org/perdidokey

The unusual spaceship-shaped Futuro House in Pensacola

PENSACOLA: INSIDE INFO

Top tip The **Saenger Theatre** (118 S. Palafox, tel: 850/444-7686; www.pensacolasaenger.com) provides a historic setting for performances by the local symphony orchestra and opera.

At Your Leisure

5 Amelia Island and Fernandina Beach

Sitting right at Florida's northern border across the river from Georgia, Amelia is the barrier island and Fernandina its only city. Recognized as the shrimp capital of Florida, it is also the only place in America to have been ruled under eight flags of domination during the past five centuries. In addition to beaches on the Atlantic coast, there's a 50-block historic district dotted with various styles of homes, plus gift shops, pubs, antiques malls and restaurants found along **Centre Street**. The **Palace Saloon** at No 117 is said to be the oldest in the state, just as the **Amelia Island Museum of History** is one of the best local museums in Florida. Lastly, visit **Fort Clinch State Park**, a Civil War-era fortress that was occupied by Union troops. Docents in costume portray the engineers stationed here in 1864 and offer tours of the fort. There are also nature trails, bird-watching and saltwater fishing from the fishing pier.

➕ 219 E3 🛈 961687 Gateway Boulevard, Suite 101G ☎ 904/261-3248; www.islandchamber.com 🕔 Mon–Fri 9–5

Amelia Island Museum of History
✉ 233 S. 3rd Street ☎ 904/261-7378

Fort Clinch State Park
🛈 Park Information, 2601 Atlantic Avenue, Fernandina Beach ☎ 904/277-7274; www.floridastateparks.org/fortclinch/

6 Jacksonville

Among the downtown areas that may be worth visiting in this large city, the Avondale, San Marco and Riverside districts offer a special mix of cafes, antiques shops and trendy boutiques. The 1927 **Florida Theatre** is a stunning example of a Mediterranean Revival concert hall. They still hold concerts here. For party central, **Jacksonville Landing** (www.jacksonvillelanding.com), on the St Johns River's Riverwalk, is a large entertainment/shopping complex. If you have time, the **Jacksonville Jaguars** (www.jaguars.com), the city's NFL football team, play their Sunday home games between August and December at Alltel Stadium.

➕ 219 E3 🛈 550 Water Street, Suite 10,000 ☎ 904/798-9111; www.jaxcvb.com

Florida Theatre
✉ 128 E. Forsyth Street ☎ 904/355-2787; www.floridatheatre.com

7 Daytona Beach

Claiming to be the "World's Most Famous Beach," this city on the Atlantic is notorious for the annual party known as Spring Break, when college students from across America descend upon it. They're just following in the footsteps of **Bike Week**, February's motorcycle meet-up, which attracts about half a million riders from around the world. While

Main Street Pier, Daytona Beach

Delightful bed-and-breakfast in Cedar Key

the beach, with its wide white sands, is the place that attracts most tourists, a few miles inland is the **Daytona International Speedway**, which offers year-round tours of the track and racing museum and also hosts the legendary Daytona 500.

➕ 221 E4 ℹ️ 126 E. Orange Avenue
☎ 386/255-0981; www.daytonachamber.com

Daytona International Speedway
☎ 386/253-7233; www.daytonaspeedway.com

🎱 Cedar Key

It's about 25 miles (40km) off the main highway (Highway 19) and 4 miles (6km) out in the Gulf of Mexico, but the remote setting of Cedar Key off Florida's central west coast appeals to a surprising number of travelers seeking a quiet hideaway. It was a vital part of Florida history when the railroad came to town and gave the tiny island a means to ship seafood and lumber north. These days, Cedar Key is a haven for artists, writers and bird-watchers, who crave the peaceful, unspoiled environment. In the center of the village are stores and galleries, while bayous and side streets lead to hidden restaurants with seafood fresh from local waters. If you like solitude, nature and history, Cedar Key may be well worth a visit.

➕ 220 A4 ℹ️ PO Box 610, Cedar Key
☎ 352/543-5600; www.cedarkey.org

🎱 Suwannee River State Park

Stephen Foster's classic song "Old Folks at Home" popularized the Suwannee River, and this 1,800-acre (730ha) park will put you right on its banks and on its waters. Outfitters can provide you with canoes and kayaks, and several two-bedroom vacation cabins can accommodate overnight guests. The natural setting of the park, where the **Withlacoochee River** joins the historic **Suwannee**, showcases a panoramic view of the rivers as well as the surrounding wooded uplands. Admission is on the honor system, with camping available for $15 per night.

➕ 218 C3 ✉️ 20185 County Road 132,
13 miles (21km) west of Live Oak, off US 90
☎ 386/362-2746 🕐 Daily 8am–dusk
🎟️ Inexpensive

🔟 Apalachicola and the Barrier Islands

The surprisingly artsy Apalachicola has several claims to fame. First, it became popular as the southern terminus for Florida steamboat travel in the mid-1800s. Second, the oysters harvested in the muddy waters offshore are known across America. A third highlights a local hero: in 1851, as physician John Gorrie was working to invent a machine that would lower the body temperature of patients with yellow fever, he accidentally invented the ice machine – a story told at the **John Gorrie State Museum**.

Off the coast is **St George Island**, a 28-mile (45km) barrier island with secluded beaches, and clear waters for swimming and fishing. On the far eastern end of the island **St George Island State Park** has 9 miles

(14.5km) of pristine shoreline, dunes and hiking trails for bird-watching.

West of St George Island is the **St Vincent National Wildlife Refuge**. This untouched barrier island, just offshore from the mouth of the Apalachicola River, boasts a preserved mix of habitats: wetlands, scrub oaks, cabbage palms and slash pines. There are also sambar deer, bald eagles, loggerhead sea turtles and peregrine falcons.

➕ 217 E2

John Gorrie State Museum
✉ 46 6th Street, Apalachicola ☎ 850/653-9347 🕐 Thu–Mon 9–5

St. George Island State Park
✉ 1900 E. Gulf Beach Drive ☎ 850/927-2111 🕐 Daily 8am–dusk 💷 Inexpensive

🄳 Marianna and Florida Caverns State Park

Thanks to the water-filled aquifer that sits just below the surface, few homes in Florida have basements. To see why Floridians face this construction challenge, stop in Florida Caverns State Park and join a ranger-led caving tour. You'll travel below ground to see limestone caverns that reveal an impressive array of stalactites, stalagmites, soda straws, columns, rimstones and draperies.

Marianna, the closest town to the park, is quite picturesque and makes a great introduction to the park, where you'll also find quiet hiking trails, campgrounds and areas for

---

STATE PARK UPDATE

Florida's state parks are open from 8am–dusk. For $43.40 per person (or $85.80 for a family), you can buy an annual pass that will get you (and/or your family) into most Florida state parks for a year. Check the latest information at www.floridastateparks. org. If you want to camp out in a state park, go to www.reserveamerica. com. The Florida State Parks Information Center is at 850/245-2157; www.floridastateparks.org.

---

fishing, swimming and canoeing on the Chipola River.

➕ 217 E4 ✉ 3345 Caverns Road (off, Highway 90 on Route 166), Marianna ☎ 850/482-9598; www.floridastateparks.org/floridacaverns 🕐 Tours Thu–Mon 9:30–4 💷 Inexpensive (not covered by parks pass)

🄲 Ponce de León Springs State Recreation Area

Spanning two sparsely populated counties in the Panhandle (Holmes and Walton), this 443-acre (180ha) park rests atop the site where two subterranean rivers meet and release 14 million gallons (53 million liters) of crystal-clear spring water each day. Ignore the neighborhood around the park (it's rather derelict) and enjoy splashing in the 68°F (20°C) waters. To see Florida in its natural state, wander across the rolling hills and floodplain forests and beside swamps leading into small creeks that flow into the Choctawhatchee River. Incidentally, there's no evidence that the Spanish explorer ever assumed this really was the Fountain of Youth.

➕ 217 D4 ✉ Off Highway 90 on SR 181A, Ponce de León ☎ 850/836-4281 🕐 Daily 8–dusk 💷 Inexpensive

🄳 Grayton Beach

Off Highway 98 and tucked into the piney woods is this 100-year-old community of narrow streets, crushed gravel paths and weather-worn clapboard cypress shacks – many of which can be rented. A small market and a few restaurants have added some modernity to this rustic village, but the most popular destination here is 1,133-acre (460ha) **Grayton Beach State Recreation Area**. Amazingly untouched, the park showcases a natural side of Florida with salt marshes, soft sand dunes covered with sea oats, and crystal-white sands meeting the blue-green waters of the Gulf. Stay awhile to enjoy swimming, fishing, snorkeling and camping.

➕ 216 C3

Grayton Beach State Recreation Area
✉ 357 Main Park Road (off 30A) ☎ 850/231-4210 🕐 Daily 8–dusk 💷 Inexpensive

Where to...
Stay

Prices
Expect to pay per room per night:

$ under $125 $$ $125–$250 $$$ over $250

ST AUGUSTINE

◊◊◊ Casa Monica Hotel $$
The hotel's original Moorish-Revival accents are visible throughout, from its 137 rooms and suites to the themed dining room, pool, cafés and shops.

✚ 219 F2 ⌂ 95 Cordova Street, ☎ 904/827-1888; www.casamonica.com

TALLAHASSEE

◊◊ Econo Lodge $
A seriously middle-of-the-road, modest retreat where you can rest and get refreshed before exploring one of the most intriguing cities in Florida. Rooms come with two double or one queen- or king-size bed, as well as free local calls, premium TV channels, and a continental breakfast. If you won't be staying in your room much, give some thought to this.

✚ 218 A3 ⌂ 2681 N. Monroe Street ☎ 850/385-6155

◊◊◊ Governors Inn Hotel $$
This restored historic warehouse is popular with politicians, press and lobbyists. After visiting nearby attractions, come home to a cozy retreat with soft beds and classic prints. A complimentary continental breakfast is served in the warm and welcoming lobby.

✚ 218 A3 ⌂ 209 S. Adams Street ☎ 850/681-6855

PANAMA CITY BEACH

◊◊ Osprey Resort Motel $$
An affordable option featuring oceanfront rooms, friendly staff and a pool. It's a good choice for families and budget travelers, but can get noisy during high season.

✚ 217 D3 ⌂ 15801 Front Beach Road ☎ 850/234-0303

PENSACOLA

◊◊ Days Inn Pensacola Beachfront $$
Located on a barrier island just off Pensacola Beach, this Days Inn offers spotless rooms with free WiFi. A continental breakfast is also included.

✚ 216 B3 ⌂ 16 Via de Luna ☎ 850/934-3300

AMELIA ISLAND

◊◊◊ Elizabeth Pointe Lodge $$
You may think you're in New England when you check in to this sprawling Nantucket-style oceanfront bed-and-breakfast. If you're not swimming or sunbathing, the historic district and Fort Clinch are close by. Wide porches are perfect for reading and resting. Complimentary breakfast.

✚ 219 E3 ⌂ 98 South Fletcher Avenue ☎ 904/277-4851; www.elizabethpointelodge.com

APALACHICOLA

◊◊◊ Gibson Inn $–$$
On the National Register of Historic Places, this inn is easily identified by its wraparound porches, fretwork and captain's watch. Rooms have four-poster beds and antique armoires.

✚ 217 E2 ⌂ 51 Avenue C ☎ 850/653-2191; www.gibsoninn.com

Where to...
Eat and Drink

Prices
Expect to pay per person for a meal, excluding drinks:
$ under $15 $$ $15–$30 $$$ over $30

ST AUGUSTINE

95 Cordova $$–$$$

Inside the Casa Monica Hotel (▶ 190) this restaurant keeps in line with the city's Old World theme. Dishes reflect the eclectic influences of American, Asian, Mediterranean, Caribbean and Moroccan cuisine. Consider trying the six-course, full table participation "tasting menu": shrimp cocktail, fresh mozzarella, lobster broth, jumbo sea scallops, filet mignon and tiramisu.
➕ 219 F2 ⊠ 95 Cordova Street
☎ 904/810-6810

A1A Ale Works Brewery & Restaurant $$–$$$

This combination microbrewery and restaurant is a very popular spot and will satisfy you whether you want regular food (with a Jamaican/Caribbean twist) or are on a liquid diet (some of the beers brewed here are award winners). It's usually crowded with young locals, who enjoy the lively atmosphere, it's also a great place to grab a balcony table and enjoy yourself with a view of the bridge and the bay.
➕ 219 F2 ⊠ 1 King Street
☎ 904/829-2977

Columbia Restaurant $–$$

The setting is right on St George Street, the popular pedestrian mall in the heart of the Old City. It features a superb tropical interior with high ceilings and palm trees. The menu includes such dishes as paella a la Valenciana, fresh Prince Edward mussels and sliced chorizo; tender baby lamb back ribs glazed with guava barbecue sauce; and spiced ground beef-filled empanadas with roasted corn and black bean salsa.
➕ 219 F2 ⊠ 98 St George Street
☎ 904/824-3341

Gypsy Cab Company $$

This independent restaurant across the Bridge of Lions near the northern end of Anastasia Island, does everything right. You can find it by looking for a line outside the door. It's worth the wait. The Gypsy style is called "Urban Cuisine," and the menu of fish, steak, veal and chicken dishes changes almost

daily. It's always good. Especially the cajun shrimp.
➕ 219 F2 ⊠ 828 Anastasia Boulevard
☎ 904/824-8244

TALLAHASSEE

The Ball Room $

Inside the charming lodge at the Wakulla Springs State Park (▶ 183) is a wide, sunny dining room that overlooks a broad lawn and clear springs. The menu is, naturally, Southern, with bean soup, home-baked muffins, fried seafood, Southern-fried shrimp and oysters, and pecan-crusted chicken.
➕ 218 A3 ⊠ 550 Wakulla Park Drive, Wakulla Springs ☎ 850/224-5950

Chez Pierre Restaurant $$$

This midtown favorite has been charming locals and tourists with its excellent Southern-meets-French menu, featuring the likes of saffron-scented lobster ravioli and beef bourguignon served inside a gorgeous antebellum mansion. The adjoining outdoor cafe, 2 Chez, offers a more casual, less-expensive menu, specializing in raw-bar seafood and steamed mussels.

⊞ 218 A3 ⊠ 1215 Thomasville Road
☎ 850/222-0936

PANAMA CITY BEACH

⚜⚜ Boars Head Restaurant $$

In a page out of a Dickens novel, the Boars Head would be at home in London. This "Olde English" style restaurant specializes in roasted and chargrilled meats and fresh seafood such as fried lobster and chargrilled grouper.

⊞ 217 D3 ⊠ 17290 Front Beach Road
☎ 850/234-6628

⚜⚜ Saltwater Grill $$

The sight of the huge aquarium indicates that seafood is the specialty here. Blue crab stuffed flounder, grilled Atlantic salmon, and grouper imperial sautéed with sherry butter and topped with fresh lump crabmeat are among your choices. But it's not only seafood – add steaks, chops and a piano bar to the mix.

⊞ 217 D3 ⊠ 11040 Hutchison Boulevard
☎ 850/230-2739

⚜ Sonny's Real Pit Bar-B-Q $

For authentic American barbecue, there's hardly a place better than Sonny's. Plates are stacked with all the things that make Southern food legendary: ribs, pork, hamburgers, chicken, sweet potatoes, banana pudding and more.

⊞ 217 D3 ⊠ 11341 Panama City Beach Parkway
☎ 850/230-4742

PENSACOLA

⚜ Barnhill's $

Americans love places like this, where an endless buffet of big food is available for one low price. Join the crowd. Grab a plate and load up on an overwhelming selection of steak, chicken, ham, fish, vegetables, breads, salads and more. Surprisingly, for such a large quantity of food, there's an equal amount of quality – it's actually all pretty good. If there's any room left, waddle over to the dessert bar.

⊞ 216 B3 ⊠ 10 S. New Warrington Road
☎ 850/456-2760

⚜⚜ McGuire's Irish Pub $$

A lively atmosphere, busy bar and ales, porters and stouts brewed on the premises make this traditional Irish pub, with an American steakhouse menu of ribs, burgers and aged steaks (plus seafood), a very popular Pensacola choice.

⊞ 216 B3 ⊠ 600 E. Gregory Street
☎ 850/433-6789

⚜⚜ Mesquite Charlie's $-$$

When you've had enough of Gulf Coast fish dishes, mosey over to this popular Western-style saloon for cuts of charbroiled meat from as small as a filet to the 32oz (0.9kg) porterhouse (you'll probably need to share it with friends).

⊞ 216 B3 ⊠ 5901 N.W. Street
☎ 850/434-0498

AMELIA ISLAND

⚜⚜ Beech Street Grill $-$$

In a cozy converted two-story 1889 home, waiters serve the freshest seafood, such as seared tuna loin or Chilean sea bass, seasoned with freshly cut herbs, homemade sauces and chutneys. The atmosphere is quaint, the meals creative but not ostentatious, and the wine list is extremely extensive.

⊞ 219 E3 ⊠ 801 Beech Street, Fernandina Beach ☎ 904/277-3662

⚜⚜ Brett's Waterway Cafe $-$$

At the northern end of Centre Street at the Fernandina harbor and overlooking the Amelia River and the state of Georgia beyond, Brett's is known for its steaks as well as (naturally) fresh Florida seafood.

⊞ 219 E3 ⊠ 1 S. Front Street, Fernandina Beach ☎ 904/261-2660

Where to... Shop

ST AUGUSTINE

The best concentration of stores is along **St George Street**, in the historic district. The popular pedestrian mall is active day and night, and here small restaurants sit beside gift shops and beachwear and candy stores. A few blocks away, in the back of the grand hotel that is now the **Lightner Museum** (75 King Street, tel: 904/824-2874), is a collection of antiques shops that have old maps, books, silver, crystal and many other fine, beautiful and quirky items. Several blocks north, **San Marco Avenue** has a string of antiques and collectibles shops, gift shops, clothing consigners, and a superb antiquarian bookseller, **Wolf's Head Books** (67 San Marco Avenue, tel: 904/824-9357).

TALLAHASSEE

There are some interesting items in the gift shops of the **Old Capitol** building and the **Museum of Florida History**. Aside from the stores of the **Governors Square Mall** (1500 Apalachee Parkway, tel: 850/877-8106), with its wide selection of fashion, sportswear, book, music and gift stores, 20 miles (32km) outside town is the old farming community of **Havana**. Old canning plants and tractor showrooms have been converted to antiques malls where a diverse collection of Americana is sold. Also outside of town is **Bradley's Country Store** (10655 Centerville Road, tel: 850/893-1647), which is known for its freshly made country sausage, grits and cane syrup.

PANAMA CITY BEACH

If you want a break from the beach visit the **Panama City Mall** (2150 Martin Luther King Jr Boulevard, tel: 850/785-9587). With more than 100 stores, it's a good place to find travel and gift items.

PENSACOLA

The Palafox District in the heart of old Pensacola may be your best bet for browsing. Art lovers will find galleries displaying art glass, wood, metal, paintings and jewelry. The **Quayside Art Gallery** (17 E. Zarragossa Street, tel: 850/438-2363) is the largest co-op art gallery in the Southeast.

There are numerous other stores in this area, while about 10 miles (16km) north is the **Cordova Mall** (5100 N. 9th Avenue, tel: 850/477-7562), the area's largest with 3 department stores, around 140 specialty stores and nearly a dozen restaurants.

AMELIA ISLAND

Centre Street in Fernadina Beach is the island's main shopping district, and here you will find the greatest concentration of bookstores, antiques shops, gift galleries, candy stores and fashion boutiques. Art galleries feature unique nautical items, and the owner-operated shops along Centre Street have a great range of one-of-a-kind items.

APALACHICOLA

The River City Trading Company (82 Commerce Street, tel: 850/653-2441) has casual beach clothing such as sandals, hats, T-shirts and board shorts, as well as home furnishings and gifts. Just get lost and roam throughout the district and chances are you'll find a shop worth visiting. A former ship's chandlery is now the **Grady Market** (76 Water Street, tel: 850/653-4099), with antiques shops, boutiques and restaurants.

Where to...
Be Entertained

ST AUGUSTINE

A1A Ale Works (▶ 191), along with the small pubs and bars found along St. George Street (▶ 181), is worth a visit. Also in the historic district is the Tradewinds Lounge (124 Charlotte Street, tel: 904/829-9336). A local icon, it's a popular watering hole (with a house band). A few blocks south is O.C. White's (118 Avenida Menendez, tel: 904/824-0808), a restaurant with a nice outdoor patio.

TALLAHASSEE

As well as being the state capital, Tallahassee is also a college town, with the Florida State University. The university's school of music (tel: 850/644-4774) has a great schedule of free concerts and performances offered by the students each year. The theater department (tel: 850/644-7234) has one of America's leading drama programs and also hosts performances on campus.

PANAMA CITY BEACH

The Martin Theatre (409 Harrison Avenue, tel: 850/763-8080) hosts traditional plays and concerts throughout the year. Definitely not a family spot is the Club LaVela (8813 Thomas Drive, tel: 850/234-3866), which claims to be the largest nightclub in America. It features 15 clubs, a pool, beach and a hedonistic feel that reaches its climax during Spring Break when students arrive in town.

PENSACOLA

The long-reigning king of Pensacola nightlife is the Seville Square Historic District (130 E. Government Street, tel: 850/434-6211), with seven different rooms, nine bars and two courtyards. Rosie O'Grady's Goodtime Emporium is a 1920s jazz club with a live band, sing-alongs and saloon girls; Phineas Phoggs is the disco, easy listening folk music, and Fast Eddie's Billiard Parlor is just that. Apple Annie's Courtyard features live listening folk music. Sluggo's (101 S. Jefferson, tel: 850/791-6501) has three floors of bars, books, games, pool tables and live music and is a hugely entertaining, downtown venue catering to all ages.

More soothing is the Pensacola Opera (75 S. Tarragona Street, tel: 850/433-6737), which showcases traditional selections, and the Pensacola Symphony Orchestra (205 E. Zaragoza Street, tel: 850/435-2533).

AMELIA ISLAND

In addition to the Palace Saloon, at the end of Centre Street in Fernandina Beach, Brett's Waterway Cafe (1 S. Front Street, tel: 904/261-2660) has an outdoor bar that's right on the Amelia River overlooking Georgia. On the north end of the island, Sandy Bottoms (2910 Atlantic Avenue, tel: 850/396-4134) is a beach bar that's right on the beach.

APALACHICOLA

The best bars here are attached to restaurants. For a more highbrow outing, consider an evening at the Dixie Theatre (21 Avenue E., tel: 850/653-3200). Opened in 1913, it was a theater for years, and after nearly disintegrating and being rebuilt, today it's a regional theater that offers a summer repertory between June and September, and other plays, musicals and music fests throughout the year.

Walks and Tours

1 WINTER PARK

Walk

Red-brick streets, the sound of the Sunset Limited rolling into the train station, a cool and pleasing park, great shops...when you're in Greater Orlando, why walk anywhere other than Winter Park? The avenue is filled with sidewalk cafes, ice-cream parlors, antiques and craft emporiums, art and gift galleries, fashion boutiques, perfumeries and jewelers.

DISTANCE 1 mile (1.6km) **TIME** 2 hours (4 if you shop. And you should)
START POINT North end of Park Avenue ✚ 224 E6
END POINT South end of Park Avenue ✚ 224 E6

1–2

To reach Park Avenue from the attractions area, take I-4 east to Exit 87 (Fairbanks Avenue) and head east 1.5 miles (2.5km) to Park Avenue. Turn left (north) and travel two blocks to park on the avenue or a nearby side street. Begin your walk at the corner of Park and Comstock avenues, and stop by the **Restoration Hardware** chain store, which sells art deco-era reproductions. Head north on the right side of Park Avenue, crossing New

Ice skating in Winter Park's Central Park

England Avenue, then Welbourne Avenue. You're cruising through the shopping district. Just after Welbourne, duck into **Greeneda Court**, a cozy courtyard featuring interior

design stores and **Brandywine Books**, a great little used-book store. Back on Park Avenue, head north again to Morse Boulevard and turn right (east).

2–3

Morse Boulevard ends at Lake Osceola, the departure point for the popular **Winter Park Scenic Boat Tour**. The casual one-hour cruise skirts past luxurious lakefront mansions, parks and along narrow interconnecting canals on Winter Park's famed chain of lakes.

3–4

Return to Park Avenue and turn right. Stop for lunch at the **Briarpatch Restaurant**. Back on the street, you'll notice chain stores such as Talbot's and Ann Taylor Loft. **The Garden Shops** includes small gift shops and decorator boutiques. A narrow garden path to your right leads to a group of delightful, interesting stores.

4–5

Return to Park Avenue and continue north until you reach Canton Avenue. Cross to the west side of the street, walk north to the **Charles Hosmer Morse Museum of American Art**. For a nominal charge, you will gain access to the world's largest collection of original Louis C Tiffany stained glass, including the only surviving Tiffany interior, a chapel designed for the 1893 Chicago World's Columbian Exposition. Also on display are paintings, sculptures, and arts and crafts created by other artists between 1850 and 1930.

5–6

Now head south on Park Avenue on the west side of the street. On your right between Canton and New England avenues is **Central Park**. The lush park is a gathering

Stained glass in Charles Hosmer Morse Museum

boutique hotel. A genteel ambiance is provided by the hotel's rich woodwork, a cozy fireplace and gift shops. In an intimate courtyard, the **Park Plaza Gardens Restaurant** is a pleasant place for a drink and a superb meal.

7–8

Keep heading south on Park Avenue, passing your car and crossing Fairbanks to enter the campus of **Rollins College**. Founded in 1885, it has consistently been a popular college for the offspring of wealthy Northern families. It also has some of the most beautiful Mediterranean-themed architecture in America. At the end of Park Avenue, you'll reach Holt Avenue. Turn left and walk down the red-brick road to **Knowles Chapel**, the favored venue for the springtime Bach Festival and visiting graduation speakers such as former President Jimmy Carter.

8–9

Remain on Holt, passing the Knowles Chapel. At the end of Holt is the delightful **Cornell Fine Arts Museum**, one of central Florida's hidden treasures. Exhibits range from Old Masters to contemporary sculptures to historically significant photographs. Behind the Cornell Museum is Lake Virginia, another soothing

setting where you can lie on the grass and watch the beautiful wildlife.

9–start

After you've had your fill of serenity, return up Holt, turn right onto Park Avenue, find your car and drive back to the hustle and bustle of the theme-park attractions.

Brandywine Books
114 S. Park Avenue, Suite E ☎ 407/644-1711
🕐 Daily 10–5.30

Winter Park Scenic Boat Tour
312 E. Morse Boulevard ☎ 407/644-4056
🕐 Daily 10–4 💲 Inexpensive

Charles Hosmer Morse Museum of American Art
445 N. Park Avenue ☎ 407/645-5311;
www.morsemuseum.org 🕐 Tue–Sat 9:30–4, Sun 1–4
💲 Inexpensive

Cornell Fine Arts Museum
1000 Holt Avenue ☎ 407/646-2526;
www.rollins.edu/cfam 🕐 Tue–Fri 10–4, Sat–Sun 12–5
💲 Inexpensive

Cornell Fine Arts Museum

place for young lovers, families and squirrels looking for handouts. It's also Winter Park's de facto town square where concerts, special events and art festivals are presented and is a good place to stop for a while and do nothing.

6–7

On the corner of Park and New England avenues, the **Park Plaza Hotel** is a charming

2 SPACE COAST
Tour

DISTANCE Round trip from Orlando, approximately 130 miles (210km)
TIME Full day for space-related attractions **START POINT** Kennedy Space Center ✠ 221 E3
END POINT Orlando or Walt Disney World® Resort ✠ 221 D3

Only 50 miles (80km) from Orlando, you can wring the most out of Florida's Space Coast with a full-day visit. **The obvious starting point is Kennedy Space Center.**

To reach it from downtown Orlando, travel east on Highway 50 and at the first light past I-95, turn right onto Highway 405/Columbia Drive. Follow Columbia past US 1 and the Kennedy Space Center is about 7 miles (11km) down on your right. **From Disney or International Drive, take the Bee Line Expressway (Highway 528, a toll road) east to Highway 407, which leads to Highway 405. Turn right and follow the signs.**

1–2

The Kennedy Space Center **Visitor Complex** (▲ 83) has the largest collection of space artifacts in the world, as well as presentations that are thoughtful, entertaining and intriguing. After paying one admission price,

you'll enter the complex where you should turn to your right to reach the bus loading dock. The tour takes you past the **Vehicle Assembly Building** and to the 60-foot-tall (18m) Launch Complex 39 Observation Gantry.

The next stop, the **Apollo/Saturn V Center**, begins at the Firing Room Theater, which re-creates the lunar mission of Apollo 8.

With a great pre-show and actual consoles from the 1968 mission, you'll feel like you're witnessing the real thing.

The simulated launch of Apollo 8 leads to the main concourse where there's an actual 363-foot-long (111m) **Saturn V** rocket built for a moon mission that never took place. It lies on its side and stretches the entire length

The dramatic Rocket Garden at the Visitor Complex

of the building. As you walk from one end of the rocket to the command module at the tip, check out other interesting displays such as the van that ferried astronauts to the launch pad, and a genuine moon rock you can touch.

The next show is one of the best in Central Florida. At the **Lunar Surface Theater** you'll revisit the amazing story of the Apollo 11 landing. A pre-show film clip plays scenes of mission control officers trying to re-establish communication with the command module Columbia as several television screens broadcast the chilling phrase "Loss of Signal" – an eerie reminder of the loss of the Columbia shuttle in February 2003. In a brilliant re-creation of the events of July 20, 1969, you'll be reminded that Neil Armstrong and Buzz Aldrin's onboard computers failed during their descent and, with less than 30 seconds of fuel to spare, Armstrong had to land the lunar module himself.

If you're feeling a little hungry now, the Moon Rock Café serves standard attraction foods.

After taking the bus back to the main entrance area, invest time in an IMAXfilm, *Hubble 3D* or *Space Station 3D*. The Space Station film is an amazing example of cinematography. Shot by astronauts and cosmonauts, and narrated by Tom Cruise, the super-crisp images place the nearly life-size International Space Station within your grasp – it may be the most realistic vision you'll ever have of space travel.

Outside the theater, KSC has planted the **Rocket Garden**, which is a collection of spare rockets and equipment from the early Atlas rockets of the late 1950s to the Saturn 1 from 1967. Leading to an Apollo capsule is the actual service arm that led to the Apollo 11. Although Armstrong, Aldrin and Collins did it first and 30 stories above the ground, it's still a privilege to follow in their footsteps.

A few feet away, a **museum of Early Space Exploration** focuses on the highlights of the fledgling days of rocketry, and features an actual-size mock-up of the first liquid-fuel rocket. There are additional exhibits on the glory days of the Mercury and Gemini space programs.

Time your schedule to catch the **Astronaut Encounter** in a pavilion near the entrance. Every day an astronaut is there answering questions and helping to explain space travel in down-to-earth terms. For an even closer encounter, "Lunch with an Astronaut" (about $60, including KSC admission) adds a meal and more time to stop and chat.

Before leaving, stop at the **Astronaut Memorial**. Sadly, the names of the crew of Columbia etched into the 60-ton marble mirror join 17 other astronauts who also gave their lives to help advance space exploration.

From the Visitor Complex take Highway 405 west to the **U.S. Astronaut Hall of Fame**, near Titusville, where you can witness the human side of space, with the sights, sounds and experiences of the famous astronauts. The Science On a Sphere exhibit provides a 3D view of the Earth and planets as if they are seen from space.

2–3

Leave the Hall of Fame for a trip to **Cocoa Beach**. Take Highway 405 east to State Road 3 and go south to Highway 528 east, which then turns into A1A at Port Canaveral. Drive another few miles to reach the intersection of Highway 520 and A1A.

You're at the most popular section of Cocoa Beach, the intersection highlighted by **Ron Jon Surf Shop**. This huge surf shop has become legendary. Tourists from far and wide head here not for surfboards but for T-shirts and Ron Jon paraphernalia. One block east of A1A is Ridgewood Avenue. For miles south or north, there are entrances to some of Florida's finest beaches. A few blocks north of Ron Jon's, the **Cocoa Beach Pier** (401 Meade Avenue, tel: 321/783-7549) contains a collection of stores, bars and restaurants.

3–4

When you're done at the beach, return to Orlando by taking Highway 520 east. About 6 miles (10km) past I-95, stop at the rustic **Lone Cabbage Fish Camp** (tel: 321/632-4199) for an airboat ride or a platter of gator tail and frogs' legs.

4–5

At the Bee Line Expressway (Highway 528), head west to return to **International Drive** or **Walt Disney World® Resort.**

Space Coast Office of Tourism
✉ 420 Brevard Avenue, Suite 150, Cocoa Village
☎ 321/433-4470; www.space-coast.com

Kennedy Space Center
☎ 321/449-4444; www.kennedyspacecenter.com
🕐 Daily 9–5.30

U.S. Astronaut Hall of Fame
✉ 6225 Vectorspace Boulevard, Titusville
☎ 321/2696100 🕐 Daily 10–6:30 (call ahead to confirm times)

Ron Jon Surf Shop
✉ 4151 N. Atlantic Avenue ☎ 321/799-8820;
www.ronjons.com 🕐 Daily 24 hours

3 SoBe and the Art Deco District

Walk

The streets and the beaches of the Art Deco District (▶ 109–110) are so gorgeous that the area deserves a closer look. While it's easy to be dazzled by the bronzed bodies, white sands, blue waters and the bright pastel colors of art deco hotels, look a little closer and you'll find cool shops, quiet bookstores and small cafes that provide oases of respite within this high-energy area. There are dozens of places that can kick your adrenaline into overdrive after dark, so here's an easy daytime walking tour that will introduce you to some comforting and peaceful zones.

DISTANCE 1.5 miles (2.5km) **TIME** 4 hours
START POINT Lincoln Road and Collins Avenue, Miami ⊞ 226 C3
END POINT Delano Hotel ⊞ 226 C3

1–2

While the Lincoln Road Mall may not be any more or less lively than Ocean Drive or Collins Avenue, it can be more interesting. By starting at the east end (Collins Avenue) you can walk up the left (south)

side of the street and enjoy window-shopping. Otherwise, this pedestrian mall has palm trees and fountains to calm things down, and galleries such as **Britto Central** are fun to visit. Romero Britto's bright pop art images have found a perfect backdrop in SoBe.

Keep walking west and at the corner of Lincoln Road and Jefferson Avenue,

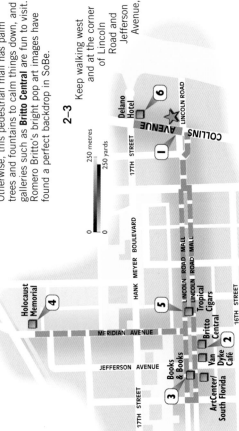

the enormously popular **Van Dyke Cafe** (▶ 138) is a great place to stop. Work off your meal by heading west, dropping into any of the eclectic shops that pique your interest. Miami inspires artists the way the Mississippi Delta inspires the blues. At the

ArtCenter/South Florida more than 40 "yet-to-be-discovered" artists have their goods on display. The gallery is located at nearby 800 Lincoln Road.

Books & Books, just across the road from the ArtCenter/South Florida, has books and magazines on nearly every topic and is worth a stop. It's a quiet yet active little store that serves snacks and coffees. Inside the door to your right is a table filled with discounted books, most of which deal with Miami art, architecture and history. Reading a good book in a cool city might just be one of the best ways to enjoy a vacation.

3–4

Before you reach your next stop, take a detour. As you head east, look for Meridian Avenue and turn left. Walk three blocks to the end of the street and the **Holocaust Memorial**. It's

worth spending some time at the memorial, so don't limit yourself to a quick glance from across the street. Pay a modest donation, walk down a hall with a timeline of the Holocaust, then turn left toward a monumental, 42-foot-high (13m) arm, the *Sculpture of Love and Anguish*, on which Jewish victims are depicted climbing to escape. The absence of all sounds, save spiritual music, makes this a chilling experience.

TOP TIP

South Beach Shuttle (tel: 305/770-3131), is a fleet of buses that runs all around SoBe, at a very nominal 25¢.

For an interesting historical perspective of the Art Deco District, take one of the excellent guided or audio walking tours that depart from the **Art Deco District Welcome Center** (1001 Ocean Drive, tel: 305/531-3484; www.mdpl.org; daily 11–6). Audio tours (90-minutes long) are available in English, German, Spanish and French. The 90-minute guided tours are offered on Thursdays at 6:30pm and rest of week at 10:30am (inexpensive), departing from the Art Deco Gift Shop. No reservations are necessary.

The Van Dyke Cafe is a prime spot for people-watching

The swimming pool of the Delano, one of Miami's coolest hotels, features soothing underwater music

5–6

Now you have only to walk to Collins Avenue, turn left and head to the corner of 17th Street and into the **Delano Hotel**, instantly recognizable by its finlike towers. This, more than any place in Miami, epitomizes the creativity and undiluted weirdness that descended upon the city. Have a drink by the poolside bar, where furniture sits in the pool and mirrors rest on the lawn. After a moment you'll start to feel as if you are in a Salvador Dalí painting!

Britto Central
⊠ 818 Lincoln Road ☎ 305/531-8821; www.britto.com
🕒 Sun–Thu 10am–11pm, Fri–Sat 10am–midnight

ArtCenter/South Florida
⊠ 924 Lincoln Road ☎ 305/674-8278; www.artcentersf.org

Holocaust Memorial
⊠ 1933–1945 Meridian Avenue ☎ 305/538-1663

Tropicana Cigars
⊠ 1933–1945 Meridian Avenue ☎ 305/673-3194

SAVED FROM DEMOLITION

In the 1980s, many deemed the colorful facades of the Art Deco District passé and the developers began to move in. Activist Barbara Baer Capitman spearheaded a movement to preserve the area, and as more and more people began to realize the value and beauty of the architecture, the district was saved.

4–5

Backtrack to Lincoln Road, turn left and drop in at **Tropical Cigars**. Miami is known for cigars and this place doesn't disappoint. Soft terracotta and earth tones enhance the setting here, that of an Italian villa. Smokers will be in ecstasy over the selection of ashtrays, cutters, humidors and a "cigar cave" where they can complement their smoke with a coffee or cocktail.

4 THE FLORIDA KEYS

Drive

The Florida Keys evoke images of an island paradise – azure blue waters, white sandy beaches and some of the best snorkeling, scuba diving and fishing in the world. It's all this – plus crowded roads, broken-down old trailers and tacky tourist shops on the 110-mile (177km) journey from Key Largo to Key West. On a casual drive to the southernmost point in mainland America you'll find parks, dive centers and restaurants to keep you entertained. Addresses along the way are clearly marked by small green and white mile markers, which start with MM 127 south of Florida City and end at MM 0 in Key West.

DISTANCE 254 miles (408km)
TIME At least 2 days
START/END POINT Miami ✚ 223 E3

1–2

To reach **Florida City**, the start for the Florida Keys, you can take one of two southern routes out of Miami. US 1 is the main road, but it has thick city traffic for several miles. Florida's Turnpike is a less trafficked and faster road, although it's a little west of Miami, and you'll pay a small toll to take it. The choice is yours.

2–3

Once you reach Florida City, a 19-mile (31km) stretch between MM 127 and 108 serves as a buffer zone between Miami and the more laid-back mood that begins in **Key Largo**, the longest of the Keys. Be cautious, because even though the speed limit is 55mph (88kph), some drivers can be reckless (they frequently pass in no-passing lanes). For safety's sake, always drive with your main beams on.

Your first stop will be on your right at MM 106. The **Key Largo Chamber of Commerce and Florida Keys Visitor Center** is well stocked with brochures, pamphlets and discount coupons for Keys attractions, and the staff can help you make lodging reservations if needed. They also carry brochures for nearly 30 nearby dive stations. Most offer similar snorkeling

Boats of all kinds line Key Largo Harbor Marina

trips and scuba-diving excursions (moderate for a half-day of snorkeling to expensive for a scuba-diving trip; certification required, equipment rental extra). Spencer Slate at the **Atlantis Dive Center** has earned a reputation for his knowledge of the waters, the underwater weddings he organizes, and the fact that he feeds moray eels fresh fish held in his mouth.

Drive farther south to MM 102.5 and look to your left for the entrance to the

John Pennekamp Coral Reef State Park

(▶118–119), arguably the most popular spot between Miami and Key West. Starting on the shoreline, the underwater preserve stretches 3 miles (5km) into the Florida Straits and runs 21 miles (34km) along the southern coast of the Keys. It is a refuge for a variety of corals and fish. After paying admission (inexpensive), you drive along a trail to the visitor center (daily 8–5), where there's a small exhibit about Florida wildlife, as well as John Pennekamp, who helped establish the preserve.

Chances are you'll be more interested in hitting the water. Next to the visitor center, there's a gift shop, snack shop and a ticket counter where you can book various water excursions. Snorkeling, diving, glass-bottom-boat tours, and canoe and kayak rentals are arranged here, and they rent out swim fins, snorkels and masks. There are lots of submerged wrecks to explore, and the popular bronze statue, Christ of the Deep. If you don't have time for a dive trip, there are small, shallow swimming areas.

Head south and consider a stop at the **Dolphin Cove Research Education Center**, on your right at MM 101.9. Swimming with

dolphins is one of the more popular (and expensive) recreational activities in the Keys, so you have to pay and book well in advance. During a boat ride and training session you learn how to interact with the dolphins before getting in the water with them. Your actual time in the water is only about 15 minutes, making this an expensive, but unforgettable, experience.

Head south to MM 100 and take a look at the boat Bogart and Hepburn made famous: *The African Queen.* It's docked on a canal next to a Holiday Inn and is free to look at, as is *Thayer IV,* the boat Hepburn used in *On Golden Pond.* When you've seen these, you've seen most of Key Largo.

Still following in the wake of Jacques Cousteau, **World Watersports** claims to be America's largest dive store. It has everything you need for a day in the water. The staff can also answer your questions about local dives.

3–4

Continue south past shopping plazas and fishing charters until you reach Windley Key and the entrance to **Islamorada**. When the Spanish arrived, they saw the violet shells of the Janthina sea snails and dubbed this "islas moradas," or purple isles – not one island, but a collection of keys. There are only a few things here worth seeing, but if you like fishing, there's plenty to do.

At MM 86.7 on your left you'll see a huge lobster statue. There's a collection of a dozen stores here, but the lobster is the real draw.

Halfway down the Keys at MM 84.5, **Theater of the Sea** (www.theaterofthesea.com) is an old aquatic attraction

Miami

Cape Florida

Kendall

Perrine

Biscayne Bay

Elliot Key

Princeton

Homestead

Florida City

Key Largo

Atlantis Dive Center

John Pennekamp Coral Reef State Park

African Queen

Key Largo

Dolphin Cove Research Education Center

Tavernier

roseate spoonbills, pelicans, seagulls and ospreys. The islands become increasingly narrow and, in a loose sense, you are driving across the Atlantic Ocean – enjoy the view. At MM 61, you'll see the entrance to a large resort, **Hawk's Cay** (tel: 305/743-7000). It has watersports rentals including power boats, wave-runners and parasailing (rates vary). They also promote a "dolphin connection," but since you don't actually get to swim with them (you stand next to them in the water) pass this one by.

where shows feature dolphins and other sea creatures. Not that impressive if you've seen SeaWorld, but worth it if you want to swim with a dolphin, kiss a sea lion or ride on a "bottomless" boat.

A few miles down at MM 82.5 is an old train car housing the **Islamorada Chamber of Commerce**, a good place to stop for local information on the area's biggest draw: sportfishing.

At MM 82, look for the huge mermaid on your right, and you will have stumbled across the **Lorelei Restaurant and Cabana Bar**. If you arrive here at sunset, the celebration is a precursor to the one in Key West. With chairs right on the sand, and killer sunset views, the Lorelei has a 1960s cabana-bar vibe, tasty cocktails and fresh seafood. Get ready for dancing after dark when live local bands rock the beach. The Lorelei can also organize sport-fishing charters and guided backcountry fishing trips.

Farther south at MM 81.1, sport-fishing anglers swear by **Tarpon Flats** for shallow water thrills. If you want to catch a tarpon – nicknamed the silver king, it's known for its majestic arcing jumps and bright armored scales – in crystal-clear saltwater flats, there's no better place in the Keys than here.

4–5

From here, the attractions of nature hold sway. Vaulting from key to key, US 1 follows the old seagoing railroad that passes emerald-green lagoons, deep-blue seas, nodding palms and an abundance of white herons,

TAKING A BREAK

After a day diving in Key Largo, if you are too worn out to drive on, the **Largo Lodge** (MM 101.7; tel: 305/451-0424; www.largolodge.com; inexpensive) epitomizes the Keys of the 1940s. This low-key collection of cottages is surprisingly inexpensive for what it offers: $95–$135 affords an in-season evening in a secluded, house-size unit complete with exposed beam ceilings, kitchenette, a large living room, bedroom and screened porch. If you're stressed out, you can calm down in the soothing setting of your room or in the grassy bayfront area out back.

Florida Bay

Theater of the Sea
Plantation Key
Upper Keys
Islamorada Lorelei
Tarpon Flats
Lower Matecumbe Key
Craig
Layton
Long Key
Hawk's Duck Key
Cay Resort
Dolphin Research Center
Marathon
Boot Key
Seven Mile Bridge
Big Pine Key
National Key Deer Refuge
Summerland Key
Cudjoe Key
Lower Keys
Pine Islands
Florida Keys
Key West
Information Center
Key West

0   20 km
0   10 miles

5–6

Just past Duck Key, you'll arrive at MM 59, Grassy Key, and the **Dolphin Research Center**. If you had to pick just one dolphin swim based on celebrity endorsements, you may have the best luck here. Jimmy Carter, Jimmy Buffett, Arnold Schwarzenegger and Sandra Bullock have latched onto the dorsal fins of these dolphins to be pulled and pushed around the lagoon. You have to book well in advance if you plan to do this, and make sure you bring an extra $190 for the privilege.

If you'd rather not swim, you can take a tour ($19.50 adults, $13.50 children) and watch sea lions and dolphins, who stare back at you with equal curiosity. The tour lasts about 30 minutes and can drag in places, and the Florida heat can wear you down quickly. Be prepared to seek refuge in the air-conditioned gift shop.

6–7

After this, the road continues south past Marathon. This is a crowded island, dense with traffic, and holds little of interest for travelers. At MM 47, the main attraction is the famous **Seven Mile Bridge,** an impressive span leading to Bahia Honda Key. There's not much to see except the Florida Straits, which stretch forever on your left.

7–8

Once the bridge has been crossed, the scenery begins to suffer. The grass is sunburned and there are numerous abandoned cars by the roadside. The only section worth observing is at MM 36.5, when you leave Bahia Key and arrive in Key deer territory. About 300 Key deer (a subspecies of the Virginia white-tailed deer) live here and are threatened by little else but speeding cars. Slow down, keep your eyes open and you may see one.

8–9

At MM 10, you can stop at the **Key West Information Center** and stock up on brochures. Otherwise, keep on heading south and into the liveliest and most popular of all the Keys, **Key West** (▶122–125).

Key Largo Chamber of Commerce and Florida Keys Visitor Center
☎ 305/451-4747; www.keylargo.org 🕐 Daily 9–6

Atlantis Dive Center
✉ Garden Cove Drive, MM 106.5 ☎ 305/451-3020 or 800/331-3483; www.captainslate.com

Dolphin Cove Research Center
☎ 305/451-4060; www.dolphinscove.com

World Watersports
✉ MM 99 ☎ 305/451-0118; www.diversdirect.com

Islamorada Chamber of Commerce
☎ 305/664-4503; www.islamoradachamber.com
🕐 Mon–Fri 9–5, Sat 9–4, Sun 9–2

Lorelei Restaurant and Cabana Bar
☎ 305/664-2692; www.loreleifloridakeys.com 🕐 Daily 7am–11pm

Dolphin Research Center
☎ 305/289-0002 or 289-1121; www.dolphins.org 🕐 Daily 9–4:30

Key West Information Center
☎ 888/222-5590; www.keywestinfo.com

Practicalities

BEFORE YOU GO

WHAT YOU NEED

		UK	Germany	USA	Canada	Australia	Ireland	Netherlands	Spain
● Required	Some countries require a passport to remain valid for a minimum period (usually six months) beyond the date of entry. Check with the embassy before you travel.								
○ Suggested									
▲ Not required									
Passport/National Identity Card		●	●	▲	○	●	●	●	●
Visa (waiver form to be completed)		▲	▲	▲	▲	▲	▲	▲	▲
Onward or Return Ticket		●	●	▲	▲	●	●	●	●
Health Inoculations		▲	▲	▲	▲	▲	▲	▲	▲
Health Documentation (►214, Health)		▲	▲	▲	▲	▲	▲	▲	▲
Travel Insurance		●	●	●	○	●	●	●	●
Driver's License (national)		●	●	●	●	●	●	●	●
Car Insurance Certificate		n/a	n/a	●	●	n/a	n/a	n/a	n/a
Car Registration Document		n/a	n/a	●	●	n/a	n/a	n/a	n/a

WHEN TO GO

Central Florida/Orlando

High season   Low season

JAN	FEB	MAR	APR	MAY	JUN	JUL	AUG	SEP	OCT	NOV	DEC
22°C	23°C	25°C	27°C	27°C	30°C	32°C	32°C	30°C	28°C	25°C	22°C
72°F	73°F	77°F	81°F	81°F	86°F	90°F	90°F	86°F	82°F	77°F	72°F

☀ Sun   ⛅ Sunshine and showers   🌧 Wet   ☁ Cloudy

Temperatures are the **average daily maximum** for each month. At night temperatures fall to 70–75°F (21–24°C). **Florida** has a subtropical climate: it is warm in the winter and extremely hot and humid in the summer. Cooling sea breezes help to dissipate the summer heat of **Miami** and **Tampa** (77–86°F/25–30°C). Winter temperatures in Central Florida are a little cooler than in the southern part of the state. In **Orlando** the summer heat is more stifling and the humidity can become unbearable. During summer (June to September), most mornings are sunny, but expect afternoon thunderstorms which cool temperatures a little. Few days in February and March are cloudy all day. Best times to visit Orlando are October and early May. For up-to-date information on storms call the hurricane hotline (tel: 305/229-4483).

GETTING ADVANCE INFORMATION
Websites
- Visit Florida: www.visitflorida.com
- Orlando Tourist Information Center: www.orlandosentinel.com/travel/
- Greater Miami C&VB: www.miamiandbeaches.com
- Kissimmee/St Cloud C&VB: www.floridakiss.com
- Tampa Bay Convention & Visitors Bureau: www.visittampabay.com
- The Florida Keys and Key West: www.fla-keys.com

GETTING THERE

By Air Many airlines serve Florida from all over the world. International flights land in Miami, Tampa, Orlando, Sanford (charter flights for Orlando), Daytona Beach, Jacksonville and Tallahassee. There are also some charter flights to Fort Lauderdale and Fort Myers. The easiest destination to reach is Orlando; in addition to its proximity to the parks, it makes a great hub to visit both coasts, South Florida, Daytona and St Augustine. US domestic airlines serve numerous local airports.

Ticket prices tend to be highest in summer and at Easter and Christmas. Check with the airlines, travel agents, flight brokers, travel sections in newspapers, and the internet for the best deals and special offers. Airlines operating **non-direct flights** may offer substantial savings on standard fares. Tickets for short stays are generally expensive unless a Saturday night is included.

Fly-drive packages are popular. These include flights and car rental, accommodations (optional) and sightseeing discounts. **Charter flights** are a good option but can be more crowded and cramped than scheduled flights.

Approximate **flying times** to Florida: Sydney (via Los Angeles) 19 hours, New Zealand 17 hours, Berlin 10 hours, London and Dublin 8 hours, Vancouver 8 hours, Montréal 2.5 hours, Toronto 3 hours.

All **airport taxes** are usually included in the price of the ticket.

By Rail and Bus Alternative options for travelers from Canada or elsewhere in the US are **Amtrak trains** (tel: 800/872-7245; www.amtrak.com). Long-distance **Greyhound buses** (tel: 800/231-2222; www.greyhound.com) serve all major cities in the United States.

TIME

Florida is on Eastern Standard Time (GMT -5), apart from the Panhandle region, west of the Apalachicola River, which is on Central Standard Time (GMT -6). Daylight Saving Time (GMT -4) applies from early April to late October.

CURRENCY AND FOREIGN EXCHANGE

Currency The basic unit of currency in the United States is the dollar ($). One dollar is 100 cents. **Bills** come in denominations of $1, $5, $10, $20, $50 and $100. All bills are green and are the same size, so look carefully at the dollar amount on them. Coins are: 1 cent (penny), 5 cents (nickel), 10 cents (dime), 25 cents (quarter) and 50 cents (half-dollar). There are also one-dollar coins but these are comparatively rare.

An **unlimited amount** of US dollars can be imported or exported.

US dollar **travelers' checks** are the best way to carry money and they are accepted as cash in most places (not taxis), as are **credit cards** (Amex, VISA, MasterCard, Diners Card).

Exchange The best place to exchange non-US currency in Florida is at a bank. There are also currency exchange offices at airports. Automated teller cards can be used to withdraw money from your bank account in US currency. Your bank will provide you with details of where your cards will be accepted in Florida. Avoid check-cashing stands – these are high-interest, money-lending operations.

In the USA
Visit Florida
PO Box 1100
Tallahassee
FL 32302-1100
☎ 888/735-2872

In the UK
Visit Florida
Roebuck House
Palace Street
London SW1E 5BA
☎ 0870 770 1177

In Canada
Consular Affairs Bureau
☎ (1800) 267-6788;
www.dfait–maeci.gc.ca
In Australia
US Consulate
☎ (02) 9373 9200

WHEN YOU ARE THERE

NATIONAL HOLIDAYS

Jan 1	New Year's Day
Third Mon Jan	Martin Luther King Day
Third Mon Feb	Presidents' Day
Mar/Apr	Easter
Last Mon May	Memorial Day
Jul 4	Independence Day
First Mon Sep	Labor Day
Second Mon Oct	Columbus Day
Nov 11	Veterans' Day
Fourth Thu Nov	Thanksgiving
Dec 25	Christmas Day

Boxing Day (Dec 26) is not a public holiday in the US. Some stores open on national holidays. Some attractions may be closed on national holidays.

ELECTRICITY

The power supply is 110/120 volts AC (60 cycles). Sockets take two-prong, flat-pin plugs. An adaptor is needed for appliances with two-round-pin and three-pin plugs. European appliances also require a voltage transformer, as well as an adaptor.

OPENING HOURS

○ Shops   ● Post Offices
● Offices   ● Museums/Monuments
● Banks   ● Pharmacies

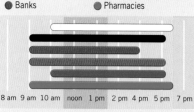

8 am 9 am 10 am noon 1 pm 2 pm 4 pm 5 pm 7 pm

☐ Day   ▨ Midday   ☐ Evening

Stores Most open Mon–Sat. Malls usually open Mon–Sat 10–9 and Sun noon–5.
Banks Some larger branches have a drive-through service on Sat 8–noon.
Post Offices Some open Sat 9–noon.
Museums Many museums are closed on Mon, but stay open late one night a week.
Pharmacies Some open 24 hours in major towns.

TIPS/GRATUITIES

Tipping is expected for all services. As a general guide:
Yes ✓   No ✗

Restaurants (service not included)	✓	15–20%
Bar service	✓	15%
Tour guides	✓	discretion
Taxis	✓	15%
Chambermaids	✓	$2 per day
Bellmen	✓	$1 per bag

LOST PROPERTY

If you lose an item in a theme park, report it to the Lost and Found office.

If something is stolen from your hotel or car, contact the police (tel: 911) and get a copy of the paperwork for your insurance company.

TIME DIFFERENCES

GMT
12 noon

Orlando
7 am

The Panhandle
6 am

USA West Coast
4 am

Spain
1 pm

Australia
10 pm

STAYING IN TOUCH

Vending machines sell stamps but at a 25 percent premium (keep small change for these). Post offices usually open Mon–Fri 9–5; hotels and major attractions often provide full postal services, including shipping.

Public telephones are found in hotel lobbies, pharmacies, restaurants, gas stations and at the roadside. Use AT&T (dial 1-800/225-5288 before dialing your main number) for inexpensive long-distance calls. Prepaid phone cards are available from drugstores and visitor centers; calls cost around 30 cents a minute from any phone. From public phones dial 0 for the operator. Dial 1 plus the area code for numbers within the US and Canada. Dial 411 to find US and Canadian numbers.

International Dialing Codes
Dial 011 followed by

UK:	44
Ireland:	353
Australia:	61
Germany:	49
Netherlands:	31
Spain:	34

Mobile providers and services Cell phones in the US operate on GSM 1900 or CDMA 800. You will need a tri- or quad-band cell phone (most smartphones including Blackberry and the iPhone have the bandwidth built in to operate in the US these days). If you have a GSM phone, check with your service provider about using it in the US. Ask if roaming charges apply, as these will mount up quickly. You can rent a GSM 1900-compatible phone with a set amount of prepaid call time – try www.t-mobile.com.

WiFi and internet Many hotels restaurants and coffee houses offer WiFi internet access. Rates vary – some hotels require you to purchase prepaid cards, others and most coffee shops offer the service free. If you have an older laptop your modem may not work once you leave your home country. Check if you will need a "global modem" before you leave.

PERSONAL SAFETY

Florida is not generally a dangerous place but to help prevent crime and accidents:

- Never open your hotel room door unless you know who is there. If in doubt call hotel security.
- Always lock your front door and/or patio doors when sleeping in the room or going out. Use the safety chain/lock for security.
- When driving keep all car doors locked.
- If lost, stop in a well-lit gas station or ask for directions in a hotel, restaurant or store.
- Never approach alligators; they can outrun a human.
- Hitchhiking is always risky and not recommended. Don't pick up hitchhikers when driving.
- Florida has been hit hard by the recession with some of the highest unemployment numbers in the country. As a result, petty theft and crimes of opportunity are up. Don't leave valuables in your car and take care when walking alone late at night.

Police assistance:
☎ 911 from any phone

POLICE	911
FIRE	911
AMBULANCE	911
HIGHWAY PATROL (from cell phone)	*FHP

HEALTH

 Insurance Medical insurance coverage of at least $1 million is strongly recommended; medical fees in the US are unregulated. If you are involved in an accident, you will be cared for by medical services and charged later.

 Dental Services Your medical insurance coverage should include dental treatment, which is readily available but expensive. Some dentists will accept credit cards, but most prefer cash or travelers' checks.

 Weather By far the most common source of ill health in Florida is too much sun. Orlando in the summer is very hot and humid, and the sun is strong throughout the state all year. Use a good sunscreen, cover up and drink plenty of fluids.

 Drugs Medication can be bought at drugstores, but certain drugs generally available elsewhere require a prescription in the US. Acetaminophen is the US equivalent of paracetamol. Use an insect repellent containing DEET, and cover up after dark to avoid being bitten by mosquitoes. Ask-a-Nurse (tel: 407/897-1700) is a free 24-hour helpline for information on symptoms and services.

 Safe Water Tap water is drinkable throughout Florida, though not very palatable. Mineral water is inexpensive and readily available.

CONCESSIONS

Students Holders of an International Student Identity Card are entitled to discounts on many attractions. Children under three are generally allowed into attractions free; children's tickets are usually available up to age 12. Teenagers often have to pay the full adult rate. Most concessions at major theme parks apply to children under 17. (At Walt Disney World® Resort, children over nine pay the full adult price.)

Senior Citizens Discounts on many services and attractions, and reductions on hotel room rates during the low season, are available to senior citizens (seniors). Qualifying age varies from 55 to 65.

TRAVELING WITH A DISABILITY

The Americans with Disabilities Act (1990) has required hotels, public transportation and attractions to make special provision for travelers with disabilities, although some theme park rides are not accessible. If you have a disability, request a specially adapted hotel room.

CHILDREN

In Orlando the larger hotels provide special children's programs. In Miami attractions are geared toward adults so you will need to be selective. Tampa's beaches and Busch Gardens are child friendly. Most theme parks provide baby-changing and nursing facilities. Many restaurants offer "Earlybird" children's meals.

RESTROOMS

The cleanest and safest lavatories are in hotels, convenience stores, shopping malls and highway rest stops.

CUSTOMS

Most foreign visitors will need a visa from a US consulate or embassy in their home country. It may mean a personal interview to which you must bring all documentation and proof of fee payment.

EMBASSIES AND HIGH COMMISSIONS

UK	Ireland	Canada	Australia	New Zealand
305/374-1522; 407/426-7855	(Washington D.C.) 202/462-3939	(Miami) 305/579-1600	(Miami) 305/858-7633	(Washington D.C) 202/328-4800

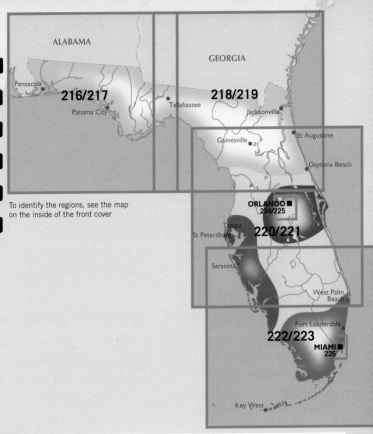

To identify the regions, see the map
on the inside of the front cover

ALABAMA

GEORGIA

Pensacola

216/217

Panama City

Tallahassee

218/219

Jacksonville

Gainesville

St Augustine

Daytona Beach

ORLANDO
224/225

Tampa
St Petersburg

220/221

Sarasota

West Palm
Beach

Fort Lauderdale

222/223

MIAMI
226

Key West

Regional Maps

10 Interstate/major route	National park/forest
90 U.S. Highway/major route	Marsh
100 State Highway/regional road	Indian reservation
— State boundary	Restricted area
■ Featured place of interest	
■ Other place of interest	
✈ Airport	

216-223   0   30 km
          0   15 miles

Area Maps

95 Interstate/major route	■ Featured place of interest
41 U.S. Highway/major route	■ Other place of interest
933 State highway/other road	Built-up area
	Park/garden

224-225   0   5 km
          0   3 miles

226   0   5 km
       0   3 miles

Atlas

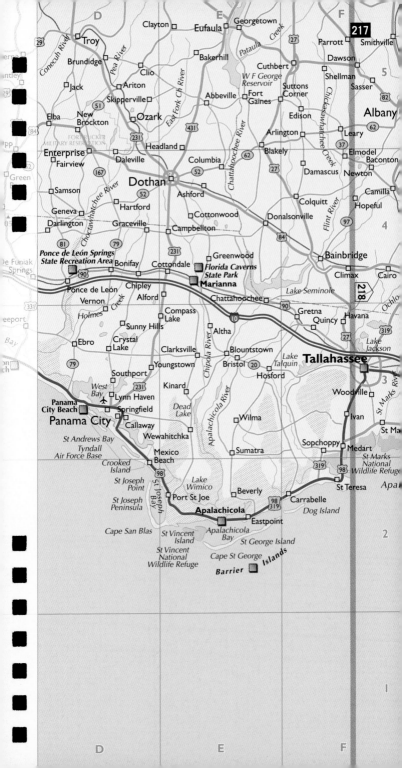

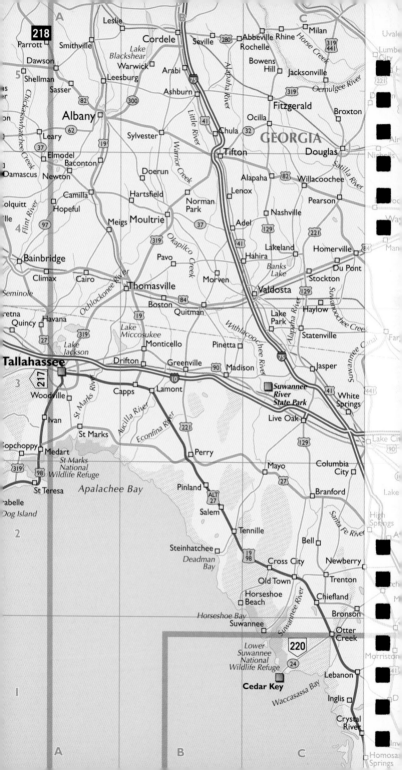

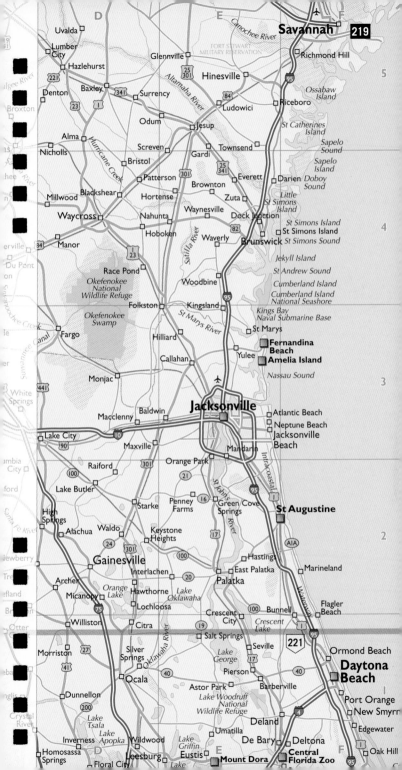

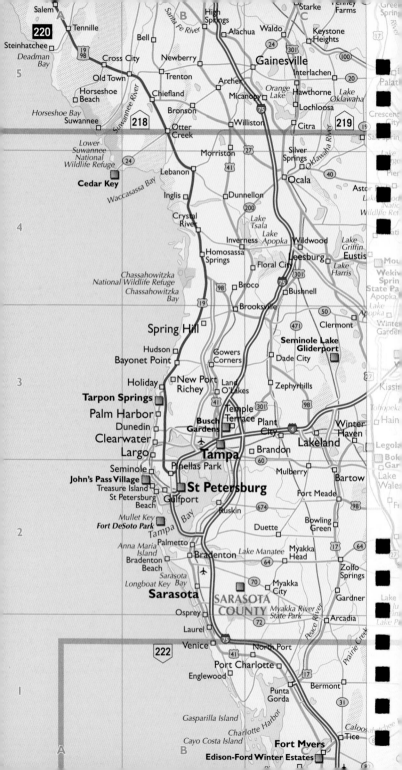

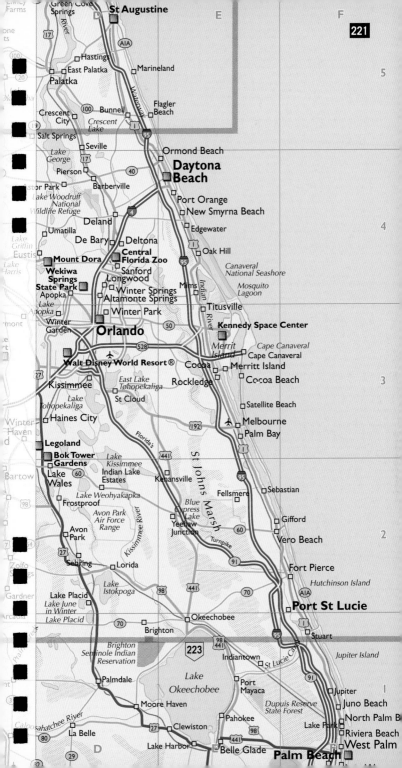

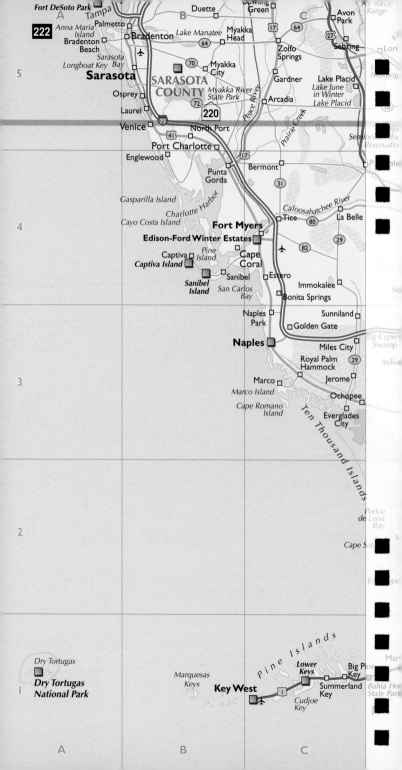

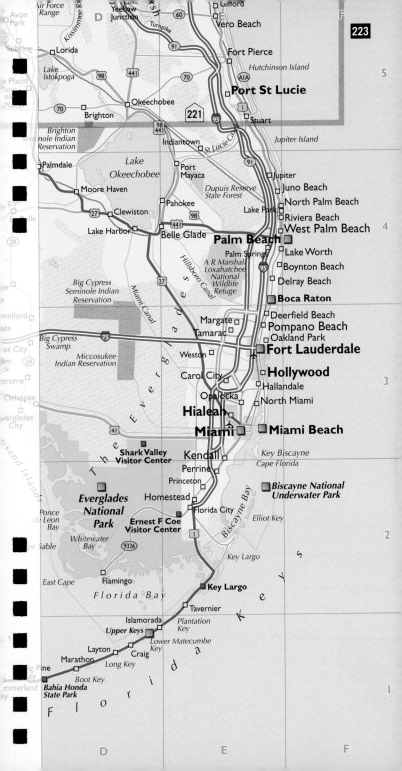

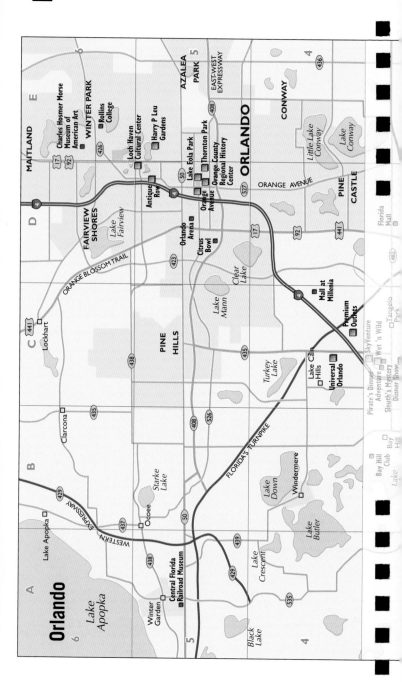

224

Orlando

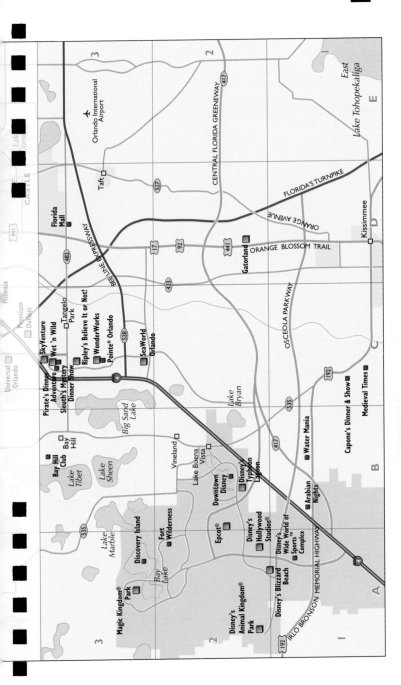

Miami

MIRAMAR
HALLANDALE
GOLDEN BEACH

Snake Creek Canal

CAROL CITY

The Cloisters of the Monastery of St Bernard

Greynolds Park

NORTH MIAMI BEACH

SURFSIDE

Biscayne Canal

MIAMI LAKES

Opa-Locka Airport

NORTH MIAMI

Olefa River State Recreation Area

OPA-LOCKA

BAL HARBOUR

Amelia Earhart Park

Little River Canal

Surfside Beach

Miami Canal

HIALEAH

Amtrak Train Station

MIAMI SHORES

NORTHBAY VILLAGE

Hialeah Race Track

MIAMI SPRINGS

Doral Park

MIAMI BEACH

Biscayne

Miami International Airport

ALLAPATTAH

MIAMI

Bay

Port of Miami

South Beach

WEST MIAMI

CORAL GABLES

LITTLE HAVANA

Maximo Gomez Park

Vizcaya Museum & Gardens

Venetian Pool

Virginia Key

COCONUT GROVE

University of Miami

Cocowalk

Museum of Science

Miami City Hall

Seaquarium

The Barnacle State Historic Site

Coconut Grove Exhibition Center

Crandon Park

Tropical Park

Calusa Park

KEY BISCAYNE

SOUTH MIAMI

Biscayne

Key Biscayne

KENDALL

Matheson Hammock Country Park

Bay

Bill Baggs Cape Florida State Recreation Area

Parrot Jungle

Fairchild Tropical Gardens

Florida State Preservation Area

Cape Florida Lighthouse

Chapman Field Park

Charles Deering Estate Park

PERRINE

CUTLER RIDGE

Picture credits

The Automobile Association would like to thank the following photographers, companies and picture libraries for their assistance in the preparation of this book.

Abbreviations for terms appearing below: (t) top; (b) bottom; (l) left; (r) right; (c) center. The Automobile Association wishes to thank the following photographers, libraries and associations for their assistance in the preparation of this book.

2 (i) LOOK Die Bildagentur der Fotografen GmbH/Alamy; 2 (ii) Ian Dagnall/Alamy; 2 (iii) © 2010 SeaWorld Parks & Entertainment, Inc. All Rights Reserved; 2 (iv) James Schwabel/Photolibrary; 3 (i) John Coletti/Photolibrary; 3 (ii) James Schwabel/Alamy; 3 (iii) Red Square Photography/Alamy; 5l LOOK Die Bildagentur der Fotografen GmbH/Alamy; 5c Sylvain Grandadam/Robert Harding; 5r Richard Cimmins/Robert Harding; 6/7 Moviestore Collection Ltd/Alamy; 8 Time & Life Pictures/Getty Images; 10 NASA; 11 NASA; 12t NASA/Kenny Allen; 12b NASA/Jack Pfaller; 13 Photo courtesy of Scott Andrews/NASA; 14/15 Raymond Forbes/Photolibrary; 15t Amanda Hall/Robert Harding; 16/17 Pepeira Tom/Photolibrary; 18l Wendell Metzen/Photolibrary; 18r Barry Mansell/Photolibrary; 19 Fritz Polking/Photolibrary; 20 Douglas Peebles/Robert Harding; 21 Peter Titmuss/Alamy; 22/23 Panoramic Images/Robert Harding; 24/25 Fraser Hall/Robert Harding; 25br Darrell Jones/Photolibrary; 27 (i) Florida Photographic Collection; 27 (ii) Library of Congress/Science Faction/Corbis; 27 (iii) Michael Ochs Archives/Corbis; 28 WireImage/Getty Images; 29 Walter Bibikow/Getty Images; 30 Mark Peterson/Corbis; 31l Ian Dagnall/Alamy; 31c AA/J Davison; 31r Marco Simoni/Robert Harding; 43l © 2010 SeaWorld Parks & Entertainment, Inc. All Rights Reserved; 43c Superstock Inc/Photolibrary; 43r NASA/Sandra Joseph; 46 © 2010 SeaWorld Parks & Entertainment, Inc. All Rights Reserved; 47t Universal Orlando; 47b AA/P Bennett; 49 RH Productions/Robert Harding; 51 Disney; 52/53 Katja Kreder/Photolibrary; 54 Disney; 56 William McAuley/Alamy; 58/59 Disney; 61 Sylvain Grandadam/Photolibrary; 62/63 Mel Longhurst/Photolibrary ; 64 Disney; 65 Dallas and John Heaton/Photolibrary; 66/67 Dennis MacDonald/Robert Harding; 68 Angelo Tondini/Robert Harding; 69 Disney; 70 Mark & Audrey Gibson/Photolibrary; 71 © 2010 SeaWorld Parks & Entertainment, Inc. All Rights Reserved; 72b © 2010 SeaWorld Parks & Entertainment, Inc. All Rights Reserved; 72/73 © 2010 SeaWorld Parks & Entertainment, Inc. All Rights Reserved; 75 2009 Universal Orlando; 76 2007 Universal Orlando Resort; 77 2008 Universal Orlando Resort; 79 2010 Universal Orlando; 80/81 2010 Universal Orlando Resort; 82 2010 Universal Orlando Resort; 83 Massimo Dallaglio/Tips Italia/ Photolibrary; 85 America/Alamy; 86 Alex Griffiths/Alamy; 87 Andre Jenny/Alamy; 88 Carrie Garcia/Alamy; 89t Richard Cummins/Superstock/Photolibrary; 89b Travel Division Images/Alamy; 90 Ian Dagnall/Alamy; 91 AA/P Bennett; 103l Jim Schwabel/Ticket/Photolibrary; 103c Juliet Ferguson/Alamy; 103r Rob Crandall/Photolibrary; 106 Franz Marc Frei/LOOK-foto/Photolibrary; 107t Gregory Wrona/Superstock/Photolibrary; 107b Arco Christian/imagebroker/Photolibrary; 108 Fraser Hall/Robert Harding; 109 Ethel Davies/Photolibrary; 110 Angelo Cavalli/Robert Harding; 111 Jeff Greenberg/Alamy; 113 ImageState/Alamy; 114 Elan Fleisher/LOOK-foto/Photolibrary; 115 Jeff Greenberg/Photolibrary; 116 Visions LLC/Photolibrary; 117 Sylvain Grandadam/Superstock/Photolibrary; 119 Robert Abrams/Superstock/Photolibrary; 120 Carl DeAbreu/Alamy; 121 Jeff Greenberg/age fotostock/Photolibrary; 122/123 R H Productions/Robert Harding; 124 Robert J Bennett/Robert Harding; 125 AA/L Provo; 126/127 Doug Boag/OSF/Photolibrary; 128 Jeff Greenberg/age fotostock/Photolibrary; 129 Lite Productions/Glow Images/Photolibrary; 130 Walter Bibikow/age fotostock/Photolibrary;133 Medio Images/Photolibrary; 134 Terrance Klassen/Robert Harding; 145l John Coletti/Jon Arnold Travel/Photolibrary; 145c Ian Dagnall/Alamy; 145r Klaus Lang/Alamy; 147 colinspics/Alamy; 148 LOOK Die Bildagentur der Fotografen GmbH/Alamy; 149t Andre Jenny/Alamy; 149c Ian Dagnall/Alamy; 150 Kelly Shannon Kelly/Alamy; 152/153 © 2010 SeaWorld Parks & Entertainment, Inc. All Rights Reserved; 154 Peter Ravallo/Alamy; 155 James Schwabel/Alamy; 156 Franz Marc Frei/LOOK-foto/Photolibrary; 157 JHP Attractions/Alamy; 158 Klaus Lang/Alamy; 159t TTL Images/Alamy; 159b Dennis MacDonald/age fotostock/Photolibrary; 160 Andre Jenny/Alamy; 161 Ilene MacDonald/Alamy; 162 Peter Horree/Alamy; 163t Don Smetzer/Alamy; 163b America/Alamy; 164 James Schwabel/Alamy; 165 malbraman/Alamy; 166 James Schwabel/Alamy; 167 nobleIMAGES/Alamy; 168 Terrance Klassen/age fotostock/Photolibrary; ;175l James Schwabel/Alamy; 175c Radius Images/Photolibrary; 175r Johann Schumacher/Peter Arnold Images/Photolibrary; 177t Richard Nowitz/Robert Harding; 177b Michael Szönyi/imagebroker.net/Photolibrary; 178c Lite Productions/Glow Images/Photolibrary; 178b Douglas Peebles/Corbis; 179 Jon Arnold Images Ltd/Alamy; 180/181 Fridmar Damm/Bridge/Photolibrary; 183 Andre Jenny/Alamy; 184 Jim Wark/LPI; 185 Danita Delimont/Alamy; 186 Peter Horree/Alamy; 187 Mark & Audrey Gibson/Photolibrary; 188 James Schwabel/Alamy; 195l Red Square Photography/Alamy; 195c NASA/Jack Pfaller; 195r Wolfgang Kaehler/Alamy; 196 Jeff Greenberg/Alamy; 197 M Timothy O'Keefe/Alamy; 198 Gregory Wrona/Alamy; 199 NASA; 203 Jeff Greenberg/Alamy; 204 Nadia Mackenzie/Alamy; 205 Rod McLean/Alamy; 209l Sylvain Grandadam/Robert Harding; 209c Richard Cummins/Photolibrary; 209r STOCKCONCEPTS/Alamy; 213t Melvyn Longhurst/Alamy; 213c AA/P Bennett; 213b Peter Steiner/Alamy;

Every effort has been made to trace the copyright holders, and we apologise in advance for any accidental errors. We would be happy to apply any corrections in the following edition of this publication.

Questionnaire

Dear Traveler

Your comments, opinions and recommendations are very important to us. So please help us to improve our travel guides by taking a few minutes to complete this simple questionnaire.

Send to: **Spiral Guides, MailStop 64, 1000 AAA Drive, Heathrow, FL 32746–5063**

Your recommendations...

We always encourage readers' recommendations for restaurants, nightlife or shopping – if your recommendation is added to the next edition of the guide, we will send you a FREE AAA Spiral Guide of your choice. Please state below the establishment name, location and your reasons for recommending it.

_____

_____

_____

_____

_____

Please send me AAA Spiral _____

(see list of titles inside the back cover)

About this guide...

Which title did you buy?

_____ **AAA Spiral**

Where did you buy it? _____

When? m m / y y

Why did you choose a AAA Spiral Guide? _____

_____

_____

_____

_____

Did this guide meet your expectations?

Exceeded ☐   Met all ☐   Met most ☐   Fell below ☐

Please give your reasons _____

_____

_____

_____

_____

continued on next page...

Were there any aspects of this guide that you particularly liked?

_____

_____

_____

_____

_____

Is there anything we could have done better?

_____

_____

_____

_____

_____

About you...

Name (Mr/Mrs/Ms) _____

Address _____

_____

_____ **Zip** _____

Daytime tel nos. _____

Which age group are you in?

Under 25 ☐ **25–34** ☐ **35–44** ☐ **45–54** ☐ **55–64** ☐ **65+** ☐

How many trips do you make a year?

Less than one ☐ **One** ☐ **Two** ☐ **Three or more** ☐

Are you a AAA member? Yes ☐ **No** ☐

Name of AAA club _____

About your trip...

When did you book? m m / y y   When did you travel? m m / y y

How long did you stay? _____

Was it for business or leisure? _____

Did you buy any other travel guides for your trip?   Yes ☐   No ☐

If yes, which ones? _____

Thank you for taking the time to complete this questionnaire.